ROBERTO BUSA, S.J., AND THE EMERGENCE OF HUMANITIES COMPUTING

It's the founding myth of humanities computing and digital humanities: In 1949, the Italian Jesuit scholar, Roberto Busa, S.J., persuaded IBM to offer technical and financial support for the mechanized creation of a massive lemmatized concordance to the works of St. Thomas Aquinas. Using Busa's own papers, recently accessioned in Milan, as well as IBM archives and other sources, Jones illuminates this DH origin story. He examines relationships between the layers of hardware, software, human agents, culture, and history, and answers the question of how specific technologies afford and even constrain cultural practices, including in this case the academic research agendas of humanities computing and, later, digital humanities.

Steven E. Jones is Professor of English and Director of the Center for Textual Studies and Digital Humanities at Loyola University Chicago. He was a Distinguished Visiting Fellow at the CUNY Graduate Center Advanced Research Consortium in 2014-2015 and a recipient of the Keats-Shelley Association Distinguished Scholar award in 2013. His most recent book, *The Emergence of the Digital Humanities*, highlights his specialties in textual studies and digital humanities.

ROBERTO BUSA, S.J., AND THE EMERGENCE OF HUMANITIES COMPUTING

The Priest and the Punched Cards

Steven E. Jones

Routledge
Taylor & Francis Group

NEW YORK AND LONDON

First published 2016
by Routledge
711 Third Avenue, New York, NY 10017

and by Routledge
2 Park Square, Milton Park, Abingdon, Oxon OX14 4RN

Routledge is an imprint of the Taylor & Francis Group, an informa business

© 2016 Taylor & Francis

The right of Steven E. Jones to be identified as author of this work has been asserted by him in accordance with sections 77 and 78 of the Copyright, Designs and Patents Act 1988.

Library of Congress Cataloguing in Publication Data
Jones, Steven E. (Steven Edward), author.
Roberto Busa, S.J., and the emergence of humanities computing : the priest and the punched cards / Steven E. Jones.
pages cm
Includes bibliographical references and index.
ISBN 978-1-138-18677-4 (hardback)
ISBN 978-1-315-64361-8 (e-book)
1. Computational linguistics—Research—United States—History—20th century.
2. Computational linguistics—Research—Italy—History—20th century.
3. Humanities—Research—United States—Data processing—History—20th century.
4. Text processing (Computer science)—History—20th century.
5. Busa, Roberto.
6. Index Thomisticus. I. Title.
P98.32.U6J66 2016
006.3'5—dc23
2015035949

ISBN: 978-1-138-18677-4 (hbk)
ISBN: 978-1-315-64361-8 (ebk)

Typeset in Bembo
by diacriTech, Chennai

TABLE OF CONTENTS

LIST OF ILLUSTRATIONS

FIGURES

INTRODUCTION

Roberto Busa, S.J. and the Emergence of Humanities Computing

On August 9, 2011, the Italian Jesuit scholar, Father Roberto Busa, S.J., died at the age of 97. Obituaries and online posts around the world celebrated him as the pioneer and founder of humanities computing and, by extension, of the more recent interdisciplinary field of digital humanities. A photograph on the *Forbes* website showed him smiling while holding an iPhone, implying a direct linear descent from his work to the latest technology of the present, the past of humanities computing meeting the present of ubiquitous mobile computers.[1] Most of the stories mentioned his signature contribution to scholarship, the *Index Thomisticus*, a massive (56 volumes in print), lemmatized concordance containing every word in the complete works of the thirteenth-century philosopher and theologian, St. Thomas Aquinas. (A lemmatized concordance is organized according to word-family, with all forms of a given word grouped under its dictionary entry or lemma.) The *Index*, in a web edition created by Eduardo Bernot and Enrique Alarcón, has by now been incorporated into the larger digital project of the *Corpus Thomisticum*, which also includes an electronic edition of the complete works of St. Thomas Aquinas with related works, an edition of his manuscripts, a bibliography, and a list of research tools.[2] This resource has its origins in Father Busa's tentative, experimental forays into creating the *Index*, beginning in the mid-1940s with his PhD research and extending to the use of punched-card machines starting with his first trip to North America in 1949.

Father Busa is an important symbol for the history of humanities computing and for digital humanities. The Alliance of Digital Humanities Organizations (ADHO) named its most prestigious award for him and presented him with the first instance of the Roberto Busa Prize in 1998. Since then, the prize has been awarded every three years. The official website (http://adho.org/awards/roberto-busa-prize) tells how Busa, "the first pioneer of humanities computing ... in 1949 began experiments in linguistic automation, with the support of the IBM offices in New York and Milan, as part of his analytical research on the writings of Thomas Aquinas." The formal citation for his own award says that it was presented "in honor of the monumental achievement of the *Index Thomisticus*, the commencement of which is generally regarded as marking the beginning of the field of computing in the humanities."[3]

In this account and others like it, the origin of using computers in humanities research is linked not only to Busa's *Index* but to his crossing the Atlantic to gain the support of the iconic American computer company, support he worked to maintain in some form for over forty years. Anyone who has followed humanities computing and digital humanities in recent decades will have heard a version of this founding narrative. Susan Hockey, a historian of humanities computing who was herself the recipient of the Busa Prize in 2004, summarizes it in this way:

> Unlike many other interdisciplinary experiments, humanities computing has a very well-known beginning. In 1949, an Italian Jesuit priest, Father Roberto Busa, began what even to this day is a monumental task: to make an *index verborum* of all the words in the works of St Thomas Aquinas and related authors, totaling some 11 million words of medieval Latin. Father Busa imagined that a machine might be able to help him, and, having heard of computers, went to visit Thomas J. Watson at IBM in the United States in search of support (Busa 1980). Some assistance was forthcoming and Busa began his work. The entire texts were gradually transferred to punched cards and a concordance program written for the project. The intention was to produce printed volumes, of which the first was published in 1974 (Busa 1974).[4]

Like other versions of this story, Hockey's is based largely on Father Busa's own accounts, especially as published in the influential article of 1980 she cites.[5] The key elements are all there: the priest and the CEO, two "founding fathers" (one a Jesuit father of the Catholic Church who is also taken as the father of humanities computing, the other the founder of the world's dominant computer company at the time), the start of a collaboration between European humanities and American global business, meanings and machines. It's a good story, and as Hockey says, "a very well-known beginning." And it has been taken by some as the beginning of digital humanities, as well, an interdisciplinary field which emerged in the past decade or so out of the longer tradition of humanities computing, with newly available government grants, new graduate programs, and new research centers. But leading digital humanities scholar Willard McCarty (recipient of the Busa Award in 2013) cautions that, although Busa may be an "intellectual father-figure" who was there from the beginning of humanities computing, "[t]here are other beginnings on offer."[6] Despite this caution, the story of Father Busa's coming to IBM remains the dominant founding myth of humanities computing and digital humanities. Busa's own predilection for vivid symbolic illustrations surely contributed to making the myth.

My aim in this book is to complicate that myth with history. I pay close attention to that influential beginning and to the human story of Busa's project in historical context. To begin, although Busa has been called the founder of digital humanities, he was more properly helping to establish a viable form of early humanities computing, or, even more precisely, humanities data processing. I focus on the first decade of Busa's work, roughly 1949–1959, and how that early work led to the uneven emergence of more extensive use of computers in the humanities. The interdisciplinary field known as digital humanities came along decades later, in the midst of a flurry of debates about how to define it. To collapse humanities computing and digital humanities is to obscure much of what's most interesting about their related histories. Throughout this book, when I do connect something Father Busa did to some aspect of today's digital humanities, I do so explicitly, and it's usually to correct what I take to be a distorted view of his legacy. It's never because I think, as one critical theorist in digital humanities recently put it, that the "boundaries" of the field of digital humanities can or should be "circumscribe[d] to Father Busa and his punch cards."[7] Quite the contrary. My own digital humanities work in textual studies, media studies, and video games, for example, was undertaken in opposition to such rigid boundaries. But the myth of the priest and the CEO remains powerful in the field even as the history behind the myth remains obscure. More history is needed.

The complicated history behind the myth can be glimpsed even in Father Busa's own accounts. For example, his often-repeated story of the initial meeting at IBM contains witty, polished dialogue, complete with jokes and subtle allusions by both men, when the actual meeting was sure to have taken place with a certain formality, perhaps unavoidable awkwardness—especially given the fact that Father Busa's English was not yet fluent by that date. Anyway, it's likely that the meeting between the priest and the CEO was at first a kind of diplomatic courtesy, probably not all that significant at the time to the Chairman or his huge company. It's clear that IBM took more convincing than Busa's entertaining and influential account from 1980 would suggest, requiring a testimonial or character reference from New York's Cardinal Spellman, for example, and H. Paul Tasman at IBM later said he thought he was expected to make the proposal "go away" (see Chapter 1). For his part, Father Busa was considering a range of possible technologies right up until an agreement was reached with IBM (as even his own published accounts indicate). In general, large forces were at work, institutional, political, and technological conditions that made that initial meeting a possibility and opened the way to further collaboration.

In what follows I attempt to fill in the picture, to detail some of those conditions, including the specific locations where the work took place and the particular technologies Busa used. From the archival record, we get a sense of Father Busa's lived experience in the 1950s: traveling on transatlantic ocean liners and merchant ships, living in New York City for months at a time almost every year, riding the elevated train, working on punched-card machines at IBM World Headquarters in Midtown and IBM World Trade Corporation near the new United Nations building, sending telegrams, and making visits to local universities, then going back to Italy, working at IBM Italia in Milan, negotiating with local industrialists to arrange for space in their buildings for his Center for Literary Data Processing in the town of Gallarate, again taking trains and holding meetings and staging experiments—all of this activity punctuated by key events, such as hosting a demonstration of his punched-card method in IBM's showroom at 590 Madison Avenue in 1952, or presenting his work to large crowds at the 1958 World Expo in Brussels. This is not a biography of Father Busa. But it is a kind of biography of his project in its first decade. That's when methods for humanities computing of this particular kind—a kind that has been extremely influential (even though it is not the only kind of humanities computing, let alone the only kind of digital humanities)—were first established from among the available possibilities.

Busa's work continued into the beginning of the twenty-first century, involving the use of powerful computers like the IBM 705 and the IBM 7090, for example, as well as personal computers, CD-ROMs, hypertext links, and the Internet. Those were the decades in which he became the eminent scholar with a worldwide reputation who lent his name to the ADHO Digital Humanities prize. Much of that happened well after the initial decade that is the focus of this book. Even many who knew him in more recent years (alas, I did not) may not be aware of the details of the early period.

So my story begins at the very midpoint of the twentieth century. This was the era just after World War II that saw the rise of the Cold War, when for example Busa acted as liaison between linguistic work underway at Georgetown University and the European atomic energy center in Ispra, near his home in Lombardy; or when Paul Tasman's and Roberto Busa's work on the Dead Sea Scrolls, recently discovered in the Judean desert, led to at least the beginnings of a collaboration with philologists around the world. The story begins in 1949 in New York City, where one large-scale calculator—with walls of vacuum tubes, electromechanical relay switches, and paper tape drives as well as punched cards—had just been built under the direction of an IBM lab uptown at Columbia University and installed for working display at IBM's Midtown headquarters at 590 Madison Avenue. The machine captured the public imagination and signified "the future" for many. But much smaller black or gray metal punched-card machines, arranged in various suites and configurations for performing specialized tasks, were the actual present at the time, a time of data processing in offices all over town (and increasingly, worldwide—notably in Milan, for example). Commonly operated by women, some of whom were also trained to set up or "program" the machines by re-cabling them using matrix-based plug boards, this was office equipment associated with accounting, and operating it was generally treated as a specialized category of clerical work, more akin to skilled bookkeeping or stenography than to later software-based computer programming.

It was an age of data processing, and New York City was at the center of the age. We see this even in an iconic avant-garde painting of the 1940s, Jackson Pollock's *Stenographic Figure*, first shown to acclaim in 1943. Later in the decade, just as Father Busa was visiting New York for the first time, *LIFE* magazine published an illustrated article on Pollock as a representative American artist.[8] By then abstract expressionism had arrived and Pollock had begun to make his famous action paintings, but this earlier work was at least partly figurative (hence the punning title). And it contains scores of calligraphic markings, layered signs and symbols suggesting a world of ambient data—with what would appear to be shorthand and numbers ("figures") among them—arrayed in multiple floating and overlapping dimensions (as was characteristic of Pollock's canvases), with what appear to be two human-like figures facing one another, even perhaps a secretary or stenographer taking dictation at a desk. This scene may represent an important aspect of the 1940s, especially in New York, the significance of "figures," seemingly cryptic data everywhere—in the air. Father Busa's own letters, documents, and photographs from 1949–1959 belong to the same moment and help to defamiliarize this mid-century milieu, with its culture of data-processing machinery and, within a few years in the new decade, the emergence of limited numbers of large-scale electromechanical calculators. Punched-card processing was part of a whole flood of data processing of various kinds at the time, almost none of it quite "computing" as we've come to know it. The application of this data-processing technology to linguistic research was really only proleptically and obliquely related to the humanities computing that would emerge (and be constructed) in the years that followed.

As late as 1971, Busa wrote from Venice to the New York academic, Professor Joseph Raben, editor of the first dedicated journal in the field, *Computers in the Humanities*, to question him about the definition in American English of the term "humanities."[9] Busa asked whether linguistics or psychology would be included, for example, under the category. In Italian, he said, "scienze umanistiche" had a broader "and less definitive comprehension"—in effect meaning "only the opposite [of] mathematics, physics, chemistry, medicine," etc. Raben replied—speaking pragmatically, as an editor—that it depended on the researcher's disciplinary and institutional affiliations, but also on "whether the philosophy of a particular project stresses the human qualities of the material and calls into play the human qualities of the investigator." For example, he says, an anthropologist performing a statistical study of physical types would not count as "humanities," but a cultural anthropologist analyzing folk tales (using computers) would. This disciplinary discussion—which sounds relatively fresh today in relation to debates about the digital humanities—reminds us that this so-called founder of humanities computing was himself still negotiating the meaning of key terms as he began the third decade of what would turn out to be over a half century of work in the field.

It also reminds us of the sometimes complicated cross-cultural nature of that work, in more than one sense—interdisciplinary, bilingual, transatlantic—even well after that first decade (the focus of this book).

That exchange with Joseph Raben is just one example of how much this book has depended on Busa's correspondence. The project would not have been possible without the Busa Archive at the Catholic University of the Sacred Heart in Milan, under the stewardship of Father Busa's former student and colleague, himself a computational linguist, Dr. Marco Passarotti, who serves as Coordinator of Research and Secretary of CIRCSE—the *Centro Interdisciplinare di Ricerche per la Computerizzazione dei Segni dell'Espressione* (Interdisciplinary Center for Research in the Computerization of Signs of Expression).[10] Busa's papers first came to the university starting in 2009 and they continued to arrive and be sorted and organized after his death in 2011. The collection is still being fully accessioned and catalogued as I write—some new materials arrived while I was working there in March 2015—but meanwhile Dr. Passarotti has generously given me and other researchers access to the collection as it stands.

Besides the Busa Archive, and of course published materials of various kinds, I've also consulted archival materials elsewhere, starting with the IBM Archives. Although I was not permitted to examine the corporate archives on site, I was sent a wide variety of materials over the course of a year, including valuable oral-history transcripts and additional photographs, by the company archivists, in particular, Reference Archivist Dawn Stanford, under the direction of Jamie Martin. I also consulted the papers of a former IBM engineer, A. Wayne Brooke, now at North Carolina State University. I viewed relevant papers at Columbia University in New York—while benefitting even more, perhaps, from the materials put online by Frank da Cruz at the Columbia University Computing History website[11]—and Fordham University. Both universities, in different ways, played crucial roles in Busa's early work in New York. On March 13, 2015, I was shown some of Father Busa's papers at another academic location, the former Jesuit college, the Aloisianum in Gallarate in Lombardy, where Father Busa taught and in the infirmary of which he was cared for in his final years. As I mentioned, some additional papers from the Aloisianum were donated to the Archive at CIRCSE while I was visiting to research this book in March 2015—a brown-paper packet tied in string was dropped off at the Director's office and she thoughtfully brought it straight to the office where I was working. There are sure to be more such deliveries and discoveries in coming years. Among the materials already at CIRCSE that have not yet been thoroughly accessioned are those related to the Dead Sea Scrolls, which I discuss in Chapter 5. In addition, there remains the possibility that some of Father Busa's papers are still in storage in various locations and may be made public at a later date. I look forward to hearing more of the story of the earliest years of this work, as other scholars engage with the materials as they continue to become available.

The basic collection in the Busa Archive, now at CIRCSE, was first prepared under Father Busa's own supervision. The core of it consists of papers and other materials he saved, copies of his correspondence, press clippings, and over 900 photographs, usually taken professionally for the press or for the purposes of general publicity. Most of the illustrations in the book are drawn from these (additional photographs have been made available online with permission of the Busa Archive: http://priestandpunchedcards.tumblr.com). The Archive also contains Busa's own handwritten notes, business cards, massive numbers of punched cards and stacks of computer printout on accordion-fold continuous-feed paper, boxes of floppy disks, and magnetic tapes with data recorded on them. For some parts of the story, we have very little documentation besides Father Busa's own accounts—starting with that famous first meeting with Thomas J. Watson, Sr., at IBM (as I explain in detail in Chapter 1). Other papers on this event (and other events) may well surface in the future. Since my interest is in the first decade of Busa's work with IBM, for the most part I've mostly consulted the materials in English and Italian that directly pertain to that collaboration. There are many additional materials in the Busa Archive (and undoubtedly some beyond it, still), in multiple languages, including Latin, a reminder of the global reach and ambitions of Father Busa's work. There are many letters and documents from other people in the Archive, as well as edited and published materials of various kinds. Readers should keep in mind, however, that it's a pre-selected and in effect a self-curated collection.

A similar caveat applies to the use of the IBM Corporation Archives, a caveat which for obvious reasons would apply to any self-curated corporate archive, but also in this case including the fact that I was only able to work remotely, with materials sent to me by the Archivist based on emailed queries. Also, among the published sources I cite are a few that count as "house organs" of IBM: *World Trade News* or *THINK*, for example. These usually serve as sources of factual reporting about internal matters, the dates of events, for example, but I also cite them as sources of the public rhetoric by which the company represented Busa's and Tasman's research or computing in general. Obviously they have to be understood as operating within a promotional mandate. Indeed, even some research publications, such as Paul Tasman's reports on literary data processing and on the Dead Sea Scrolls project, were published by IBM, and should be read as falling within a similar promotional mandate. For that matter, a parallel caveat applies to some of the Catholic publications I cite, or to Father Busa's own watershed publication, the *Varia Specimina Concordantiarum*, which was published by his home institution, the Aloisianum Jesuit college. All of these publications—of obvious historical importance and often demonstrating perfectly admirable intellectual integrity, are nonetheless by their very nature not quite fully peer-reviewed materials in the usual scholarly sense. I've tried wherever possible to confirm reports among multiple sources, comparing IBM-related documents in the collection of retired engineer A. Wayne Brooke, for example, and published accounts by former employees and others. Still, some portions of the story remain obscure: for example, the exact itinerary of Father Busa's initial visit to Canada and the U.S. in 1949, before his arrival in New York and the famous meeting at IBM, how precisely the arrangements were made for that meeting, and the specifics of the formal agreement he reached with the company (I mean contemporary documentation, rather than accounts from later years by the parties involved). Once again, papers may well come to light in the future that will enrich these and other aspects of the story.

I should add that, although I was not allowed to browse the IBM Archives directly, I'm very grateful for the generous expenditure of her time and effort by IBM Reference Archivist Dawn Stanford, under supervision of the IBM Corporation Archivist, Jamie Martin. I owe an enormous debt to Lilian S. Wu of IBM, for facilitating much of my access to IBM materials and for encouraging my research at various stages, as well as to my own Dean of the College of Arts and Sciences at Loyola University Chicago, Father Thomas Regan, S.J., for putting me in touch with Ms. Wu in the first place.

In terms of approach, wherever possible, I tell adjacent stories of technology and culture in shared contexts: of Father Busa's work in linguistics alongside IBM's punched-card business after the Second World War, for example; or of his presentation at the 1958 Expo in Brussels, the first major world's fair held after the war, literally adjacent to both IBM's RAMAC computer on display and a film by Eames Studios about the humanistic promise of computing, and as an immediate precursor to his leveraging of Cold War funds dedicated to machine-translation research, at Georgetown and at the European Atomic Energy Community at Ispra. The point is not only to place what Busa did (and didn't do) in historical and cultural contexts (which include specific technologies and institutions), but to sketch part of the general milieu within which he acted from 1949 to 1959, including roads he did not take and possibilities he could not realize, but which nevertheless add historical depth to our understanding of the research project as a whole.

From one vantage, this is a story about the history of technology. But technology does not "evolve," or "descend," in a linear way. It's worth recalling what Michel Foucault said of his own approach:

> Genealogy does not resemble the evolution of a species and does not map the destiny of a people. On the contrary, to follow the complex course of descent is to maintain passing events in their proper dispersion; it is to identify the accidents, the minute deviations—or conversely, the complete reversals—the errors, the false appraisals, and the faulty calculations that gave birth to those things that continue to exist and have value for us; it is to discover that truth or being does not lie at the root of what we know and what we are, but the exteriority of accidents.[12]

This book is not a Foucauldian genealogy. But my descriptions of punched-card and computing technology were inspired by recent theoretical discussions of media archaeology, an approach that owes something to Foucault's methodological suspicion. Like many media archaeologists, I've tried to write with an awareness of the inevitable discontinuities of history, the epistemic gaps that separate us from the past, no matter how assiduous our reconstructions or archival explorations. I pay special attention to marks in the record of "the exteriority of accidents," the contingencies that have shaped history—as opposed to received myth, with its clean and direct lines of descent as destiny.

At every stage, I look for adjacent possibilities, alternative lines of descent and potential influence. For example, I shift attention in more than one instance to the women operators who often appear in the background of the main narrative (or literally in the visual background of documentary photographs). As I've said, the story is about two founding fathers, in more than one sense, and I try to read both of their stories critically, for example by placing the patriarchal roles played by Busa and Watson, then by Watson's familial and corporate heirs, in relation to the stories of some of the mostly anonymous and uncelebrated women with whom they worked. In many of the photographs in the Busa Archive, we see young women operating the punched-card machinery (interestingly, this is less the case once the photographs shift to large electronic calculators in the 1960s and after). Julianne Nyhan and Melissa Terras, of University College London, were the first to turn the spotlight on these young women, first in blog posts about the Busa Archive starting in 2013, and they have since begun to write accounts that place the formerly anonymous operators at the center of Busa's project.[13] I'm grateful to them for sharing the results of their research in progress while this book was also in progress. In Chapters 2 and 4, especially, I connect Busa's operators to the ambiguous feminization of computing, at the transitional moment in which Father Busa was establishing the first modern Center for Literary Data Processing. At the time, computing was obviously a male-dominated realm built on a foundation of mostly female labor. This became increasingly the case in the early 1960s, as the pragmatic arrangements made during World War II were left behind (and male veterans returning from the war were often given jobs that had been held by women before 1945). But this gendered dynamic is best understood through specific relations of power, specific skills, and particular job descriptions. The specifics are crucial to any general historical understanding of the role of women in computing—and in the accounting and data processing activities that preceded actual computing and continued for many years to overlap with it.

I've said I aim to demythologize Father Busa's story in favor of a more detailed sense of his lived history. This is not to deny that Busa was indeed among the first to imagine and institute in material form specific interdisciplinary methods for humanities computing, from linguistic data processing to experiments with a wide variety of technological platforms, to founding the earliest dedicated humanities computing center. The founding myth expresses these real achievements and his very real historical influence. It's not my aim to debunk it, but only to provide a more complicated picture of its history, to fill in some of the rich contexts out of which the myth arose in the first place.

On the other hand, this is no hagiography. Father Busa emerges from the archival record (and I hope in these pages) as a deeply human scholar as well as a priest, a canny negotiator and a shrewd fundraiser, fully conscious of the risks and the stakes in the deals he brokered in order to accomplish his purposes (and of course the higher purpose he served). In 2014, the parody Twitter account, @DHDarkSider, tweeted: "Roberto Busa wasn't merely the first DH [Digital Humanities] enthusiast. He was the first in a long line of enthusiasts working for The Man." The tweet was meant sarcastically, but behind the mockery is a plain historical truth—which I'm sure Father Busa himself would not have disputed. Especially in the first decade, he assiduously and openly negotiated and collaborated with representatives of power and authority. As a Jesuit priest, he necessarily worked within the patriarchal hierarchy of his order and the Catholic Church. And as a "pioneer" who crossed the Atlantic from Europe, he collaborated with one of the iconic American corporations of the mid-twentieth century, which had continued to do business with Germany during the war, faced antitrust suits, and in the latter half of the century, for many, became synonymous with multinational capitalism and technocracy itself. The paper punched card, IBM's signature mid-century product, is very near to being a cultural cliché. It inspired the oppositional slogan of the Berkeley Free Speech Movement in the 1960s: "I am a human being; do not fold, spindle, or mutilate" (FSM stands for Fold, Spindle, or Mutilate as well as Free Speech Movement). At the end of that decade, IBM lent its name (transparently encrypted with one alphabetic shift) to the fictional, dystopian computer, HAL. It was famous for the corporate uniform of its sales force, and the image of Father Busa in his Roman collar, dark suit or long cassock, is met from the other side by all those IBMers in white shirts and navy-blue suits (and when he first arrived in New York, many still wearing fedoras).

The problematic nature of this collaboration with institutional power would not have been lost on anyone, even at the time, least of all on Father Busa himself. He claimed that the alliance with big business pragmatically served to further the greater glory of God.[14] From a secular point of view, however, the @DHDarkSider tweet just states the obvious in comic terms: he was not exactly (or exclusively) "working for The Man," but Busa was working with forms of power that were in the most literal sense patriarchal. And aspects of the ideology and agenda of mid-century American business are interwoven with his own research agenda—from the general celebration of the power of data and data-processing machinery, including its applications within traditionally "humanistic" arenas, to his participation the 1958 World's Fair against the backdrop of the Cold War, to securing an actual contract for preparing Russian texts for experimental processing on behalf of the U.S. military-funded work in machine translation.

Beyond IBM, Father Busa actively sought the support of government agencies (especially in the U.S. but also in Italy), corporations (starting with local textile companies in his part of Northern Italy), and, just to point to one obvious example, cultivated the support of the well-known Cold Warrior, Francis Cardinal Spellman, who as Archbishop of New York vouched for him at the beginning of his project and attended his first important demos. Busa's collaborations with authority of various kinds are obvious and overdetermined, to say the least, and have to be taken as central to the history of his project. This is not the same as the history of all of humanities computing, or even less so, of the digital humanities, but it is at least a (celebrated) part of the history of both, a kind of tributary prehistory. Humanities computing, even relatively more than traditional humanities—given the internal tensions of its interdisciplinarity and the material basis of the technologies with which it engages—has depended on industry and government, for technology, for funding, and, more often than some humanities academics might like to admit, for intellectual impetus and research questions. Busa's arrangement with IBM changed over time, but it mostly involved the company's making machines and support available on a points system—free rent, basically, for machines and personnel at IBM locations in New York and Milan and (beginning in earnest in 1956) in the new Literary Data Processing Center in Gallarate (CAAL). By then Busa had also secured some financial support from business leaders in the area of Milan, mostly from the textile industry (one of them donated the use of the former factory that became the headquarters of CAAL). He also received some funds from the Italian government, and in the 1960s, CAAL seems likely to have secured money from Euratom, the European Atomic Energy Community, as part of a deal he brokered bringing IBM and Georgetown linguists there for work in machine translation. Father Busa was a tireless fundraiser who worked pragmatically to create a worldwide network with many strong and weak ties connecting various centers of activity. His story, in the era following the Second World War and Vannevar Bush's famous call for intensive government funding for research,[15] illustrates how these dependencies and potential complicities have functioned in academic research in general and humanities computing in particular for the better part of a century.

In that context, by way of disclaimer: I have my own personal and professional connections to both IBM and the Jesuits. A member of my family is a long-time IBM employee and I teach at a Jesuit institution, Loyola University Chicago. I'm also a founding Director of the interdisciplinary Center for Textual Studies and Digital Humanities at Loyola (CTSDH). All of this undoubtedly shaped my interest in the topic in the first place. I'm anything but disinterested. I don't pretend to be able to rise above my own interests, but I've tried to keep them in the foreground and to write curiously, self-consciously, and critically about the entangled forces at work on all sides.

Another issue: I'm not Catholic, and because my take on the topic is a secular one—the humanities-computing aspect of Father Busa's work—this book may seem to some to distort his work. I hope not. Readers should remember that of course Father Busa saw his scholarship in linguistics as falling within his vocation and mission as a Jesuit priest. He sometimes wrote about the spiritual aspect of what he was doing, often in closing perorations of essays or lectures (I discuss some of these in what follows). But he also addressed different audiences with different emphases. I make an effort in the book to attend to relevant Catholic contexts for the research questions, models, and material resources that were made available to Father Busa. And at times the intellectual contexts of the work necessarily touch upon theological and philosophical questions.

In a 1962 essay, Father Busa acknowledged: "I was unaware of the fact that I was placed in the sequence of events by which the automation of accounting caused the worldwide evolution of the means of information."[16] Although his best-known humanities computing publications rarely discuss it explicitly, he always understood developments in computing as part of a larger divinely ordered co-evolution of the world and humanity. Take the example of the essay I've just cited. Despite its religious framing, the evolution Busa describes is worldly in its causes and effects. In the postwar period after 1945, he says,

> The development of communications and organizing techniques allowed the great enlargement of firms that were able to operate worldwide. Equally rapid was the increase of the reciprocal influence of the markets, and between politics and the market. With such a development it has become indispensable for a manager to be able to review a great number of particulars and quickly synthesize them, and at the same time to check and perhaps modify the great masses of small and extensive peripheral phenomena. Calculators answered this need and provided economics with industrial and commercial accounting.[17]

His analysis mentions industry, defense, and the "deepening of the relationship between industrial production and scientific research," then cites as an example his own involvement in Euratom, which "has felt obliged to acquire for its own Centro [Center] of Ispra the IBM 7090 calculator, which costs about three million dollars, or about two thousand million lire."[18] In fact, Father Busa himself apparently arranged for the deal between Euratom and IBM, by way of Georgetown's center for linguistic research. Writing at the end of his first decade of intense collaboration with IBM, Busa sees the confluence of "production, trade, and defense" and the consequent "demand" for "the automation of 'information retrieval,' as "an opportune tracing system of useful knowledge."[19] Pragmatically, he sees an opportunity to leverage business and government interests in favor of intellectual (and spiritual) interests. While his intellectual interest in the translation experiments, or in Goethe's texts, or in the non-biblical Dead Sea Scrolls is evidently genuine, it's also clear that his anchor project remained though the decades the *Index Thomisticus*.

Busa's focus on the work of St. Thomas Aquinas is itself historically significant when we consider it in context. It can ultimately be seen as one result of the encyclical of Pope Leo XIII in 1879, *Aeterni Patris*, which called for Catholic philosophy to re-establish its foundation in medieval scholasticism, and particularly in the work of St. Thomas Aquinas.[20] The document argues for the necessity of connecting faith and reason in a dialectical process, and observes that even the medieval scholastics were not opposed to science. This dialectical view of human knowledge, the idea of seeing the rational pursuit of scientific truth as a legitimate road to divine truth, is in keeping with Father Busa's own published work, which he often articulated in playful rather than homiletic tones, as in the following example (from the essay I cited above): "Aristotle, therefore, purposefully set about looking into language, and in its folds discovered metaphysics. . . . Even the good and gentle St. Thomas Aquinas stood and admired him, wondering, with his head in the clouds, at the power with which a pagan from this earth had been able to enter into heaven."[21] There's no question that Busa saw the enumerative study of words, his kind of linguistics, as contributing to a greater understanding of the logos, the metaphysics of presence. But in practice, his own published and publicly demonstrated research focused on human language and technology, and the peers who reviewed it were philologists and cyberneticists as often as they were Thomists (or theologians of any kind). His own humanistic focus when it came to his linguistic research helps to justify the secular and humanistic focus of the chapters that follow.

Another important papal encyclical, published at the very commencement of Busa's doctoral research, was Pope Pius XII's *Divino Afflante Spiritu* (1943). It called for new translations of the bible from source texts in Hebrew, Aramaic, and Greek (rather than only from the Latin Vulgate), and necessarily encouraged the kind of documentary textual criticism and analysis we associate with textual studies and modern philology. Busa's work on the Dead Sea Scrolls in the later 1950s, which amounted to data processing and analysis of those ancient source texts and their languages, followed directly from this call. (The CAAL production facility in a former textile factory in Gallarate was decorated with what I take to be puzzle-piece-shaped "fragments" inscribed with signs, some of which were recognizable as Greek or Hebrew letters). I argue in Chapter 5 that this work on the Dead Sea Scrolls is an example of what Busa called a "new philology," a computerized philology—and, given his calling, this too has to be read in the broader context of the 1943 encyclical. On the one hand, it may be a sign of his caution in this regard that Busa's Center worked only on the non-biblical scrolls (as he repeatedly specified). His computerized philology was never directly applied to the bible. On the other hand, he publicly recognized as his "great ally" the Episcopal scholar, the Rev. John W. Ellison, who used the UNIVAC to build a concordance to the Revised Standard Edition of the bible at about the same time that Father Busa was working on the non-biblical Dead Sea Scrolls (and on a range of secular literary texts).

While I'm interested in the Catholic contexts in which Father Busa pursued his work on St. Thomas Aquinas and philology, and how he might have seen his work as enriching the dialogue between reason and faith, and even seen the collaboration with IBM as for the greater glory of God, it's not the aim of this book to focus on religion. Nor am I qualified to write about Thomistic theology (the topic of Father Busa's dissertation). At any rate, Busa's engagement with problems of language and computing (and the precursor to computing *per se*, data processing) was as intense and persistent as his theological pursuits—the worldly side of a long interdisciplinary career. He was committed to the idea of a dialectical relationship between science and faith, but in practice this meant that he engaged fully in each side of the dialectic, on its own terms. For this book, the focus is on the scientific or humanistic side—on how his interests in data processing, cybernetics, and literary and linguistic analysis contributed to the emergence of at least one important form of humanities computing. Nevertheless, it should be kept in mind that this way of defining the topic necessarily represents only one aspect of this remarkable scholar-priest's work.

Even within my defined topic, the religious aspect of the story is complicated in multiple ways, just considered institutionally. For example, the culture of the Jesuit order has historically characterized itself as facing outward, toward an engagement with the social and material world, often including the worlds of industry and government. The religious order's culture differs fundamentally from the culture of (public or private) secular universities with which Busa also interacted for decades in conducting and presenting his research, not to mention the business and technical cultures with which he was involved. The authority he ultimately recognized was his order and the Church, and he had to seek approval—turning inward to his Jesuit superiors—at every stage of his research career. The Archive illustrates his sense of being held accountable, both to the Jesuit hierarchy and to the worldwide scholarly community. But his sense of mission as outward-facing led him to engage with business, government, technology, and scholarship. The engagement with IBM is therefore representative of this outward turn on the part of the scholar-priest.

When it comes to IBM, I focus in this book on selected parts of the story of the company between 1949 and 1959, not for the sake of business history in itself, but as a way to better understand the material and institutional contexts of the technologies and methods with which Father Busa worked. I'm interested in the way technology—and the culture that produced and marketed it—intersected with and shaped his humanistic research. As the record shows, the influence flowed in both directions. The most important IBMer in the story is not Thomas J. Watson, Sr., or one of his sons, though they authorized and continued to support the collaboration. It's the redoubtable H. Paul Tasman, a senior engineer in charge of a good deal of the nascent World Trade Corporation who became Busa's collaborator and friend until his death in 1988. Near the end of their first decade working together, Busa referred to him as "the ingenieur who was my great friend and the key of all our project [sic]."[22] Indeed, one could argue that Tasman, as much as Busa, helped to found a language-based humanities computing. From the day they met, he served as mediator between the priest and the punched-card machines. Tasman like to use the term "language engineering" to describe their collaborative work, and he may have helped to coin the term "literary data processing," presciently seeing its connection to the emerging field of information retrieval. Twenty years after their first meeting, he characterized his relationship with Busa as a kind of "mixed marriage," by which he seems to have meant a difficult union of two cultures, European and American, surely, but also a union of linguistics and engineering, humanities and computing. In this context, IBM's culture of data processing helped to orient emergent humanities computing, directing it towards the treatment of natural language as a source of data. The consequences of this orientation are still being felt today in the digital humanities, most recently in terms of the implications of so-called big data and the general "datafication" of humanities research.[23]

One subject of this book is in effect the prehistory of these implications, how humanities computing turned toward the processing of data in the first place. In a paper for the 2014 international Digital Humanities conference, Geoffrey Rockwell and Stéfan Sinclair briefly considered Father Busa's work along with other examples of "the period of technology development around mainframe and personal computer text analysis tools, that has largely been forgotten with the advent of the web . . . ."[24] They advocated a media-archaeology approach as a way to question simple narratives of inevitable triumphal progress and to begin to "understand how differently data entry, output and interaction were thought through" in the mainframe era. In this regard, I follow their lead. My account of Father Busa and IBM, and of punched-card machines, large-scale calculators, and related technologies, is influenced by the perspective of media archaeology, shaped by what Lori Emerson has called the "sobering conceptual friction" of that approach.[25]

It's a suggestive coincidence that Siegfried Zielinski's media archaeology includes a close look at the inventions and designs of the Renaissance Jesuit polymath, Father Athanasius Kircher, S.J. (1602–1680), in the context of his worldwide "network of clients and patrons."[26] Much of what Zielinzki says of Father Kircher—"obviously an extremely industrious and gifted communicator"—applies as well to Father Busa, including the role played by Jesuit culture and its infrastructure in determining his use of technology:

> The operating method of the Societas Jesu in the seventeenth century can be described from a media-archaeological perspective as governed by two principles, which were also of decisive importance in Kircher's own work. These principles were the international network of a thoroughly hierarchical and centralistically structured system of religious faith, knowledge, and politics, combined with the development of advanced strategies for the mise-en-scène of their messages, including the invention and construction of the requisite devices and apparatus.[27]

Kircher was a polyglot linguist who studied hieroglyphics and cryptology, and even designed "combinatorial boxes," mechanical calculating machines based on narrow slats of wood on which "units of information" were "inscribed" for recombination[28]—among the many possible early ancestors of Jacquard's and Hollerith's punched-card mechanisms in the nineteenth century, and of twentieth-century punched-card data processing systems like those used by Father Busa. The parallels between Kircher and Busa are not accidental. They grow out of a shared Jesuit culture, even across the differences of three centuries, which encouraged the use of newly invented devices for education and research, and which organized itself into far-flung centers of activity in a worldwide network (as I say in Chapter 4).

In my descriptions of punched-card and computing technology, I apply the related approach known as platform studies, as outlined by Nick Montfort and Ian Bogost for their series at MIT Press (to which I contributed a co-authored book in 2012).[29] Platform studies looks at specific technology platforms in their layered material particulars, examining relationships between hardware, software, interface, human agents, and cultural and historical contexts, at every level. It asks: how do technologies afford and constrain cultural practices and expressions, including in this case academic practices like humanities computing? But also: how are technologies shaped by, selected by, and defined by those practices? Media archaeology, as seen in work by Zielinski, but also by Lori Emerson or Jussi Parikka, for example, can provide a historical frame for the detailed analyses of platform studies. Together, these two complementary approaches inform key moments in my narrative, when I zoom in on machinery in detail, but always with an eye to wider contexts. Technical descriptions of specific platforms in cultural context help to particularize the history of technology, and help to challenge the myths of progress and the simplifications of official histories by calling attention to quirks and discontinuities as well as continuities between past and present, and to the abundant excess of platforms and devices that are excluded by most histories of technology.[30] To be sure, in this book I trace certain continuities, for example, Busa's treatment of verbal texts as data, which has come to the fore again in recent digital humanities work (and in IBM's Watson, for example). But, there are always multiple potential continuities, alternative histories, lines of descent in the history of technology and culture broken by chance or circumstance, which reappear from time to time as seemingly anachronistic or forgotten platforms and methods. Alternative possibilities provide an opportunity for better historical understanding. As Lori Emerson puts it, the goal is not to "seek to reveal the present as an inevitable consequence of the past," but to "describe it as one possibility generated out of a heterogeneous past."[31]

Again, there are multiple possible genealogies for humanities computing and digital humanities. One line runs through film and media studies and includes video games, for example; another can be traced through hypertext theory in the 1990s and electronic literature (the production of scholarly editions or online text archives has been closely connected to this line); still another runs through the social sciences and public history, for example, with their use of maps, graphs, and trees long before they showed up in the analysis of textual corpora. Some lines of descent remain possibilities never fully realized. Alternative genealogies include supposedly outdated technologies that remained available and useable, even shaping developments just outside the spotlight, in lines that are orthogonal to the received story of technological progress but affected it in profound ways.

This is how I view punched-card data systems—with their plug-board setups, clacking machinery, and flurries of perforated rectangular cards—which coexisted for many years with electromechanical calculators and electronic computers, helping to define, delimit, and shape the possibilities for research applications, including humanities research applications like Father Busa's. Because these systems were connected to computers, they have become part of the story of humanities computing. But in many ways, the first decade of humanities *computing* can more accurately be described as an era of humanities *data processing*—in the historically specific sense of that term—which applied to literature and linguistics, for example, the punched-card machines developed for business accounting and tabulating, and adapted for government censuses, defense calculations, archival management, and information processing of all kinds.

Because media archaeology looks at forgotten or discounted technologies (presumed to be superseded by what has come to dominate the present), and replaces a triumphal narrative of technological progress with messier stories, it can check and complement the laser focus of platform studies. Together, they allow for richer, more detailed views of the changing cultural and historical conditions within which technologies emerge and jostle for prominence. This is for me a fruitful approach for understanding the technologies with which Father Busa worked, as well as those from which he swerved away, technologies adjacent to his own program, but which, because of his awareness of them or even through the consequences of ruling them out, affected the trajectory of his research. The emergence of humanities computing in the mid-twentieth century involved many such adjacent possibilities, at various stages. It was never a simple application of the best tools, or a matter of simply solving clearly defined problems. Specific technology platforms, whether they were employed directly or not, afforded and constrained human researchers, institutions, and communities in non-trivial ways. Humanities computing emerged in a complex cultural milieu at the midpoint of the twentieth century. Father Busa himself said that, although he was called by some "the pioneer of the computers in the humanities," there were a number of earlier examples of the idea of mechanizing humanities research. If he is to receive credit, he said, it should be for the hard work of "cultivating the idea." He suggests, "isn't it true that all new ideas arise out of a *milieu* when ripe, rather than from any one individual?"[32] It's a question worth keeping in mind in the case of this researcher so often cited as founding "father" and "pioneer." His work arose out of a milieu of its own, one that was anything but unified or linear in its organization.

The book spans roughly a decade and is organized chronologically, beginning in New York City in November 1949. Chapter 1 tells the story of Father Busa's legendary first meeting with Thomas J. Watson, Sr., CEO of IBM. As I explained above, it's a story often retold (almost always based on the same source, a text by Busa himself), but often with little attention to the contexts or detailed particulars of the visit. I trace Busa's preparations for his first trip to North America, then apply the metaphor of an "exploded view" of the meeting in order to explore the radiating contexts of postwar conditions, transatlantic travel, cultural references (including a poster Father Busa appropriated from IBM that turns out to have military origins), and punched-card technology. I look at the machines in detail, but also in the context of the larger data-processing culture. The result is to complicate the story of the legendary meeting in productive ways.

For Chapter 2 I step back a year, to the creation in 1948 of the IBM SSEC (Selective Sequence Electronic Calculator), a giant room-sized machine that for a short time, just before the more famous UNIVAC, signified "computer" in the public imagination. It was featured in magazine ads and starred in a film, and helped to inspire various cultural representations of computing—which was always part of its point, from IBM's perspective. It provides a useful example, as well, of the role of women in computing, a topic broached here and taken up again in Chapter 4's discussion of Busa's Literary Data Processing Center. The SSEC was on display at 590 Madison Avenue from 1948–1952, the exact years of Busa's initial deal with IBM and the development of his technique of literary data processing (demonstrated at IBM in 1952). Although he wasn't able to use it, Father Busa had to have seen the large-scale calculator working in the IBM showroom during his early visits, and he and Paul Tasman used one of its successors, the IBM 705, in the mid-1950s. The SSEC is an early and vivid example of how what circumstance (and IBM) made available—technologies, material support, even ideas about and representations of computing—constituted the adjacent possible, determining the direction and shape of Father Busa's research, as well as how his research fit into a larger contexts of technology and culture.

Chapter 3 is about the first major humanities computing demonstration, held by Father Busa and Paul Tasman at IBM World Headquarters in June 1952 before an invited audience of academics from a number of institutions and multiple disciplines, as well as representatives from scholarly societies, IBM, and the Church. The event, which I refer to as "the mother of all humanities computing demos," was the climax of the start-up phase of what would turn out to be a multi-decade research program. Only in retrospect has the demo of the punched-card method for literary data processing come to seem quite so historically significant, but it illustrates the importance for Busa's early research of building institutional and social networks, and of what we now call scholarly communications.

Chapter 4 continues the theme of networking, the social and institutional support for Busa's founding of the first Literary Data Processing Center in Gallarate, Italy: CAAL or *Centro per L'Automazione dell'Analisi Letteraria*, in 1956. The center was in reality one node in a dynamic network made up of multiple centers of activity, created and maintained for varying periods. When it comes to understanding the history of humanities computing, these institutional and organizational precedents matter as much any specific technology or method. CAAL was influenced by Jesuit, business, and academic cultures. Industrially organized, it was also conceived of as a laboratory and a training school and production apprenticeship for mostly young women, who worked for two-year stints on scholarships, learning to process the punched cards with IBM machines in exchange for a certificate and help with job placement, including at the new Euratom atomic energy center at nearby Ispra. Another center but of a different kind, Euratom, it turns out, was deliberately connected by Father Busa to his own center (by way of Georgetown University and IBM), in ways that illustrate the complex and ambiguous entanglements and collaborations by which Busa's kind of humanities computing emerged in the Cold War era. The chapter concludes with a look at another key demo by Father Busa, this time at the IBM Pavilion at the World Expo 58 in Brussels, the first major world's fair since the end of World War II. The fair itself provides illuminating contexts for the emergence of humanities computing (though it was not yet called that)—starting with the theme of the Expo, "a new humanism"—out of the technologies, institutions, and cultural representations of the period.

Finally, Chapter 5 focuses on Roberto Busa's and Paul Tasman's collaborative attempt starting in the late 1950s to apply their punched-card indexing methods to the texts of the newly discovered Dead Sea Scrolls. It was an intense and complicated effort that, unlike the *Index Thomisticus*, never resulted in publication—except for papers and presentations on the method itself—and it led Father Busa to what he himself called a "nervous breakdown" in the final year of the decade. I argue, however, that in retrospect this work was important as a process, as a set of experiments in computerized philology. In the 1950s and 1960s Busa repeatedly called for a new philology. The Dead Sea Scrolls work in the late 1950s (and continuing into the early 1960s) shows how a philological approach, the attempt to interpret microscopic materialities of language in relation to broad cultural contexts, more than simply being automated or made more efficient by the introduction of computing, was conceptually re-shaped, becoming an experiment in human–computer collaboration, thus opening up new dimensions for humanities research.

Father Busa began his work in the late 1940s along strictly instrumental lines. The machinery of automation was intended simply to increase the speed and efficiency of indexing. By the end of the 1950s, however, he had begun to speculate more widely about cybernetics and a new philology, and to suggest that computers could prompt (indeed, require) "new thinking" on the part of humanistic researchers, and reveal "new dimensions" in the cultural materials with which they worked. By 2004, he famously declared:

> Humanities computing is precisely the automation of every possible analysis of human expression (therefore, it is exquisitely a "humanistic" activity),

in the widest sense of the word, from music to the theater, from design and painting to phonetics, but whose nucleus remains the discourse of written texts.[33]

Looking closely at the first decade of Father Busa's work provides a better understanding of the mid-century emergence of humanities computing as something more than a merely instrumental or practical application of tools, as a set of institutional arrangements, self-representations, and practices engaging theoretical and methodological questions that remain important today.

A brief word about the place of physical and geographical settings in this book. Buildings and locations are not inert and neutral sites—they're extensions of the institutions and technologies that matter to this story. With that in mind, my research involved paying close attention to where things happened, as part of establishing context for Father Busa's work. So in March 2015, I stood with my guide on the quiet via G. Ferraris in Gallarate, Italy, outside the gate of the building that once housed a small textile factory, and was then converted into the headquarters for CAAL, arguably the first humanities computing center, referred to at the time as a Literary Data Processing Center. We confirmed the address plate (no. 2) and, although scaffolding obscured much of the structure, and the distinctive "sawtooth" roof of factory-floor skylights had been replaced, when the lone construction worker on duty allowed us into the courtyard, I was able to identify the arched windows and decorative brackets under the eaves that I had seen in photographs. The building appeared to have been altered and rebuilt many times over the years, renovated in successive layers. But an old fireplace and tiled floor in the front room showed the building's true age. (Later in 2015, it was demolished.) This was the place where Father Busa organized CAAL at its peak at the end of the 1950s and the beginning of the 1960s, with a sizable team of trainee-operators on the floor, working in long lines to process punched cards containing linguistic data on the *Index Thomisticus*, the Dead Sea Scrolls, and various related projects in humanities computing.

I had come to Milan and Gallarate from New York City, where I was living for the year. Back in New York, I stood in the middle of 116th Street to take a cellphone picture of the building that had housed the Thomas J. Watson Scientific Computing Laboratory at Columbia University in the 1940s, when Father Busa first visited New York. Now Columbia's Casa Hispanica, the tall townhouse stands in sight of the IRT subway stop at the main gate of the university on Broadway. As it happens, I had passed the building every day for years when I was a graduate student in the 1980s. But 65 years ago, a team of scientists, programmers, and keypunch operators worked there to design IBM's SSEC, the Selective Sequence Electronic Calculator, a room-sized machine that had captured the imagination of the public when Busa arrived at IBM World Headquarters for the first time in autumn 1949. The machine was installed in the ground floor showroom at 590 Madison Avenue in Midtown Manhattan, where passersby could watch its tape drives and punched cards and blinking lights operating day and night. Father Busa would have walked past it on his way to his first appointment in that building with the CEO.

While working on this book I spent a good deal of time around that location at the intersection of 57th Street and Madison Avenue. Today IBM only leases space in the imposing building, but it's still known locally for its association with the company. The wedge-shaped glass and steel high-rise replaced an earlier brick and stone skyscraper that stood on the same spot, which was the IBM building that Busa visited. Thanks to photographs in the Busa Archive I know that the watershed demo in 1952 took place in the ground-floor showroom, adjacent to the room that housed the SSEC. One image shows principal guests listening to Paul Tasman (Father Busa stands around the circle to his left), sitting in a circle by the windows at the corner of Madison and 57th. Nowadays, that spot is occupied in the new building by a multistory atrium, a public space containing tall bamboo plants, large sculptures, and a mozzarella bar, standing almost exactly where the circle of chairs were arranged that the summer of 1952. Sitting by the bar in early 2015, I looked up at the "IBM building" towering above me, seeing it through the atrium's glass skylights, arranged in an accordion-fold series of peaks, not unlike the skylit roof of the former textile factory in Gallarate (and like similar "sawtooth" roofs still visible everywhere in the light industrial area outside Milan). Upstairs in IBM's leased office space, I had seen vintage posters on the walls, some of them dating from Father Busa's time in that same geographical location.

On another afternoon I rode the subway up to Fordham University in the Bronx to examine papers in the library's Special Collections (on a previous visit I had found some early correspondence of Father Busa there). Taking a break later, I left the library and walked across the quad to the Jesuit residence where Busa had lived during some of his extended visits to the city. I went around the building to look down the street toward the location of the former "El" stop he would have used to commute into Manhattan to work at IBM headquarters. On my own trip back into Midtown on the subway, I thought about that commute in the early 1950s and the many ways New York and the world in general have changed since then—and how difficult it is sometimes to really understand those changes.

I'm not a historian. But as someone who studies literature of the British Romantic period I'm used to working with 200-year-old texts, both printed books and archival manuscripts, and trying to place them in often elusive historical contexts. Of course specialists in Shakespeare or Medieval literature—not to mention classicists and ancient historians—deal with much older materials. 65 years is a relatively brief period of time in the scheme of things—less than a full lifetime. And yet, it's just long enough for many of the people who knew and worked with Father Busa, who played important roles in the story of his project, to be gone, now. I'm painfully aware of several just-missed opportunities in this regard, starting with the fact that, during my own work in humanities computing and digital humanities over many years I somehow never met Father Busa face to face. In one sense, the mid-twentieth century was only yesterday; in another sense, it was a long time ago, long enough for the losses of history to be felt. We collapse the distance of 65 years in our collective imagination at our peril. It's too easy to forget the strangeness of the technology and methods involved in the earliest years of humanities computing, the period when in fact such work was done without actual computers, when "computer" was still a job description and the dominant platform for calculation and data processing was electromechanical punched-card machinery. My descriptions of buildings and locations and modes of transportation, among the details of biography and history, are meant to place the punched-card platform in a suitably rich context in the first postwar decade, an era further away from our own ideas about computing and humanities computing than we often realize. To reimagine the culture and technology of that mid-century moment calls for self-consciousness about what we are sure to be missing, what we cannot recover, and this is true even for the diminishing number of witnesses who were there at the time.

My work on this book was made possible by a year's leave of absence from Loyola University Chicago, in support of a fellowship at the Advanced Research Collaborative (ARC) of the City University of New York (CUNY) Graduate Center for the academic year 2014–2015. The Director of ARC at CUNY, Professor Donald Robotham, generously supported my research, including trips to Milan to consult the Busa Archive, and encouraged the writing in an atmosphere of collegial interchange. Matthew K. Gold was a warmly supportive colleague at CUNY, despite having extensive commitments of his own, and fellow ARC Fellows Andrew Stauffer and Elizabeth Maddock Dillon, among others, were willing to listen to Busa stories and inspire me in turn with examples of their own work. Invited talks at CUNY, Fordham University, and Columbia University provided smart audiences and challenging questions at just the right time. At Fordham, Micki McGee served as a liaison and host and Patrice M. Kane, Head of Archives and Special Collections, helped me discover early correspondence with Busa. (Back in Chicago, my colleague Thomas Kaminski graciously helped me translate those first Latin letters.) At Columbia, my old stomping ground, Alex Gil invited me to give a talk at the Studio@Butler, but also gamely accompanied me one afternoon into the archives in Butler Library to examine materials related to IBM, the Watson Computing Laboratory, and the SSEC. The earliest research for the book began at Loyola University Chicago with the helpful assistance of Lowell Wyse. It continued during the year with the financial assistance and moral support of the Dean of Loyola's College of Arts and Sciences, Thomas Regan, S.J. (who, along with my English department chair, Professor Joyce Wexler, supported the leave of absence that allowed me to write the book). As I mentioned above, I was greatly aided by Lilian S. Wu of IBM, as well as Dawn Stanford in the IBM Corporation Archives, under the supervision of Jamie Martin, the IBM Corporate

Archivist. At North Carolina State University in Raleigh, NC, I was assisted with the A. Wayne Brooke Papers by Gwyneth A. Thayer, Associate Head and Curator, Special Collections Research Center.

For timely cultural advice, I thank my English department colleague, Mark Bosco, S.J. At CIRCSE, the Università Cattolica del Sacro Cuore in Milan, Dr. Marco Passarotti offered seemingly tireless hospitality, facilitating my research in the Busa Archive and sharing his memories of Father Busa. I'm very grateful to him and to his colleague, Professor Savina Raynaud, Director of CIRCSE, as well as to the patient Archivist and Librarian, Paolo Senna. Others at CIRCSE shared office space or told me stories about Father Busa. (I remember in particular one convivial afternoon of coffee and conversation with Paolo Frasca.) My spring visit to Milan included two side trips to Gallarate, one hosted by Busa's final secretary, Danila Chairati (as I describe above and in Chapter 4), who very kindly drove me to key sites and confirmed details over the phone with Busa's first secretary, Gisa Crosta. Marco Passarotti's initiative and translating over the telephone made this connection possible. For my trip to the Aloisianum in Gallarate I was met at the station and driven to the college by local residents Signor and Signora Passarotti. Once there, I was met by the Archivist, Father Diego Brunello, S.J. As I've said, when I commenced my research, preliminary work in the newly accessioned Busa Archive in Milan had already begun by Julianne Nyhan and Melissa Terras of University College London. Nyhan's interviews with some of Busa's women punched-card operators and her general early reconnaissance of the Archive, both undertaken along with her colleague, Melissa Terras, have been invaluable for my research, as have the regular conversations with Nyhan to share our findings and compare notes.

For their gracious responses to my inquiries, I wish to thank the grandchildren of Paul Tasman, Ms. Amy Sklar and Professor Jordan Nash. Professor Nash shared photos of Paul Tasman's copy of the *Varia Specimina Concordantiarum* inscribed by Father Busa, as well as an interesting letter from Busa to Arthur K. Watson about God's approving the collaboration between the businessman and the priest. I quote from both the inscription and the letter with the permission of Professor Nash. At Routledge, I'm lucky to have been able to work again with Publisher and Editor, Erica C. Wetter, who, with the assistance of Simon Jacobs, made it seem easy (though of course it was not). I also owe a debt to four anonymous peer reviewers for their helpful feedback on the manuscript. Of course, no one I've mentioned here is responsible for any errors or limitations in the book. That responsibility is mine alone.

This project had its origin in the drinks line at a digital humanities conference reception at the University of Nebraska in 2013. Father Busa had recently died and I was discussing his work and its legacy with Stephen Ramsay, a leading digital humanities scholar whose own work can in part be seen as extending what Busa began (as I argue in this book). Waiting for our cocktails, we wondered about the fate of the *Index Thomisticus* punched cards themselves as material objects and historical artifacts, and we speculated about how a curious scholar might get to see them. Just over a year later, on a visit to Milan in October 2014, I was handed a deck of those cards, held one up to the light, and squinted to see if I could make out the pattern of its punched holes. Days later, I began to draft this book.

Notes

1 Roberto Bonzio, "Father Busa, Pioneer of Computing in Humanities with Index Thomisticus, dies at 98," *Forbes*, August 11, 2011, http://www.forbes.com/sites/ robertobonzio/2011/08/11/father-busa-pioneer-of-computing-in-humanities-dies-at-98/#2715e4857a0b23954bc875d0. (Busa was born November 28, 1913; he would have turned 98 in November, 2011.)

2 *Corpus Thomisticum*, http://www.corpusthomisticum.org/wintroen.html.

3 "The Roberto Busa Award Winners," European Association for Digital Humanities, http://eadh.org/awards/busa-award/busa-award-winners.

4 Susan Hockey, "The History of Humanities Computing," in *A Companion to Digital Humanities*, eds. Susan Schreibman, Ray Siemens, and John Unsworth (Oxford: Blackwell, 2004), http://www.digitalhumanities.org/companion.

5 Roberto Busa, "The Annals of Humanities Computing: The *Index Thomisticus*," *Computers and the Humanities* 14.2 (1980), 83–90.

6 Willard McCarty, "What does Turing have to do with Busa?," in *Proceedings of the Third Workshop on Annotation of Corpora for Research in the Humanities* (ACRH-3, December 12, 2013), eds. Francesco Mambrini, Marco Passarotti, and Caroline Sporleder (Sofia: Institute of Information and Communication Technologies, Bulgarian Academy of Sciences, 2013), 1–14; http://www.mccarty.org.uk/essays/McCarty,%20Turing%20 and%20Busa.pdf.

7 Roopika Risam, "Revise and Resubmit: An Unsolicited Peer Review," blog, April 20, 2015, http://roopikarisam.com/2015/04/20/revise-and-resubmit-an-unsolicited-peer-review/. In the post Risam responds to an essay by Adeline Koh, "A Letter to the Humanities: DH Will Not Save You," *Hybrid Pedagogy* (April 19, 2015), http:// www.hybridpedagogy.com/journal/a-letter-to-the-humanities-dh-will-not-save-you/, which she charges with limiting the definition of DH in this narrow way, to Busa and his machines only. The dispute behind these essays includes the question of what counts as the intellectual ancestry and central narrative of digital humanities. I emphatically do *not* claim an exclusive status for Father Busa or his research in this regard. I agree that there are multiple possible alternative narratives or lines of descent for the interdisciplinary practices called digital humanities today, some of them not at all focused on linguistics or the processing of verbal texts.

8 "Jackson Pollock: Is he the greatest living painter in the United States?," *Life*, August 8, 1949, 42–45. Although *Stenographic Figure* remained in the hands of Lee Krasner and only ended up at the Museum of Modern Art decades later, it was shown and admired by Piet Mondrian and others in 1943. See Sue Taylor, "The Artist and the Analyst: Jackson Pollock's 'Stenographic Figure'," *American Art* 17.3 (Autumn 2003), 52–71 (53). An image of the painting is available at the Museum of Modern Art website: http:// www.moma.org/collection/works/79686?locale=en.

9 Letter from Roberto Busa to Joseph Raben, December 10, 1971, and reply from Raben to Busa, January 6, 1972, Busa Archive (Rel. Cult. USA 1 1952).

10 The present-day CIRCSE research center is in effect a descendant of CAAL, the *Centro per L'Automazione dell'Analisi Letteraria* (or, especially later, *Linguistica*): the Center for the Automation of Literary (or Linguistic) Analysis.

11 Frank da Cruz, Columbia University Computing History, http://www.columbia.edu/cu/computinghistory/index.html.

12 Michel Foucault, "Nietzsche, Genealogy, History," in *The Foucault Reader*, ed. Paul Rabinow (New York: Pantheon Books, 1984), 76–100 (81).

13 Melissa Terras, "For Ada Lovelace Day–Father Busa's Female Punch Card Operatives," blog, October 15, 2013, http://melissaterras.blogspot.com/2013/10/for-ada-lovelace-day-father-busas.html; Julianne Nyhan, "What is in the archive of Fr. Roberto Busa S.J. (1913–2011)?," Arche Logos blog, April 29, 2014, http://archelogos.hypotheses.org/127.

14 Copy of letter from Roberto Busa to Arthur K. ("Dick") Watson, October 30, 1960 (personal copy of Professor Jordan Nash), forwarded to Paul Tasman. Quoted by permission of Professor Jordan Nash. See Chapter 3.

15 Vannevar Bush, *Science, the Endless Frontier: A Report to the President* (Washington, D.C.: U.S. Government Printing Office, 1945), http://www.nsf.gov/about/history/vbush1945.htm.

16 Roberto Busa, "L'analisi linguistica nell'evoluzione mondiale dei mezzi d'informazione," in *Almanacco Letterario Bompiani 1962* (Milan: 1962), 103–107; trans. Philip Barras in Marco Passarotti, A. Ciula, and Julianne Nyhan, *One Origin of Digital Humanities: Fr Roberto Busa S.J in His Own Words* (forthcoming, Springer Verlag), 106.

17 Busa, "L'analisi linguistica nell'evoluzione mondiale dei mezzi d'informazione," 106.

18 Busa, "L'analisi linguistica nell'evoluzione mondiale dei mezzi d'informazione," 106.

19 Busa, "L'analisi linguistica nell'evoluzione mondiale dei mezzi d'informazione," 106.

20 The importance of this papal encyclical and the one from 1943 I discuss below as contexts for Father Busa's work was called to my attention by an anonymous peer reviewer, to whom I'm grateful.

21 Busa, "L'analisi linguistica nell'evoluzione mondiale dei mezzi d'informazione," 104.

22 Roberto Busa letter to William Le Saint, S.J., March 16, 1957, Busa Archive (Rel. Cult. 1940, USA tab).

23 Besides self-conscious reflections on data in digital humanities, published or presented in various fora by practitioners working in humanities data analysis, text mining, and visualization—such as Elijah Meeks, Miriam Posner, Geoffrey Rockwell, Scott B. Weingart, and Ted Underwood—see Christine L. Borgman, *Big Data, Little Data, No Data: Scholarship in the Networked World* (Cambridge, MA and London: MIT Press, 2015), esp. Chapter 7; Johanna Drucker on data versus "capta" in "Humanities Approaches to Graphical Display," *DHQ* 5.1 (2011), http://www.digitalhumanities.org/dhq/vol/5/1/000091/000091.html; and Matthew L. Jockers, *Macroanalysis: Digital Methods & Literary History* (Urbana, Chicago, Springfield: University of Illinois Press, 2013). Jockers places his own work in relation to Busa's, especially at the beginning of chapter 3, "Tradition."

24 Geoffrey Rockwell and Stéfan Sinclair, "Past Analytical: Towards an Archaeology of Text Analysis Tools," Digital Humanities 2014 conference, Lausanne, Switzerland, October 7, 2014, http://www.researchgate.net/publication/273449857_Towards_an_Archaeology_of_Text_Analysis_Tools. They cite Sigfried Zielinski in particular, *Deep Time of the Media: Toward an Archaeology of Hearing and Seeing by Technical Means* (Cambridge, MA: The MIT Press, 2008); I would add Jussi Parikka, *What Is Media Archaeology?* (Cambridge, UK: Polity, 2012); and Lori Emerson, *Reading Writing Interfaces: From the Digital to the Bookbound* (Minneapolis: University of Minnesota

Press, 2014)—and more generally Emerson's work at the Media Archeology Lab, http://loriemerson.net/media-archaeology-lab/.

25 Emerson, *Reading Writing Interfaces*, xii.
26 Zielinski, *Deep Time of the Media*, 101–57 (113).
27 Zielinski, *Deep Time of the Media*, 118.
28 Zielinski, *Deep Time of the Media*, 141.
29 Bogost, Ian and Nick Montfort. "Platform Studies," http://platformstudies.com.
30 As pointed out by Sarah Werner and Matthew G. Kirschenbaum, "Digital Scholarship and Digital Studies: The State of the Discipline," *Book History* 17 (2014), https://muse.jhu.edu/journals/bh/summary/v017/17.kirschenbaum.html. Their useful summary of media archaeology (434–38) connects it to the tradition of book history but also emphasizes, as I am doing, its affinity with platform studies.
31 Emerson, *Reading Writing Interfaces*, xiii.
32 Busa, "The Annals of Humanities Computing: The *Index Thomisticus*," 84.
33 Roberto Busa, "Foreword: Perspectives on the Digital Humanities," in Susan Schreibman, Ray Siemens, John Unsworth, eds., *A Companion to Digital Humanities*, http://digitalhumanities.org/companion.

1

PRIEST WALKS INTO THE CEO'S OFFICE

The Meeting between Father Roberto Busa, S.J. and Thomas J. Watson, Sr. of IBM, November 1949

The end of the war with Japan in 1945 was celebrated by one of New York City's signature ticker-tape parades, with people throwing paper generated by stock-ticker machines out of windows on lower Broadway, making flurries of confetti that floated in the canyon of tall buildings and fell onto the street below. Besides those discarded paper tapes—some of which were printed with abbreviated and encoded stock prices that had been sent along telegraph wires—other office paper was thrown out in these parades, for example, piles of tiny rectangles of paper "chads" (or sometimes collectively plural, "chad") from punched cards used in accounting and data-processing machines in the offices along the route. In earlier decades, these offices would have included IBM, the company responsible for those punched cards themselves, which were widely called simply "IBM cards." The chads (inside IBM they were often called "chips") could be collected and sold back to the paper manufacturer. But, according to Thomas J. Watson, Jr., the eldest son of the company's founder, when there was a parade on Broadway, "the clerks would dump some of this stuff out the window," and he recalled that he "loved to throw handfuls" of punched-card chips himself when he got the chance.[1]

Watson's parade memories were located at an early IBM location in down-town New York. By 1938, the company's World Headquarters had shifted up to Midtown, just a few blocks from the Plaza Hotel and Central Park, at 590 Madison Avenue, on the corner of 57th Street. Today, a newer building stands on that corner, but it's still known to many as the IBM building (though the company now only leases space there), a dark-glass 41-story skyscraper with a multistoried atrium at its base. When it opened in 1983 it replaced the earlier IBM World Headquarters, which had stood on that same corner for 45 years. A 1948 photograph of the first stone and brick 20-story building shows an "International Business Machines" marquee across the façade above large metal and glass windows on the first two floors. From the street, passersby could see into the ground floor showroom where a diverse collection of IBM equipment, old and new, was on display. In the 1948 photograph, along with other vehicles parked outside the building, an old-fashioned truck stands double parked, with "ICE" painted in capitals on its side panel. The image of that ice truck is a useful reminder of the uncertain and uneven distribution of new technologies, contrary to popular narratives of inevitable, unitary progress with each new release. Until the middle of the last century, before refrigerators were universal, what we think of as the advanced technology of accounting and calculating machines coexisted with ice boxes and icemen to deliver to them.

Just over a decade after the opening of that building at 590 Madison Avenue, in November 1949, the aging founder of IBM, Thomas J. Watson, Sr., held a brief meeting with a visiting Italian Jesuit priest, Father Roberto Busa, S.J. That meeting in the Chairman's office on the 17th floor wasn't recorded in Mr. Watson's formal datebook. That may be because it was scheduled at the last minute, perhaps based on a phone call, and it may have been fitted in between existing appointments.[2] The 36-year-old priest visiting from Milan (and its vicinity) had been sent to IBM at the suggestion of Professor Jerome Wiesner, director of the Research Laboratory of Electronics at MIT. He had been referred to Wiesner in the first place by Harry J. Krould, Chief of European Affairs at the Library of Congress.[3] Father Busa had come to the U.S. looking for financial and technical support for an ambitious research project. He planned to create a massive concordance to the 13th-century philosophical and theological Latin writings of St. Thomas Aquinas, and he had decided to explore the possibility of using "some type of machinery" to automate the laborious process.[4]

The goal was to make a reference work, but this concordance was more than a simple word list with reference numbers. It was meant to be fully *lemmatized*, eventually to include every word from everything written by St. Thomas (over 10 million words), each word organized according to its multiple forms and the linguistic context in which it appears, grouped according to each base-word or *lemma* (the dictionary entry under which the forms of each word are collected). All 10 million words would be in alphabetical order, grouped according to lemma, all inflected forms grouped together, with the verbal context in which each word occurs noted by page and line number.

For his thesis at the Papal Gregorian University in Rome, Father Busa's research on "The Thomistic Terminology of Interiority," had focused on a linguistic point of departure: the Latin preposition "in" and its meanings in context. The dissertation work, based on the evidence of language, was published in 1949. He had begun by writing out thousands of individual index cards by hand. Between 1946 and 1948, facing the limitations of this method, he had come to suspect that new kinds of "gadgets" (as he would call them later)—for example the kind of calculating and accounting machines normally used in business or government offices—might save enough labor and time to make possible the enormous project he had begun to imagine, an organized index to the entire corpus. Sometime around 1947–1948, as he was completing work on his thesis, he looked into the possibility of support from the Italian office machinery company, Olivetti, and the French company, Bull (the two of which were on the verge of forming a joint company, Olivetti-Bull, in 1949). Probably because of postwar economic conditions in Italy, he decided he would do better to make inquiries in Canada and the U.S., and he began to make arrangements for an overseas journey, in order to meet with scholars and technologists and to explore the possibilities. Although he later emphasized that the main purpose of his trip was to search for useful technology, it's clear from his correspondence that it was also an opportunity to consult with other Thomistic scholars in North America about the feasibility of the planned index and, in a kind of informal preliminary peer review, to determine to what extent there might be support for such work in the international scholarly community. The humanities subject matter and guiding questions of his research, focused on the texts of St. Thomas, were always closely bound up with the search for appropriate technology to aid the research. At every stage, material, practical, and social considerations shaped the pace and form of the project. As a Jesuit, Father Busa first had to gain the permission of his superiors even to make such a long journey, but he also had to work out a plan for funding, a way to finance the trip across the Atlantic and around the States and Canada, a major undertaking for a priest. So he began to network, as we'd now say.

Among the letters of inquiry about the project, the earliest I've seen is an exchange with the President of Fordham University in the Bronx, Father Lawrence J. McGinley, S.J.; it gives a sense of the terms on which Father Busa was able to make the trip.[5] The first letter of May 19, 1949, states his "need to travel to America to visit the centers for Thomistic studies, whether in the States or in Canada. I am doing preparatory work for a project on the text of St. Thomas." With the permission of his superiors, Busa says, he has secured financial support from a wealthy family from the area in the textile industry, in the person of Mrs. Lucia Ferrario (née Crespi), from the town of Busto Arsizio, near Milan, who wishes to send her young son, Giulio Ferrario, on a supervised trip abroad. The letter bluntly spells out the terms of the arrangement—"A rich family here will provide me with the money I need for travel and for my stay as long as I bring with me their 15 year old son"—and asks Father McGinley for information on possible vacation rentals or summer camps where the boy might spend two months beginning in July, interacting with other boys his own age, playing sports and practicing his English, which until then he had learned only from books. He's to be chaperoned by Father Busa, who needs a separate place to stay nearby and who says that he too intends to spend those summer months learning English. The letter to his fellow Jesuit is in Latin. The Crespi-Ferrario family is "willing to undertake even large expenses as long as the experience contributes to their son's physical and spiritual well-being. A place directed by our Order (or at least one in which we have the care of souls) would be desirable," Father Busa explains to his fellow priest.

Decades later, Busa's own accounts mention Giulio Ferrario's supervision as the occasion for his own first trip to America, but these letters give us a sense of the particulars involved, and provide unequivocal evidence of the social and financial arrangements on which the scholar's own intellectual program depended. "Afterwards, when the young man has become familiar with the language and the customs and can be left alone at school or with a family, I will be able to begin my journey in pursuit of my own ends," the letter concludes. His own goals were already clear—the ends, if not yet the means: the "preparatory work for a project on the text of St. Thomas." Their pursuit would be possible only through the cultivation of a social network on two continents (and eventually worldwide), the usual intellectual and academic networks required for any scholarship but with something additional—a collaboration with business and its multinational resources, both technical support and hardware, as we'd now say, donated or borrowed wherever possible, which Busa saw as necessary for the long-term collaborative work. It's unlikely he knew the full scope and difficulty of the task he was facing when he began,[6] but he clearly understood the essential components: intensive textual data—marked, sorted, and re-organized records of the words in the corpus—along with some kind of mechanization for processing all that data, including the ability to machine-print pages of the concordance as output (a non-trivial matter at the time, we may need to remind ourselves).

Father Busa and young Ferrario sailed from Genoa in July 1949, although by then the plans had shifted a bit, since his patrons for the journey, the boy's family, preferred to accept another invitation from a Jesuit in Canada, as Busa wrote to Father McGinley on July 5. So it would seem that they arrived at a port in Canada and a little later crossed the border into the U.S., probably by rail. Father Busa promises to write to Father McGinley once they arrive in Toronto: "I shall greatly be in need of Your Reverence's help and advice in achieving the purpose of my journey, of which I will inform Your Reverence" (after the arrival in Toronto). Their exact itinerary between July and November 1949 remains obscure. But according to Father Busa's own later account, he traveled around by train, visiting many North American universities, "from coast to coast," as he said, as well as government agencies in Washington, D.C., such as the Library of Congress.[7] At any rate, a map of his travels in the final months of 1949 would sure be heavily marked. The correspondence suggests a flurry of trips and plans for trips in November and December. In one exchange he mentions a planned visit to St. Louis University for two days only, December 1 and 2, 1949.[8] He did indeed contact numerous centers of Thomistic studies and visited some of them, to explain his plans for an index and sound out the support such a project might have. He joined the American Philological Association in November and, along with his membership card, received from the Secretary the usual materials, including a list of

APA publications, an invitation to contribute to the bibliography, and a copy of the Proceedings with a full list of the membership, which gave him an important set of professional contacts.[9]

Besides meeting scholars in philology, theology, classics, and linguistics, Busa also examined a range of potentially useful machines. He doesn't seem to have made a clear distinction between the two kinds of inquiries: both were necessary for his relatively unprecedented research program. For example, he spoke with Frank H. Towsley, an inventor of a cataloguing and retrieval system based on photographic micro-cards. In a letter from Italy on May 11, 1951, he alludes to the earlier discussion, mentions the limitations of the system and offers to help Towsley seek a patent attorney in Milan, even perhaps a manufacturer, and says that he has discussed it with contacts at the Vatican Library.[10] It's a small but significant example of a common thread in Father Busa's work over the decades: his hands-on interest in basic engineering, the nuts and bolts of technologies that might be useful to scholarship. A better-known example is the machine called the Microfilm Rapid Selector, which he saw in operation at the Department of Agriculture in Washington, D.C. in November 1949 (I'll have more to say below about that machine).

By the end of the year, when he wasn't traveling, he established a kind of home base at Fordham University: whether or not he actually stayed there on that first visit, he certainly did in later years, and by late November 1949 he was receiving mail there, care of the Jesuit Father Provincial on Fordham Road in the Bronx; within a few years his standard New York address would become the Jesuit residence on campus, 501 East Fordham Road.[11] Sometime in November, probably under pressure from the looming deadline for his return to Italy, Father Busa was able to arrange a meeting with the founder and CEO of IBM, the world's dominant supplier of data-processing equipment.

How did the meeting come about? It seems likely to have started with a series of referrals, introductions, and references, first from within the Church, beginning with Robert I. Gannon, S.J., retired president of Fordham University, who made the connection to Francis Cardinal Spellman of New York, who in turn recommended or formally introduced Busa to IBM; one account suggests that the referral to IBM came from MIT.[12] At any rate, the trail of referrals included Italian industrialists, extended to American universities, clerical figures, a government library, and, finally, the corporation itself (with its own fledgling university lab)—a trajectory across the institutions that began and ended with his own Jesuit order and the Roman Catholic Church. Decades later it would come to seem like fate, the origin of humanities computing; for Father Busa of course it was providential. But the record shows how far he flung the nets, how many miles he traveled, how many letters he wrote, and how many visits he made in order to achieve that "fateful" meeting, treated later as a key event but clearly dependent on hard work and chance, the material contingencies of time, place, and available resources. The surviving correspondence and published accounts read in relation to that correspondence reveal just how uncertain and provisional the prospects for that initial meeting must have been. IBM's support remained for a brief time just one possibility among others for the implementation of his plan to automate the work of index building.

Here is Father Busa's own account of the meeting at 590 Madison Avenue, published over thirty years later:

> I knew, the day I was to meet Thomas J. Watson, Sr., that he had on his desk a report which said that IBM machines could never do what I wanted. I had seen in the waiting room a small poster imprinted with the words: "The difficult we do right away; the impossible takes a little longer," (IBM always loved slogans). I took it with me into Mr. Watson's office. Sitting in front of him and sensing the tremendous power of his mind, I was inspired to say: "It is not right to say 'no' before you have tried." I took out the poster and showed him his own slogan. He agreed that IBM would cooperate with my project until it was completed "provided that you do not change IBM into International Busa Machines." I had already informed him that, because my superiors had given me time, encouragement, their blessings and much holy water, but unfortunately no money, I could recompense IBM in any way except financially. That was providential![13]

Priest walks into the CEO's office: it sounds like the beginning of a joke.[14] And there were jokes exchanged by both parties before it was over, but this 1980 account of the late 1949 meeting (which must have seemed relatively insignificant to IBM at the time), has come to be widely treated as the founding myth of humanities computing and the digital humanities. The purpose of this book is to complicate the myth with history, to demythologize Busa's work through an attention to the human story in context—starting with that initial meeting—in order to understand what happened, but also how what happened has been constructed as the origin story of humanities computing.

I want to pause for a moment on the scene of that meeting. Father Busa, a crewcut 36-year-old Italian priest with limited English, was sent into the spacious office of Thomas J. Watson, Sr., at 75, one of the world's most famous industrialists. Watson was presumably sitting at his wooden desk with an iconic "THINK" sign mounted high on the wall, an icon that had been his own invention and was ubiquitous at IBM locations around the world, translated into many languages. I imagine freezing that scene, forensics-style, as in the special effects of TV shows and film, or better: like the exploded-view diagrams used by engineers and patent attorneys (sometimes today produced in computer assisted design software, in interactive 3D form). This kind of drawing shows the parts of a device or system as if blown apart and suspended, so that each component can be clearly seen and understood in relation to the whole. Everyone's familiar with this kind of diagram from instruction sheets for assembling Ikea furniture or Lego blocks.

Appropriately enough, this kind of exploded view is often said to descend from Father Busa's fellow Milanese, Leonardo da Vinci, whose notebooks are full of such drawings illustrating his speculative inventions.

In the imagined exploded view, every detail of that meeting is rich with meaning. Like the labels on a diagram, each detail is surrounded by a cloud of implied questions and connections radiating out to wider contexts: the IBM site at 590 Madison Avenue; its relation to the new laboratory uptown at Columbia University; the network of Church, government, and academic contacts and collaborators that Father Busa had to activate in order to get to the meeting in the first place and to continue the research for decades afterwards; his Jesuit scholar's background and history; the American company's own history; New York City and Milan in 1949; institutional forces, postwar technology, nascent multinational capitalism, the emergent Cold War, with its competing technologies and propaganda; what Dwight Eisenhower—then President of Columbia University (thanks in large part to the support of Mr. Watson) and soon to be President of the U.S.—would in his farewell address of 1961 name the "military–industrial complex"; the troubled relationship between science and the humanities in the postwar period, examples of what would come to be characterized as "the two cultures"; and, more concretely, machines—punched-card machines, paper tape, magnetic tape, vacuum tubes, the whole complicated, ripe moment of transition from accounting and tabulating machines and calculators to stored-program computers at the midpoint of the twentieth century. All of that makes up the multilayered context—at different scales, from telling detail to larger historical sweep, what has been called the long zoom[15]—within which to understand the birth of humanities computing. It was barely noticed at the time, even within the academy. And it was never merely an academic event. It was a set of opportunistic responses to changes in technology and (linked to those) changes in the larger culture.

The story of Father Busa as pioneer of humanities computing isn't the only possible genealogy for humanities computing and the digital humanities. Willard McCarty, recipient of the 2013 Roberto Busa Award from the Alliance of Digital Humanities Organizations, reminds us that, while Busa remains an "intellectual father-figure," there from the beginning of humanities computing, "[t]here are other beginnings on offer."[16] There are indeed alternative genealogies, other possible lines of descent besides computational text analysis; for example, there are lines running through film studies, "new media studies, postcolonial science and technology studies, and digital [and quantitative] research on race, gender, class, and disability and their impact on cultures around the world,"[17] not to mention the kind of information and library science in which Father Busa and his collaborator at IBM, Paul Tasman, were interested. It's important to continue to explore these and other alternative histories. But the story of the meeting of the priest and the CEO in 1949 has been highly influential, often retold (usually paraphrasing Father Busa's own later accounts) with little attention to its wider resonances and cultural implications. My imagined exploded view is meant to call attention to those resonances and implications, to begin to paint a more complex picture and provide a more critical understanding of that meeting and what it signifies, including its later use as a founding myth.

Again, every detail in the imagined exploded view has a history. Take the seemingly trivial detail of that poster. Father Busa says he carried it into the executive office and it carries the burden of persuasion in his story. He uses it in a Socratic way to turn Mr. Watson's words back on himself, with the gently sardonic aside, "IBM always loved slogans," as we imagine him sitting in the office looking up at the CEO's "THINK" sign, the famous one-word slogan for the company. The small poster, we are told (probably printed as a flyer or even on a handheld card), read: "The difficult we do right away; the impossible takes a little longer." It sounds like a familiar kind of workplace motivational cliché (as it presumably was). But it too has a history. Just a few years before the meeting you could have seen it everywhere in the European and Asian theaters of war. It's the motto of the Seabees, for "CB" or Construction Battalions of the U.S. Navy, an engineering group created early in World War II for building airstrips and bridges and roads. The Seabees are famous for their engineers' "'can do' philosophy," *their* official slogan, and for the slogan on Father Busa's appropriated poster, as well, which is so closely associated with the group that a version of it is engraved on their national memorial at Arlington: "The Difficult We Do At Once, The Impossible Takes A Bit Longer."[18]

This is a typical engineer's perspective, really, marking the gap between user expectations and the more skeptical view of specialists whose work is in demand. A recent stick-figure XKCD cartoon, for example, a favorite web comic among technology specialists, shows a ponytailed programmer sitting at a computer and being asked for an app that would check the location of a photographer, noting "whether they're in a national park." She replies, "Sure, easy GIS lookup. Gimme a few hours." " . . . and check whether the photo is of a bird," the questioner adds, provoking the response: "I'll need a research team and five years." As the caption says, "In CS [computer science], it can be hard to explain the difference between the easy and the virtually impossible."[19]

In 1949, the slogan about doing the (virtually) impossible versus the merely difficult would inevitably have carried with it the context of the war, still, and in that meeting, one has to imagine, it would also have reinforced the already-present context of the relationship between Italy and the U.S. during the period of reconstruction and the Marshall Plan. Though prompted by my imagined exploded view, this requires no stretch of the imagination. On the contrary, it's a *de*contextualized and "timeless" (or presentist) interpretation of the slogan, as if it were merely an inspirational cliché, or even *merely* a harbinger of today's techno-solutionism, that would be forced (though I believe the slogan does foretell that latter ideology, too, if in a subtly different sense, as I'll explain in the next chapter). More immediately, the slogan would have invoked the war and its troubled aftermath. The seat of Mussolini's government, Milan was a target of heavy Allied attacks, as any visitor today knows—the city still bears the scars of bombings. Milan was also the heart of the Resistance movement and what amounted to civil warfare that expanded after 1943.[20] Decades later, Father Busa himself invoked these contexts in telling the story of his research program. He said that he spent the final years of the war primarily concerned with "philosophy and philosophical texts," while he was "surrounded by bombings, Germans, partisans, poor food and disasters of all sorts." But in fact he was rather more closely embedded in the conflict than this makes it sound. He was an auxiliary chaplain in the Italian Army and then, after 1943, like so many others, served with the Partisan Resistance. Just days after Busa first wrote to Father McGinley about coming to America (May 19, 1949), the anniversary of Italy's Liberation Day—or Anniversary of the Resistance—on April 25, 1946, was recognized by law as a national holiday.

IBM had its own disturbing wartime history, including as we now know the use of its punched-card machine systems—already in place in Germany since the days of Herman Hollerith and established in the IBM subsidiary, Dehomag, by the 1930s—by the Nazis to enhance the censuses and tracking that enabled, or at least made more efficient, the Holocaust.[21] Indeed, T. J. Watson, Sr. had received awards from both Hitler and Mussolini for his internationalist economic policies in the decade leading up to the war.[22] Racial and religious data had been included in census-taking for decades already, and the persecution of Jews made use of conventional lists as well as punched-card tracking, but it's true nonetheless that IBM's mechanized efficiencies accelerated the reach and pace of the violence. And IBM equipment was fully integrated into the German government due as much to IBM's business decisions as to appropriations by the regime. Thomas J. Watson, Sr. had openly called for cooperation with Hitler's Germany early on, and in 1937, the American chief executive traveled to Berlin for an International Chamber of Commerce ceremony where he received a medal from the Nazis. He returned the medal in June 1940. After the U.S. went to war in 1941, IBM in New York lost financial control of the German subsidiary, but IBM continued to do business with it through its other European subsidiaries, including delivering supplies of punched cards. IBM also supplied the U.S. military during the war, and promoted a policy of receiving no more than 1% profit from U.S. military contracts.[23]

IBM's was not a unique case when it came to doing business with Nazi Germany or Fascist Italy, but the example of its involvement is historically significant for its extent and persistence, under shifting relations with local European subsidiaries, and even in the face of evidence for atrocities. Because of the company's history and reach, it's a particularly vivid example of the logic of global capital, the way claims of amorality or neutrality can serve to justify entanglements with immoral actors and regimes. In fact, IBM did business with everyone it could during and after the war—that was the practice called for by its internationalism. The U.S. military relied heavily on IBM systems, too, for everyday payroll as well as more sophisticated ordnance-trajectory calculations. Thomas J. Watson, Jr. recalls seeing punched-card machines late in the war, brought into combat zones in the Pacific on Army trucks as mobile data processing centers.[24] The business in Germany in the early 1930s had been propelled in the first place by the notion of the supreme value of commerce, and of trade, which supported a kind of European common market created a decade before the fact, to the continuing benefit of IBM,[25] supported by the ideology expressed in another favorite motto of Thomas J. Watson Sr.'s: "World Peace Through World Trade." The motto predated the war, and Watson seems to have been a sincerely dedicated internationalist. A plaque inscribed with the phrase was mounted on the World Headquarters at 590 Madison Avenue when it was constructed in 1938. Between the date of the plaque, 1938, and the 1949 visit by Father Busa, however, the war had altered the connotations attached to the slogan. The economic, diplomatic, and cultural internationalism was in 1949 in the process of mutating into a new kind of multinational global enterprise. On a practical level, this meant recovering and making use of wartime assets and resources wherever possible, and shoring up ties with Europe where they had been tested during the conflict. When in 1946 the European demand for machines became evident, and IBM found it difficult to deliver new machines due to postwar shortages and import restrictions, it began selling "as-is" equipment, decommissioned punched-card machines from the U.S. military—"some with the mud of the battlefield still on them"—that were refurbished in European plants.[26] Even a brief meeting with an Italian Jesuit priest about his speculative research project (involving medieval Latin texts, of all things) might have seemed, or come to seem after the meeting and subsequent discussions, like a kind of fruitful diplomatic "outreach" putting to work essentially surplus equipment, and in that capacity might have seemed a potentially valuable contribution, however small, to IBM's larger postwar strategy in both Europe and the U.S.

One motivating factor Edward Vanhoutte puts directly: after the war, companies were "prospecting for new markets. . . . This is why key players like Remington Rand and IBM teamed up with humanities scholars and funded conferences and projects that explored new applications of computing."[27] Only months before the meeting with Father Busa, IBM had created as a wholly owned subsidiary its World Trade Corporation, first at the 590 Madison Avenue headquarters but eventually (in summer 1954) placed under the direction of Watson's second son, Arthur K. ("Dick") Watson and moved to a separate headquarters at 807 United Nations Plaza, across from the UN Headquarters. (The UN had been established as an organization, with Watson Sr.'s support, in 1945, and the New York headquarters was completed in 1952; the cornerstone was laid in October 1949, just a month before the meeting between Busa and Watson.) The creation of the World Trade Corporation, with Dick Watson set to lead it, was part of a general shift at the top of the company in 1949, with Watson, Sr. elected Chairman of the Board in order to make way for Watson, Jr. to become Executive Vice President (and President three years later).

The existence of the brand-new World Trade Corporation is another likely motivating factor for IBM's agreeing to support the Italian scholar's project. It was to World Trade that Father Busa was sent after the meeting with Watson Sr. There he met his assigned collaborator at IBM, Paul Tasman, who was newly in charge of engineering in IBM World Trade. Thus a decades-long collaboration was established, conducted under the aegis of that organization. Tasman's Associated Press obituary in 1974 was dominated by a summary of his work with Busa, saying that he "spent nearly 30 years helping to prepare a computerized index of the writings of St. Thomas Aquinas." In 1968, just before retiring, Tasman recalled in an extended interview for IBM's oral history project that he believed the company expected him to dismiss Father Busa in 1949, whatever Watson had told the priest in their meeting: "I believe that the company expected me to shake hands with the Jesuit and things would disappear."[28] But, Tasman jokes,

> If you have dealt with Jesuits in the past, they don't just disappear. He had a tenacity of purpose on this thing and a mission to accomplish and the result was that he wasn't going away without at least an answer or at least some indication that an answer could be or could not be forthcoming.[29]

An agreement was reached and experiments were begun. But the historical forces behind the meeting were larger and more complex than might first appear, and they involved IBM's shifting relations with Europe during the postwar period—including perceptions about its business in Europe and, practically speaking, its ability to repurpose outdated or surplus machines freed up after 1945. On Father Busa's side, the forces at work included what seems to be his canny, if limited, understanding of those contexts, as well as his grasp of the potential resources and opportunities.

One additional anecdote, here, will suggest the complicated historical and cultural contexts. In the summer of 1947, Thomas Watson, Jr., the eldest son of the founder, just back from the war and within five years of taking over as President of IBM, went on a management junket (Watson, Jr., 1990, loc. 2410–14).[30] One of the two cars they used was a Cadillac that had been dismantled at IBM France during the invasion of Paris and hidden in a basement from the Nazis, then welded together again after the liberation. Watson and another executive, with their two wives and the head of operations in Brazil, Valentim Fernandes Bouças, drove across Europe inspecting the state of IBM facilities and equipment in the wake of the war. At one point they reached what Watson describes only as "a poor town near Milan." Bouças pranked the locals, telling them that Watson's wife was a famous movie star from New York. An excited crowd gathered around the Cadillac asking for autographs. At this distance, the story is like a movie cliché, with uncomfortable reminders of American privilege and cultural condescension.

The scene is an emblem of the postwar situation in Italy, the dramatic inequality of resources—of wealth and power—between America and Europe, highlighted by reconstruction efforts that would in 1948 be codified as the Marshall Plan for "European Recovery." The anecdote is reminiscent of darkly comic scenes in neorealist films from the same period, *Miracle in Milan* (1951), say, or *Rome, Open City* (1945): the American-based entourage on the streets of a "poor" town, the naive crowd, eager for contact with Hollywood, behind them the ruins of bombed-out buildings.

Father Busa was away in Spain at the time, in the final stages of his Jesuit training, but this encounter happened somewhere near his home base in Gallarate, also a town near Milan, and only two years before he was to travel to New York on his own reconnaissance mission, culminating in the meeting with the father and CEO, Thomas J. Watson, Sr. A small-world coincidence, to be sure, the incident is also a reminder of the global connections IBM already had and was working to shore up after the war, just as Busa was negotiating his own relationship with the company. IBM had been deeply involved in Italy for decades, and especially in Milan, where there was a national headquarters and a manufacturing plant. This involvement accelerated rapidly during the postwar period. Seen from a wider perspective, the timing of Father Busa's visit to IBM World Headquarters in New York was no accident. It could hardly have come very much before that moment. The late 1940s were full of such transatlantic agreements, on varying scales. The company's willingness to support a small project like Busa's was surely part of a larger program for its new World Trade Corporation, with potential benefits for public relations and for strengthening ties with Milan (and, for that matter, possibly with the Vatican). IBM obviously needed to set relationships with Italy on a firm footing after the war, and even a small alliance of this sort would have made a kind of business sense quite apart from profitability. For the first few years, Busa worked mostly at IBM Italia in Milan; it would have cost the company little to allow the scholar-priest to use what was to some degree surplus machinery, even with the addition of technical support. Without knowing that it would continue for decades, of course, IBM would likely have seen Busa's project as an easy-enough investment to make at the time, and one with a kind of philanthropic value, besides.

That telling detail in the imagined exploded view of the meeting, the poster with the slogan borrowed from the American military about doing the "impossible," is marked by these wider contexts. Father Busa's comments in the meeting, "it is not right to say 'no'" and "IBM always loved slogans," are perhaps more pointed—at least, they're much more contextually rich—than has been realized. When I first visited the Center for Interdisciplinary Computerization of Research in the Signs of Expression (CIRCSE) in Milan in October 2014, I happened to see posted on a bulletin board a printout of a quotation attributed to Seneca: "Non é perché le come sono difficult che noi non osiamo; é perché non osiamo che le cose sono difficili" ("It's not because things are difficult that we do not dare; it's because we do not dare that things are difficult"). I was told that the motto had been posted there, in the center where Father Busa had worked, for as long as anyone could remember. In the context of the work he did and the story of his meeting at IBM, it's at least an interesting philological coincidence, the kind of classical epigram that the Seabees motto about doing the difficult and the impossible seems to echo.

Even doing the possible is contingent on what's available. It means exploiting what Steven Johnson has called the "adjacent possible" (borrowing and loosely adapting the more specialized use of the term by evolutionary biologist Stuart Kaufman).[31] Like invention, research and discovery, whether in science or the humanities, depend on the exploitation of adjacent possibilities and ideas, but also on models and provocations in relevant published research, as well as material resources, including personnel, funding, machinery, and other equipment. This is not a matter of inevitable "progress" in methods and technologies. Pathways through adjacencies can take researchers in many different directions, some of them turning out to be "stubs" or apparent dead ends in terms of later developments. But even those historical pathways can affect practical research and the theories around it in unexpected ways. Once we acknowledge the affordances and constraints of cultural and material conditions, we can see that any number of adjacent possibilities exist at any given juncture, providing latent alternative genealogies for research practices and even for fields and disciplines.

Thomas J. Watson, Sr.'s joke about not renaming the company "International Busa Machines" (with a partial pun on the first three letters of "Business") reminds us that access to those expensive-to-rent machines was the driving purpose of the visit. At every stage, the search for useful and interesting machines drove work on the *Index Thomisticus* (and related projects it helped to spawn). Postwar surplus inventory at IBM afforded greater access than would have been possible just a few years earlier.[32] Paul Tasman would later admit the extent to which mere availability shaped the technological designs of his research with Father Busa. In at least one case, the team was able to use a particular model of machine precisely because it had become difficult for IBM to rent it to commercial customers, in this case because it was too flexible and therefore too complex for users.[33] It required too much on-site technical support for programming and operation. Idle and thus available, it was an adjacent possibility for the priest and the engineer's earliest experiments. At every stage, over the ensuing thirty years, Busa's work was a bootstrap process, as Tasman later said.[34] Available machines were used to move the project to a new stage, where other newly available machines could be employed to take it further. And there were always paths not taken. Father Busa was acutely aware of technical possibilities just out of reach toward which he aspired, but there were also several technologies that he investigated and turned away from.

A vivid example is the Microfilm Rapid Selector that he saw working in November 1949 at the Department of Agriculture in Washington, D.C. It was based on an experimental design by Vannevar Bush at MIT in 1940 for an automated information retrieval system, the memex, as described in Bush's famous 1945 essay, "As We May Think."[35] The hypothetical memex is essentially a desk or workstation with a built-in motorized microfilm reader, where a vast library of documents could be very rapidly searched and viewed. Interestingly, the essay begins by raising the question of what scientists should do next, now that the war is over. The answer, for Bush, is to turn to data. The challenge is to radically improve "methods of transmitting and reviewing the results of research," of following links and associations in the "growing mountain" of scientific information: "The summation of human experience is being expanded at a prodigious rate, and the means we use for threading through the consequent maze to the momentarily important item is the same as was used in the days of square-rigged ships."[36] The record of human knowledge has to be extended, stored, and rendered easy to consult, and new technology seems ripe for the task, now that "the world has arrived at an age of cheap complex devices of great reliability; and something is bound to come of it." The availability of new technology leads to the focus on what it does best: manage data.

Bush proposes that microphotography and facsimile reproduction are key technologies for addressing the problem, and mentions as an example of mechanized inscription the "punched-card machines long ago produced by Hollerith for the census, and now used throughout business. Some types of complex businesses could hardly operate without these machines." For his general readership Bush sums up the future of computing, "advanced arithmetical machines" that "will be electrical" and much faster than those available among 1945's "mechanisms and gadgetry." Because they will be "far more versatile" (he is likely thinking of applied versions of the universal Turing machine), they will be "readily adaptable for a wide variety of operations."

> They will be controlled by a control card or film, they will select their own data and manipulate it in accordance with the instructions thus inserted, they will perform complex arithmetical computations at exceedingly high speeds, and they will record results in such form as to be readily available for distribution or for later further manipulation. Such machines will have enormous appetites. One of them will take instructions and data from a whole roomful of girls armed with simple key board punches, and will deliver sheets of computed results every few minutes. There will always be plenty of things to compute in the detailed affairs of millions of people doing complicated things.[37]

That last sentence sounds like a harbinger of the surveillance state to come because its premise is the ubiquity of data and data-processing machinery. Bush's imagined memex is an extension of these improvements in scale and efficiency, for augmenting "repetitive processes of thought," which, by analogy with a mathematician using a calculator, should be "turn[ed] over to" a "mechanism."

And this mechanism should allow for sorting and retrieval of information by way of trails of association. The memex's library contains all sorts of knowledge: "[b]ooks of all sorts, pictures, current periodicals, newspapers," not just numbers but natural-language documents. The contents must be indexed, so that the operator can access them directly or by way of a "mesh of associative trails." Among the imagined users Bush cites patent attorneys, physicians, and historians, not just scientists. In this way, "science may implement the ways in which man produces, stores, and consults the record of the race."

The memex is often said to foreshadow the World Wide Web. But in the more immediate scale, we see that it was a product of its own time, the era of data processing and punched-card systems, with a sense of electronic calculators then emergent. Competing devices were being imagined in the late 1940s that extended the achievements of the wartime calculating machines used to crack codes and calculate weaponry, to more general and more broadly humanistic arenas. But accounting machinery was still at the heart of the imagined future. Technologies of information retrieval were already in the mid-twentieth century conceived as potentially serving the needs of humanities research, and Father Busa's complex index of a large natural-language corpus was among these conceptions. It's no surprise, therefore, that he took seriously the possibility of using the Microfilm Rapid Selector. The machine was developed in 1948–1949 by Engineering Research Associates and Ralph Shaw, Director of Libraries for the U.S. Department of Agriculture. As I've said, it owed much to Bush's 1940 prototype for the memex—which in turn was preceded by a design for an optical reader by Emanuel Goldberg in Germany in the 1920s.[38] In the Rapid Selector, a fast strobe light allowed for capturing document images quickly while the film was scanned, and a system of dots like the pattern of punched holes on a punched card (in fact derived from annotations made with punched cards), was linked to the documents, allowing for automated optical recognition by photoelectric sensors during scanning.

Father Busa mentions the Rapid Selector in the *Varia Specimina Concordantiarum*, explaining why he had first considered it and then decided it was not suitable for his purposes.[39] "Its principal feature is the whirlwind speed with which it explores the reels of microfilm—10,000 photograms per minute—and instantaneously rephotographs on another microfilm strip all and only those photograms which bear a determined item," he says.[40] The chief problems were that it didn't allow for automatic printing of the results, that it required the use of photosensitive paper, and, perhaps most damning, that it required prohibitively expensive hand encoding of every word in the massive text.[41] It's also likely that the limited number of such machines (there was really only the one prototype), the matter of practical availability, played a role in Busa's decision to turn to the more traditional punched-card system instead, making the Rapid Selector an adjacent possibility away from which Busa swerved.

Both the microfilm system and punched cards involved encoding language in order to facilitate processing it. Significantly, the Rapid Selector applied a kind of "standoff" metadata layer to whole documents captured photographically in their print forms, a separate series of patterned dots running alongside the micro-photographed texts, the encoding to be read by the photosensitive machine. Despite the visual resemblance and shared conceptual origins of the different printed dot or punched-hole encoding systems on the film or on paper cards, the punched-card system did something different: it "atomized" the Latin text of St. Thomas, as Stephen Ramsay describes it, dissolving it into its constituent words, de-forming the text in order to apply algorithmic instructions for re-constituting it in new forms.[42] The "founding moment" of humanities computing, as Ramsay puts it, "was the creation of a radically transformed, reordered, disassembled, and reassembled version of one of the world's most influential philosophies . . . ."[43] The intellectual result, however, was potentially like the goal described by Vannevar Bush: to reveal new meshes of association, patterns of meaning otherwise inaccessible to unassisted human readers.

By early 1950 Busa was back in Italy and conducting a letter-writing campaign, soliciting references in his support to be sent directly to IBM. He had clearly decided against using the microfilm-based Rapid Selector in favor of the punched-card data processing system. He had already by then made arrangements to return to New York later that year for proof-of-concept experiments with IBM, "the most important" of the three large companies making and vending such systems (with Remington Rand and the French Bull, soon to form Olivetti-Bull in Italy).[44] By July, he (or someone acting on his behalf) had placed a brief prospectus-announcement in *Speculum*, the journal of the Medieval Academy of America, stating his intention to pursue an index to the works of St. Thomas and soliciting suggestions from the scholarly community.[45] It specifies that the planned work will have two parts: a file of thirteen million cards (which must have got the attention of readers of the announcement!), and "indices and concordances to be drawn from such a file." Each card is to contain a specific word from the lexicon of St. Thomas, below which will be a reference to its location with a contextual sentence. Already Busa has in mind the need for some kind of automation, briefly remarking (in the odd third-person style of the prospectus, an indication perhaps that it was translated and submitted by someone else) in a concluding comment that "Father Busa has been in contact with IBM in New York, the RCA laboratories in Princeton, the Library of Congress and the Library of the Department of Agriculture, in Washington."[46]

From July 13, 1950 to November 30, 1950, he was back in New York "for research at IBM."[47] The research involved first using as a testbed texts by Dante and St. Thomas. Working with Tasman and others, including at IBM Italia in Milan after his return in late 1950, Father Busa established a basic procedure for building the *Index* using punched cards. He was able to publish the results of these experiments as a kind of pamphlet in August 1951, with a parallel text in Italian and translated into English, *Sancti Thomae Aquinatis Hymnorum Ritualium, Varia*

Specimina Concordantiarum: A First Example of Word Index Automatically Compiled and Printed by IBM Punched Card Machines. After an introduction reviewing the field of concordance-making and explaining his own search for appropriate technology, Father Busa describes in technical detail the "first series of experiments carried out with electronic accounting machines operating by means of punched cards." They used a limited sample text, first a single canto (the famous third) of Dante's *Inferno*, then four hymns of St. Thomas, in a multi-stage, iterative procedure. Operators began by creating 136 punched cards containing every word in Dante's canto, then put the cards through a series of machines for further processing. The bulk of the *Varia Specimina*, roughly pp. 50–175, contains the experimental results, starting with the data—the Latin texts of the *Hymns* of St. Thomas—and including word lists, indexes, and concordances produced from that verbal data. This is surely one of the first formal publications in the field of humanities data processing, the precursor to humanities computing and one precursor to digital humanities. It's significant, therefore, that it includes both discursive and quantified, tabular forms of data and analysis, bound together in the same pamphlet.

It's true that the "materiality of the punch cards was what enabled and constrained what could be done."[48] Soon new media for storage and even instructions, first paper tape and then magnetic tape, as well as magnetic drums, would become available, but at the inception of Busa's work everything depended on an endless supply of flexible and vulnerable rectangular cards of stiff paper, often called simply IBM cards, given the company's dominance of the worldwide market for them. In a 1956 consent decree IBM agreed that within seven years the company would control no more than half of punched-card manufacturing in the U.S.[49] In fact, differently formatted Remington-Rand cards, for example, did compete to some degree. In an unpublished document written in 1975 (rev. 1980), Father Busa estimated that, by the time the *Index Thomisticus* was completed in the 1970s, the massive stack of all the punched cards used would have weighed 500 tons.[50] Being close to the supply of cards and to machines designed to process them had to have figured into Busa's decision to approach IBM in the first place—a decision not unlike those made by many of IBM's commercial customers at the time.

Using punched cards to control machinery goes back to the eighteenth and nineteenth centuries, most famously in controlling the patterns woven by the Jacquard loom and in the designs for calculating engines by Charles Babbage. Modern systems for processing data are usually said to descend from Herman Hollerith's patented machines, such as those used for the 1890 U.S. census.[51] Hollerith's Tabulating Machine Company merged in 1911 into the Computing Tabulating Recording Company, which became International Business Machines in 1924. Punched cards of the kind he patented were called Hollerith cards for many years. Thomas J. Watson, Sr., who had started as a salesman at NCR, effected a shift in the primary use of the technology, from statistical processing of the kind seen in the census to more general accounting, creating "a punched-card system for bookkeeping that became the industry's de facto standard."[52] There were alternative formats (notably by the Powers company, which became Remington

Rand), but the proprietary design for 80-column cards with rectangular rather than round holes (which allowed for better reading of the cards and made them structurally stronger after being punched), first developed by IBM in 1928, quickly grew to dominate the worldwide market.

By the 1940s, IBM had become closely associated with the cards (all punched cards were often called "IBM cards") and with electromechanical machines designed for punching, sorting, and tabulating them, even after the company's move into large-scale electronic calculators and stored-program computers in the 1950s. Indeed, punched cards remained an important medium for input and output for decades, and became a widespread cultural symbol of computing and its use by managerial organizations. In 1964, for example, the Berkeley Free Speech Movement made punched cards a symbol of the institutional "machine" and adopted as an ironic motto the words printed on many IBM cards: "do not fold, spindle, or mutilate."[53]

By the time of Father Busa's work, the rectangular IBM cards (7⅜ inches X 3¼ inches) were divided into arrays with 12 rows and 80 columns. Encoding was a matter of the position by row and column in which the rectangular holes were punched. Punching a hole in positions 0–9 represented digits; two holes punched in a column indicated letters. (Added holes could be punched in the top two positions in a column to record additional information.) The encoding took various forms, depending on the system being used, a flexibility Busa would exploit. The well-known EBCDIC (Extended Binary Coded Decimal Interchange Code) standard didn't come into use until 1964. For the purposes of the *Index*, however, simpler systems were adequate, since limited data were to be punched on each card: one word with surrounding context words. In this case, for perhaps the first time in IBM's research, the "words" in the code (the term "word" was used for any discrete string of digits making up a unit of data) represented actual natural-language *words*—linguistic data. As we'll see in Chapter 5, when Father Busa and Paul Tasman expanded their work to include the Dead Sea Scrolls in the late 1950s, they made use of a custom-printed version of a new kind of punched card with a column of machine-readable "bubbles" at its edge, the "mark reader" card. A specially leaded pencil was required to bubble-in the ovals to allow for hand revisions to the data on a card.[54] (At least one complaint to the IBM Pure Science staff from a chief engineer, October 2, 1951, asks them not to carelessly walk away with these expensive mark-sensing pencils.[55]) One 1958 source reported that "[o]ther systems, proposed or in various stages of development, use jets of air, light rays, or fluorescent, radioactive or magnetic spots and shapes for actuating the mechanisms."[56]

The materiality of punched cards was distributed across the system as a whole, the big machines needed to punch, read, stack, and sort them. To begin with, the holes in the cards had to be read by a system of metal brushes and contacts; as the cards passed through at high speed, the brushes could make electrical contact and the current could register the pattern without stopping, thus actuating switches for various mechanical operations—the actual physical movement of the cards, passing through readers, sorters, and tabulators, required mechanization. Different machines handled the cards in different ways in order to produce different results. In the experiments by Busa and Tasman of the early 1950s, this meant having a suite of specialized machines, a kind of pre-mainframe setup that took up the space of an office, one for each stage in the process. These are machines "commonly used in Europe up to 1950," as Father Busa says in the *Varia Specimina Concordantiarum* (1951). But he expects soon to have access to "new model IBM machines already in public use in the United States . . . ."[57] He means in this case the IBM Cardatype in particular, which he and Tasman were soon to use. That system combined components in a single workstation, making it possible for the operator to use prepunched cards or go from punching cards to output of printed documents. Otherwise, in their initial trials between 1949–1951, as the description of the process in the *Varia Specima Concordantiarum* indicates, the team used a standard suite of accounting and tabulating machines like the kind then in use in offices all over the world. It's important to remember that the process was only partially automated. People—the operators mentioned in the manuals of the time—were very much needed to handle the cards, including carrying them from machine to machine between each stage of processing. Maybe at this early point in the project this was done almost entirely by Tasman and Busa, with the help of IBM staff, but within a few years Father Busa would begin to train operators for this task, as we'll see in Chapter 3.

Here are the kinds of machines they used and the order of operations undertaken in processing the punched cards, based on the description in the *Varia Specimina*:

A *keypunch* or *card punch*, used for recording alphabetic, numerical, or special character data on the cards by operators using a typewriter-like keyboard. What's typed gets encoded as a pattern of punched holes on the cards. In this case, the source text was entered, one word at a time. (Either there or on a separate *interpreter* machine, human-readable natural language could also be printed directly on the face of the cards, matching the encoded data of the punched holes.)

A *reproducing punch*, which copies the encoded information from one set of cards to another. In this case, operators ran cards through the machine in order to multiply them, such that they ended up with cards containing one contextualized entry each.

A *sorter*, for grouping together cards with related word classifications. In this case, it was used first to alphabetize the card deck. An operator fills the feed-hopper with a deck of cards and the machine rapidly reads them and drops them into separate hoppers or "pockets," sorted.

A *tabulator*, used to read the data on the cards and print them on continuous-feed paper. Although it could also perform other operations, Tasman and Busa seem to have used the tabulator to compose pages of the *Index* and print them as the output of the whole process. The ultimate goal, remember, was a printed and bound final copy of the concordance. Among other, later formats, from CD-ROM to a version on the Internet, the *Index Thomisticus* was indeed eventually produced in this way, thirty years later, as 56 printed volumes.

Additionally, a *collator* was sometimes used to check the accuracy of the transcriptions (using two sets of cards from two different operators, just as in the collation of variant texts in traditional textual studies). Also, the collator could be used to automatically insert header cards into the stack of word cards at the proper places.

Besides processing the cards according to their punched encoding, the machines could be programmed more precisely by rearranging the wires in plugboards, like those of telephone switchboards. (In fact the connections on the plugboard were called switches.) Setting the plugboards, a simple form of hardware "programming" before the advent of software programming, required a good deal of skill. In some cases, a removable plugboard allowed a set configuration to be transferred from one machine to another; an operator would simply move and reinstall the whole prewired board in a different machine.[58] The advantages to customers of using punched-card machines included the ability to use business data (about sales or personnel, or example) in various ways, once it was encoded on decks of cards. Of course, maintaining those card files of data required special cabinets with wide drawers and the clerical workers to file them. In the U.S. and some European countries, especially, early to mid-twentieth-century business culture became punched-card culture. As we saw in the Introduction, even the chads or chips that were the byproduct of all those punches joined the traditional New York ticker-tape parades on Broadway (as Thomas J. Watson, Jr. recalled), a kind of symbolic reminder of the huge numbers of punched-card machines that were still everywhere in the offices of the time when Busa visited in 1949. (It would stay that way for many years, even as large-scale calculating machines were introduced here and there.)

Father Busa quickly made the technology his own. By June 1952, he and Paul Tasman led a formal demonstration at IBM headquarters of the process they had developed, working with punched-card machines (including some other models in addition to those first used in 1950) before an audience that included scholars and a number of invited dignitaries, stopping at various points to display the cards and explain what was being done (an event I describe in greater detail in Chapter 3). Four years later, in 1956, he successfully established a training school for operators and a research center in Italy, and Father Busa was photographed in his dark cassock, standing by the massive card file already accumulated for the *Index*, a cabinet lining a wall in Gallarate, three rectangular drawers standing open: the priest leans on one elbow behind one of the open drawers and looks steadily at the camera; a companion photograph from the same session shows Busa lit dramatically against a dark background, a tableau like that of an Italian Baroque painting, his arm uplifted, holding up one card by the lower corner so the light shines through the holes and he can read the pattern punched there (see Figure 1.1).[59]

FIGURE 1.1 Roberto Busa examines a punched card at CAAL, Casa Sironi, Gallarate, Italy, June 1956 (Busa Archive #25).

Punched cards have remained a symbol of Father Busa's project, and I was excited when I had the opportunity to handle and examine decks of the original cards at the Busa Archive. But they were in fact an eminently practical, even mundane, choice at the time for the kind of sorting and tabulating the project required, and they remained so even after more advanced machinery, including stored-program computers that used tapes and magnetic drums and disks, became available during the 1960s. A 1958 source declares the common wisdom of the previous two decades:

> The fundamental reason for using punched cards is that their use facilitates many routine and repetitive operations involved in the solution of certain intellectual problems. This is particularly true of problems in which large masses of data are involved. The machines can do some things which, due to their complexity and the amount of labor involved, could hardly be undertaken otherwise.[60]

And yet, notice how the merely assistive, labor-saving utility of punched cards quietly gives way in the end of the passage to doing things that "could hardly be undertaken otherwise." This is also a fundamental trajectory in the first decade of Father Busa's research, as we'll see in the chapters that follow.

The next chapter looks at a very different platform, however, a symbolically important adjacent possibility—literally adjacent to Father Busa as he was learning to use the punched-card machines—but which he never used for the *Index Thomisticus*. Yet, as we'll see, this large-scale electronic calculator, the SSEC, would have been for him a kind of conceptual precursor to the large-scale data-processing machines that he did eventually use. And the SSEC tells us a good deal about the technology milieu at that transitional moment, the same moment of the meeting with the CEO upstairs at 590 Madison Avenue, and about the mixed platforms and other conditions which, directly or indirectly, shaped Father Busa's linguistic data processing.

Notes

1 Thomas J. Watson, Jr. and Peter Petre, *Father, Son & Co.: My Life at IBM and Beyond* (New York: Bantam Books, 1990), Kindle edition, loc. 539.
2 Thomas J. Watson, Sr., datebook, IBM Archives, consulted by Reference Archivist, Dawn Stanford, November, 2014.
3 Roberto Busa, "The Annals of Humanities Computing: The *Index Thomisticus*," *Computers and the Humanities* 14.2 (1980), 83–90. Busa's article is the source of almost every later account of the meeting at IBM.
4 Busa, "The Annals of Humanities Computing: The *Index Thomisticus*," 83.
5 Letters between Roberto Busa and Lawrence J. McGinley, S.J., May 19, 1949; July 5, 1949, McGinley Papers, Fordham University Library Rare Books and Manuscripts (Box 11, folder: Foreign, 1949). A letter from Father McGinley to Mr. John E. Cullum, Camp Notre Dame (Union City, N.J.), June 2, 1949, reads, in part: "One of our Jesuit Fathers in Rome has written to me to say that a very cultured family there wishes to send one of the sons (15 years of age) to a summer camp in the United States. . . . The family wishes him to be accompanied by a young priest, who would live in the same camp, or near it, and act as a sort of guardian for the boy. I doubt if the priest speaks English. As far as I can judge from the correspondence, the family would pay for the board of the priest as well as of the boy." A letter from Father McGinley to Father Busa, June 7, 1949, shared the details of the arrangements he had made for the camp, prompting Busa's report of a change of plans (Box 11, folder: Foreign 1949).
6 H. Paul Tasman of IBM, about whom I'll say much more below, looking back in 1968, said that he did not think Busa understood the full extent of the problem he was facing. Transcript of Paul Tasman interview by Lawrence Saphire for IBM Oral History of Computer Technology (interview TC-99, August 14, 1968), 15. IBM Archives, courtesy of International Business Machines Corporation. I wasn't able to listen to the audio recordings of interviews in the series, but relied on IBM transcripts. I was sent two versions of this transcript, one a correction of the other. Citations are to version 1 but incorporate the corrections of version 2. Thomas Nelson Winter says: "One cannot but note that Father Busa knew the nature of the task and knew what he was looking for," in "Roberto Busa, S.J., and the Invention of the Machine-Generated Concordance," *The Classical Bulletin* 75.1 (1999), 3–20, available online, http://digitalcommons.unl.edu/classicsfacpub/70/. Winter's essay was the first full treatment of Busa's methods. Compressed but thorough, it also mentions key contexts I've found useful, such as the significant role played by wartime surplus, for example.
7 Busa, "The Annals of Humanities Computing: The *Index Thomisticus*," 83–84.

8   Letter from B.T. Lukaszewski, S.J. to Roberto Busa, November 27, 1949, Busa Archive (Gall. Rel. Cult. 1940, USA tab).

9   Letter from Howard Comfort to Roberto Busa, November 29, 1949, Busa Archive (Gall. Rel. Cult. 1940, USA tab).

10 Letter from Roberto Busa to Frank H. Towsley, May 11, 1951, Busa Archive (Gall. Rel. Cult. 1940, USA tab).

11 Letter from Werner Jaeger to Roberto Busa, February 11, 1950; letter from Harry J. Krould (Library of Congress) to Roberto Busa, November 28, 1949, "c/o Rev. Fr. Provincial, 501 East Fordham Road, New York 58 / New York," Busa Archive (Gall. Re. Cult. 1940, USA tab). 501 East Fordham Road is given as Busa's American address on at least two ship's manifests, for the Queen Elizabeth in April 1952 and for the Queen Mary in April 1954. As I write, the building remains a Jesuit residence, Kohlmann Hall.

12 National Catholic Welfare Conference Press release, June 20, 1964, Busa Archive (Stampa Estera 1700, 1950–1963). Paul Tasman said that it was Jerome Wiesner of MIT who referred Busa to IBM, in Paul Tasman interview by Lawrence Saphire for IBM Oral History of Computer Technology (interview TC-99, August 14, 1968), 1. IBM Archives, courtesy of International Business Machines Corporation.

13 Busa, "The Annals of Humanities Computing: The *Index Thomisticus*," 84.

14 The joke was first noted in print by Meredith Hindley, "The Rise of the Machines," *Humanities* 34.4 (July/August 2013), http://www.neh.gov/humanities/2013/julyaugust/feature/the-rise-the-machines. In her version: "A priest and a scientist walk into a computer lab."

15 Steven Johnson, "The Long Zoom," *The New York Times Magazine* (October 8, 2006), http://nytimes.com/2006/10/08/magazine/08games.html/.

16 Willard McCarty, "What does Turing have to do with Busa?," in *Proceedings of the Third Workshop on Annotation of Corpora for Research in the Humanities* (ACRH-3), eds. Francesco Mambrini, Marco Passarotti, Caroline Sporleder, 1–14, http://www.mccarty.org.uk/essays/McCarty,%20Turing%20and%20Busa.pdf.

17 Adeline Koh, "Niceness, Building, and Opening the Genealogy of the Digital Humanities: Beyond the Social Contract of Humanities Computing," *differences* 24.1 (2014), 93–106, accessed online, DOI: 10.1215/10407391-2420015.

18 Seabee Memorial, Arlington, VA, http://www.seabeesmuseum.com/history.html.

19 Randall Munroe, XKCD web comic, http://www.xkcd.com/1425/.

20 Tony Judt, *Postwar: A History of Europe Since 1945* (New York: Penguin Books, 2005).

21 The full extent of the use of IBM equipment and resources by the Nazis only came to light with the publication of Edwin Black's *IBM and the Holocaust: The Strategic Alliance Between Nazi Germany and America's Most Powerful Corporation* (New York: Crown, 2001; Dialog Press, 2009). Claims made for IBM's exceptional status, however, and some sensationalist or tendentious language, starting with the subtitle ("strategic alliance"), at times obscure the book's real contributions to historical understanding.

22 Robert Sobel, *IBM: Colossus in Transition* (New York: Bantam Books, 1983), 88.

23 "Thomas J. Watson [Sr.]," Wikipedia: https://en.wikipedia.org/wiki/Thomas_J._Watson. After the appearance of Edwin Black's *IBM and the Holocaust*, articles on Wikipedia about IBM and the Nazis, as is usual for controversial topics at the site, have sometimes been arenas for conflicting edits.

24 Watson, Jr. and Petre, *Father, Son & Co.*, loc. 1853–56.

25 Watson, Jr. and Petre, *Father, Son & Co.*, loc. 2886.

26 Watson, Jr. and Petre, *Father, Son & Co.*, loc. 2869.

27 Edward Vanhoutte, "The Gates of Hell: History and Definition of Digital | Humanities | Computing," in *Defining Digital Humanities: A Reader*, eds. Melissa Terras, Julianne Nyhan, and Edward Vanhoutte. (Farnham, Surrey, UK: Ashgate, 2013), 119–56 (128).

28 Transcript of Paul Tasman interview by Lawrence Saphire for IBM Oral History of Computer Technology (interview TC-99, August 14, 1968), 12. IBM Archives, courtesy of International Business Machines Corporation.

29 Tasman interview by Lawrence Saphire, 12.

30 Watson, Jr. and Petre, *Father, Son & Co.: My Life at IBM and Beyond*, loc. 2410–14.

31 Steven Johnson, *How We Got To Now: Six Innovations That Made the Modern World* (New York: Riverhead Books, 2014), Kindle edition, 62–64, loc. 730–35.

32 Winter, "Robert Busa, S.J., and the Invention of the Machine-Generated Concordance."

33 Tasman interview by Lawrence Saphire, 25.

34 Tasman interview by Lawrence Saphire, 30.

35 Vannevar Bush, "As We May Think," *Atlantic Monthly* (July 1, 1945), 101–108, http://www.theatlantic.com/magazine/archive/1945/07/as-we-may-think/303881/.

36 Bush, "As We May Think"

37 Bush, "As We May Think"

38 On the development of this photoelectric microfilm platform, see Michael K. Buckland, "Emanuel Goldberg, Electronic Document Retrieval, and Vannevar Bush's Memex," *Journal of the American Society for Information Science* 43.4 (May 1992), 284–94.

39 Roberto Busa, *Sancti Thomae Aquinatis Hymnorum Ritualium Varia Specimina Concordantiarum: A First Example of Word Index Automatically Compiled and Printed by IBM Punched Card Machines* (Fratelli Bocca: Milan, 1951), 22.

40 Busa, *Sancti Thomae Aquinatis Hymnorum Ritualium Varia Specimina Concordantiarum*, 22.

41 Busa, *Sancti Thomae Aquinatis Hymnorum Ritualium Varia Specimina Concordantiarum*, 22.

42 Stephen Ramsay, *Reading Machines: Toward an Algorithmic Criticism* (Champaign: University of Illinois Press, 2011), 1–2, 6.

43 Ramsay, *Reading Machines: Toward an Algorithmic Criticism*, 1.

44 Busa, *Sancti Thomae Aquinatis Hymnorum Ritualium Varia Specimina Concordantiarum*, 22.

45 Roberto Busa, "Complete *Index Verborum* of Works of St. Thomas" ("Announcements"), *Speculum* 25.3 (July 1950), 424–25.

46 Busa, "Complete *Index Verborum* of Works of St. Thomas" ("Announcements"), 425.

47 Roberto Busa, unpublished autobiographical manuscript. Cited with the kind permission of Marco Passarotti, CIRCSE, Milan.

48 Rockwell, Geoffrey and Stéfan Sinclair. "Past Analytical: Towards an Archaeology of Text Analysis Tools." Digital Humanities 2014 conference, Lausanne, Switzerland, October 7, 2014. http://www.researchgate.net/publication/273449857_Towards_an_Archaeology_of_Text_Analysis_Tools.

49 James W. Cortada, *Before the Computer; IBM, NCR, Burroughs, and Remington Rand and the Industry They Created, 1865–1956* (Princeton: Princeton University Press, 2000), 232.

50 Quoted in Edward Vanhoutte, "The Gates of Hell," 127.

51 See Lars Heide, *Punched-Card Systems and the Early Information Explosion, 1880–1945* (Baltimore: Johns Hopkins University Press, 2009), esp. Chapter 4 on IBM. As I write, the Wikipedia article, "Punched card," provides an accessible and well-illustrated general summary for non-specialists: http://en.wikipedia.org/wiki/Punched_card. My basic descriptions of punched cards are based on that article and on Heide, as well as other sources as noted.

52 Heide, *Punched-Card Systems and the Early Information Explosion, 1880–1945*, 105.

53 Steven Lubar, "'Do Not Fold, Spindle, or Mutilate': A Cultural History of the Punch Card," *Journal of American Culture 15.4* (June 4, 1992), 43–55, DOI: 10.1111/j.1542-734X.1992.1504_43.x. (Fold, Spindle, Multilate = FSM = Free Speech Movement.)

54 As described and illustrated in Paul Tasman, *Indexing the Dead Sea Scrolls, by Electronic Literary Data Processing Methods*. (New York: IBM World Trade Corporation, 1958), 4–5.

55 A. Wayne Brooke Papers, MC 00268, Special Collections Research Center, North Carolina State University Libraries, Raleigh, NC (Box MC 268, folder 1).

56 Robert S. Casey, James W. Perry, Madeline M. Berry, Allen Kent, *Punched Cards: Their Applications to Science and Industry* (New York, Amsterdam, London: Reinhold, 1958; Second Ed., 1967), 6.

57 Busa, *Sancti Thomae Aquinatis Hymnorum Ritualium Varia Specimina Concordantiarum*, 34.

58 Charles J. Bashe, "The SSEC in Historical Perspective," *Annals of the History of Computing* 4.4 (October–December 1982), 296–312 (297).

59 Photographs #26 and #25, Busa Archive. Identified (via captions in the finding aid written by Busa) as having been taken at CAAL, Casa Sironi, June 1956.

60 Casey, et al., *Punched Cards: Their Applications to Science and Industry*, 10.

2

ORACLE ON 57TH STREET

The IBM SSEC Large-scale Calculator, Representations of Computing, and the Role of the Adjacent Possible, 1948–1952

When Father Busa arrived at IBM World Headquarters in November 1949, he would have had to walk past a machine on display in the ground-floor showroom facing 57th Street, a giant, room-sized calculator with spinning tape drives, arrays of blinking lights, and several sleek modern consoles, always attended by at least one human operator. The SSEC, or Selective Sequence Electronic Calculator, would have been running, processing actual data for customers. It ran around the clock. It had been on public display for over a year by then, and (as IBM intended) it had attracted a good deal of attention. That was the idea. If, as I suggested in Chapter 1, we imagine an exploded view of the meeting between Father Busa and T.J. Watson, Sr., up in the CEO's office on the 17th floor, in this chapter I want to focus on the SSEC as a contextual detail just outside the view of that meeting, downstairs on the ground floor. But it's a very large detail, and it's a richly suggestive one.

Only a few years after the first meeting, Father Busa and Paul Tasman were able to use a different large-scale machine, the IBM 705—part of the line which replaced the SSEC in the showroom, beginning with the 701 "Defense Calculator" in 1952—to process punched-card data from their work on the Dead Sea Scrolls. Photographs from the later 1950s show the priest at the console, in front of the tape drives (for example, Figure 2.1). (Interestingly, sitting there at the console, Father Busa is in effect in the position of the system operator, rather than an end-user, researcher, or customer.) In a different photograph, Father Busa poses in front of the tall cabinets of the 705 with Dick Watson, Cardinal Spellman, and an Italian diplomat.[1] But, as far as I can tell, Busa and Tasman never used the earlier machine, the SSEC, before it was taken offline in 1952, in part because it was explicitly defined as for scientific calculations (business users had to pay to

FIGURE 2.1 Roberto Busa at the console of the IBM 705 EDPM, IBM World Headquarters, New York, 1958 (IBM Archives).

cover expenses) and their work was linguistic and humanistic, but also because their work with punched cards was at too preliminary a stage to require such a large-scale machine. IBM's creation of the SSEC grew out of the need to enhance the company's public profile and to redefine its machines as tools of science and general human knowledge. Similar motives probably lay behind the modest support the company provided for Father Busa's work. The SSEC in the showroom was literally adjacent to his work at IBM during the start-up phase, between 1949 and 1952, and he would have quickly come to understand its significance; he clearly aspired to use machines of its kind and scale. The giant electronic calculator had already by late 1948 come to signify "the computer" (or "electronic brain") among many in the general population.

Whether or not it counted as the first stored-program computer is another question. An engineer who worked on it, A. Wayne Brooke, maintained that it did, since it could technically store some instructions, which had been fed into it from punched cards or punched paper tape, in its electronic memory, if only for a brief interval.[2] Brooke argued that the SSEC "was operating this way before the ENIAC was modified to two digit instruction words. The ENIAC was only a large electronic numerical integrator and calculator." He admits that even IBM never claimed the SSEC was a true stored-program computer, but he disagrees, since it was in theory—though on a limited scale—"dynamically modifiable".[3] Wallace Eckert, who was in charge of developing the machine for IBM, was asked in 1967 whether "the SSEC was in effect the first general purpose store[d] program electronic computer," and he answered in a qualified way: "[e]lectronic in the sense that the fast operations were all done electronically" (the calculator was a hybrid of electronic, electric, and electromechanical technologies).[4] But earlier in the same interview Eckert described the "store" (or memory) of the SSEC in a way that could support Brooke's contentions, observing that in theory there was "no difference between the instructions and data as far as the storeroom was concerned."[5]

That debate didn't matter to the press and the general public in 1948. For a year or two, the SSEC represented the cutting edge of computing. As an adjacent possibility Busa was actually able to see in person and watch working, it helped to form the context of his own research, between the meeting with the CEO and the successful demonstration held at IBM in June 1952, coincidentally, almost the exact lifespan of the SSEC (dedicated in January 1948, it was decommissioned in August 1952). Given its potential significance, it's worth understanding the big machine in some detail and in historical context, and that's the aim of this chapter.

It's said that the SSEC marked IBM's transition from electromechanical punched-card machines to electronics. That distinction is perhaps too clean. Though the SSEC used paper tapes, electromechanical relays, and electronic tubes, it also continued to use standard punched cards. Three punches were part of the system. It was a hybrid design, considered by many an anomalous, unsuccessful one. An engineer who had been involved in developing it later characterized it as "somewhat of a failure," but also "a glorious machine. . . . a glorious failure," and, more precisely, a "transitional thing that was necessary at the time."[6] The fact that it used punched cards was not unusual. Every large-scale machine at the time was transitional in that respect. Punched cards remained part of computing in one form or another for decades, and traditional punched-card data processing in offices continued to be a viable business for IBM for many years to come. This remained the case even as large-scale calculators were introduced, attracted public attention, and were adopted by government agencies and some large business clients.

The introduction in the 1930s of data-processing equipment, punches, sorters, and tabulators, helped to create demand for large calculators and computers later on, once they became available and companies could afford them.[7] IBM controlled the market for the punched-card systems in the business world and in many sectors of government. When calculators and computers came along, customers who could afford to were primed to adopt them. Like punched-card systems, the first computers also consisted of component machines linked together in suites. Where once the human operator had served as the link between the different machines and had performed each stage in processing, literally carrying decks of cards from one stage to the next, with large computers, more of the connections were made by electrical and mechanical components in the increasingly automated systems.[8] In the late 1940s and early 1950s, punched-card sorting and tabulating machinery was combined with electronic calculator technology in hybrid systems.[9]

Rather than a linear transition from one technology to another, it's more accurate to think of uneven combinations of emerging and converging technologies at the time, existing technologies being recombined in new, sometimes awkward, configurations, with new devices. It was less a smooth trajectory than a series of opportunistic responses to constraints and possibilities expressed in feedback from commercial and government clients. The SSEC is a vivid example of this messy process. A machine that combined emerging and converging technologies, it was a system with its seams exposed. It cost $750,000 and required two operators to keep it running.[10] It was made with over 12,000 large vacuum tubes as electronic switches, which had first been used in this way in the Colossus computers at Bletchley Park during the war (they were called "valves" in Britain) and on the 1946 ENIAC. In addition, the SSEC contained over 21,000 electromechanical relay switches with physically moving parts.

As we've seen, the SSEC also used tape. One of its distinctive features was its wall of tape drives. Today we think of tape as a thin magnetic medium, but the SSEC tapes were made at IBM's Endicott plant from continuous paper card stock, the same heavy gauge used for punched cards, so that the tapes were as wide as the cards were long, 7⅜ inches, and had 80 tracks, like the cards' 80 columns. Rolls of this tape weighed 400 pounds, and a kind of winch had to be used to hoist them into place; to move the heavy rolls to the punch machine (nicknamed the Prancing Stallion because of its stylized metal case), operators had to roll them up a ramp.[11] Tape drives were installed behind glass and steel panels around a 25 × 50-foot room, protecting them from dust and interference while also exposing them to view. There was a raised floor, designed to conceal all the wiring, one of the first instances of that feature, which would become ubiquitous in computer rooms in the coming decades. In these features of its physical layout, quite apart from its hardware and system architecture, the SSEC was the ancestor of IBM mainframe systems to come—after the ASCC (Automatic Sequence Controlled Calculator) or Mark I, that is. IBM had built that machine with researchers at Harvard using a team led by Howard Aiken and including Grace Hopper. T.J. Watson, Sr. believed that IBM had subsequently been given insufficient credit for the machine. Competition with its own Harvard Mark I was the impetus for IBM's building the SSEC—and the new computer was pointedly created through a new arrangement with another Ivy League institution, Columbia, in a collaboration between IBM engineering in Endicott, New York, and the newly formed (1945) Watson Scientific Computing Laboratory at Columbia.[12]

The lab at Columbia was directed by the first Director of Pure Science at IBM, Wallace Eckert (no relation to Presper Eckert, the well-known developer of the ENIAC), an astronomy professor at the university. In 1944 T. J. Watson, Sr.

recruited Eckert as the first IBM employee with a PhD and Eckert helped to hire a team that included the second PhD at IBM, another astronomer, Herb Grosch, as well as Robert R. ("Rex") Seeber, who had worked on the Harvard Mark I. After a brief interim period in Pupin Hall on the Columbia campus, the lab was located in a former fraternity house that IBM purchased, at 612 West 116th Street, just off Broadway. This initiative was part of a new emphasis at IBM on pure scientific research in addition to engineering. One anecdote illustrates the tension behind the shift (and between the university and the technology corporation): when T. J. Watson, Sr. tried to supply portraits of "American scientists" to decorate the 116th Street lab—Edison, for example, and the Wright Brothers—Herb Grosch declared them mere inventors and told the IBM representative to hang them at Endicott, but not at Columbia.[13] This comic conflict between the two cultures within technical culture led to the lab's getting a portrait of Isaac Newton. The staff had faculty privileges at Columbia, and even offered some of the earliest computer science classes at an American university, but they were IBM employees and shuttled back and forth between the Upper West Side and Midtown (with some trips, sometimes by air, to IBM's Endicott plant upstate).

As a condition of its charter, the Watson Lab was expected to build the large-scale electronic calculator. Eckert was made its first scientific "customer." Designed at Columbia and IBM, it was built at Endicott in just over a year, ending July 1947. After testing, it was disassembled, transported, and reassembled in the newly configured showroom at "590" (as IBMers called the Midtown World Headquarters). Partly because it was built so quickly, the calculator used mostly off-the-shelf parts. Engineers sent runners down to Cortlandt Street, the downtown electronics district known at the time as "Radio Row," to search shops for surplus electronics; according to one engineer, "the major factor in choosing vacuum tube types for the buffer memory and arithmetic unit of the SSEC was availability. . . ."[14] In this case, the adjacent possible was literal—what was available for purchase downtown.

The SSEC team included twenty-seven programmers based at IBM headquarters (at least eight with names that would appear to be female[15]), whose work involved setting plugboards and working with the keypunches and paper tapes, sometimes making them into literal loops, hung vertically in the drives. The machine required a team of skilled operators. Many of the publicity photos and images for news reports feature Chief Operator Elizabeth "Betsy" (Oram) Stewart, of IBM's Department of Pure Science, sitting at the console like the captain of a ship, sometimes with a group of men in business suits standing around her, sometimes alone (Figure 2.2). The Marketing department obviously saw Stewart as photogenic, and this is one reason she so often showed up in the publicity shots. But she was actually also running the machine, a technical specialist in charge of operation who reported directly to the chief engineer, Rex Seeber. That kind of ambiguous position was common for women in data processing

FIGURE 2.2 Chief Operator Elizabeth ("Betsy") Stewart at the console of the IBM SSEC, IBM World Headquarters, 1948 (IBM Archives).

at the time: skilled operators of important machinery whose work was often framed by sexist assumptions about the nature of "clerical" work and by a reductive treatment of the women in the field. Many women held positions in a gray area that comprehended clerical data workers, "computers" (the job description), and operators. Their contributions were as significant in their way as those of the few exceptional women programmers, such as Grace Hopper, for example.[16] Statistically speaking, most women's contributions to early computing remained in the arena of machine operations, and the operators remained mostly anonymous and uncelebrated.

With the exception of Betsy Stewart, none of the women workers at IBM show up in the publicity surrounding the SSEC's debut. In one photograph in the IBM Archives, a group of suited men stand gazing upward at a plaque mounted just inside the door of the SSEC showroom, quoting Thomas J. Watson, Sr.'s signed declaration that the machine was meant to "assist the scientist in institutions of learning, in government, and in industry, to explore the consequences of man's thought to the outermost reaches of time, space, and physical conditions." Machine time was free for pure science; government and industry had to cover expenses (the rent was reportedly $300/hour).[17] An initial demonstration of the machine's capabilities was run at the dedication event on January 28, 1948. Designed by Eckert, it was a complete calculation of the lunar ephemeris, or the exact shifting position of moon among the stars. It was said later that the specific results were eventually used by NASA for the Apollo program. This application in quantitative astronomy required what was at the time massive computing power. Like the space program to come (and the weapons program during the war), it was an example of what came to be known as big science. Eckert's calculations were chosen to fulfill Watson's lofty commission, as seen on the dedicatory plaque, to apply computing to problems at "the outermost reaches of time, space, and physical conditions." Another job was to run calculations for the hydrogen bomb, codenamed "Hippo." (The Soviet Union exploded a nuclear weapon August 29, 1949, and the arms race accelerated in reaction.) The programming took almost a year, running on the SSEC around the clock. As George Dyson puts it, the SSEC was "immediately obsolete, but the Hippo code continued to be used by Los Alamos for many years."[18]

Every program for the SSEC, whether for industry or government, ran live in the showroom, so the public could watch the computing being done in real time. At the dedication ceremony, Watson Sr.'s speech highlighted the feature everyone involved would continue to repeat for years: visitors and IBMers that day stood "within the structure of this new electronic calculator." Starting with the press release, and including write-ups in in-house publications (e.g., *Business Machines* 30.11 [1948]), the description was repeated for many years. Decades later, remarkably enough, people were still repeating that language as they described the SSEC, including for example, A. Wayne Brooke, Chief Operating Engineer: "when the visitor stands in this area, he is literally inside the calcula-tor."[19] And Wallace Eckert used the same image in a 1967 interview for IBM's oral histories: "the operators and the people who were watching were inside the calculator."[20] The idea of standing inside the machine was also used for decades to describe other large-scale calculating machines and computers of the era, the ENIAC, for example: "Now we think of a personal computer as one which you carry around with you. The ENIAC was actually one that you kind of lived inside."[21]

On the one hand, this is only a widely shared image, a meme, as we now say, a way to express the increasing size of computers in the late 1940s. But it's a highly suggestive image. The SSEC was designed to run scientific calculations, but it was also meant to *represent* computing to the scientific community and the public. For a few years it did just that, just at the moment of Father Busa's arrival and the start-up phase of his research. The image of inhabiting the machine was mostly an insider's view, as it were. The engineer's comments, the IBM press release, the

CEO's ceremonial remarks, later reports in company organs, all reflect something in the air around computing culture, something different from the dominant and repeated images in the press and among the public when it came to how computing was represented metaphorically and emotionally.

The image of humans standing inside the machine goes beyond the banal idea that people are mere cogs or industrial components; that's as old as the industrial revolution itself. The new image is a figure for the way human "computers" and the artificial computers they build co-inhabit a shared abstract space of possibility, defined by mutual affordances and constraints, interconnected in a dynamic relationship. In other words, it's an image of cybernetics. Like the SSEC, Norbert Wiener's famous essay on cybernetics (about "communication and control in human and machine"), dates from 1948.[22] N. Katherine Hayles has argued that the human relation to computers in the mid-century was characterized by the cybernetic model, which later, in the age of the Internet, gave way to the paradigm of virtual reality, and then, in the past decade or so, to mixed reality, the combination of virtual and physical realities.[23] But the meme of humans standing inside the computer—a figure which is at the same time a literal description—on closer inspection also expresses feelings about computing at the time that, at least among non-specialists, may have been obscured by sublime rhetoric about the growing autonomy of the machines. Most computing in 1948 was still done by human "computers," and behind their glass panels and molded consoles, the shiny new calculating machines (which were still very rare) looked like Rube Goldberg contraptions, with wheels and ramps, a flurry of paper punched cards, short pieces of stainless steel pipe as weights for glued paper loops, surplus radio tubes, and everywhere people moving around, to transport the data where they were needed and to read the results, setting plugboards, hauling unwieldy reels of tape, and moving decks of punched cards from one machine to another. There used to be a joke in the early days of the Internet about the necessity at times for human messengers to carry printed documents or floppy disks the last mile or the final ten feet, from one machine to another, or from a machine to a human user: they called it the "sneakerNet." The word "computer" in the late 1940s, ambiguously both a job description and a machine, carries similar connotations. Both terms are ways of acknowledging the persistence of the central role for people in these emerging systems, over and against fears about robots, artificial "brains," and autonomous mechanisms.

In truth, a room-sized system like the SSEC was already less like an idealized system for "steerage" or control of the machine by a human intelligence (to return to the etymology of Wiener's "cybernetics"), and more like what N. Katherine Hayles has called a "dynamic heterarchy characterized by intermediating dynamics," a two-way relationship based on feedback and feedforward loops, giving rise to the potential for "emergent complexity."[24] The repeated image of standing in the machine is an implicit recognition, by those who knew the system literally from the inside, of the necessary involvement (in the literal sense of being rolled up in or enwrapped) of humans in the new kinds of computers. Freud's theory of the uncanny comes to mind, the presence of something that we fear is alien because it has been denied or repressed within us, close to home, within the supposedly protected space of the self. The meme about standing inside the computer is like an inversion of that theory: the uncanny presence of the human inside the machine persists despite the widely held assumption that the machine is increasing autonomous. Seeing the people inside the machine may signify a fear that technology will devour humanity; or, at the same time, it may reveal the limits of that apocalyptic vision and the stubborn persistence of "the human factor," as mid-century ergonomics put it.

This is the material reality drowned out by popular rhetoric about the electromechanical monster or giant brain as something superhuman, or inhuman, as in a cartoon on the cover of *Time* magazine for January 23, 1950, captioned "MARK III: Can man build a superman?" The image depicts a giant computer with military-uniformed arms and officer's cap, reading its own output tape with a single bulging eye. After Turing, and after the use of computing at Los Alamos, in the era of increasing power in the military–industrial (-university) complex, such fears were of course legitimate. But the popular stories told about and arising out of those fears shifted early on into a narrative not about the politics of computing power, and the ethical decisions needed as a result, but about inevitable dehumanization, and an inevitably autonomous Technology, driven by an internal logic of progress beyond human control. The rise of the machines is just the inverse of techno-utopian narratives of unstoppable progress. A more detailed understanding of the actual mixed human-computer systems as they emerged in the period of experimentation between the end of the war and the mid-1950s can provide a useful counter to both dystopian and utopian narratives of technology's "rise" and humanity's coming self-transcendence (and consequent freedom from responsibility).

The complicated hybrid systems of the era, the "sedimented and layered"[25] computing history and computing culture at that moment of transition (which was anything *but* a simple linear succession) from electromechanical accounting machines and calculators to electronic computers, allows us to better appreciate the emergence of *humanities* computing at the same moment. Humanities research had a range of new opportunities in the late 1940s and early 1950s to experiment with calculating and computing machines at the periphery as it were of better-funded big science. The generally smaller-scale questions of humanities research, just in terms of its typical datasets and relatively delimited quantification, and its philological orientation—tied to natural language processing with a focus on the historical particulars of human cultural expressions—made humanities work amenable to opportunistic use of not-quite cutting-edge technologies, and these were the kinds of resources more likely to be made available in any case.

Yet, there were also opportunities for humanities researchers to contribute to the theory and practice of computing, though the contributions were not always recognized as such at the time: in machine translation, natural language processing, and information retrieval, for example. This is not to deny that much of the early work, including Father Busa's, aspired to the same kind of quantitative certainty and labor- and time-saving efficiency then associated with computing. Tasman and Busa repeatedly called attention to the merely utilitarian role of the machines, perhaps in part to defuse anxieties about redundancies and displacement, and in strategic contrast to the sophisticated intellectual work they meant to enable human researchers to pursue. (We'll see in the chapters that follow examples of the computer being described, for example, as "maidservant" or "skivvy" to human expertise and human thought.) But the transitional moment I've been describing offered new adjacent possibilities for smaller-scale experiments using computers in humanities research, in relatively peripheral areas that would in later decades move closer to the center of computing in general, and to humanities computing in particular.

Looking back on the initial support for automated grading at Columbia, Wallace Eckert said that "Mr. Watson was interested in novel uses of his equipment as long as it was socially useful. . . . he was interested in education and science and when he heard that those [punched-card] machines could be useful in this area, even though not profitable, he was willing to sponsor this experiment."[26] Similarly, Paul Tasman said that Watson was interested in "humanistic" applications at the time, specifically putting Father Busa's work in this same category of socially valuable work IBM supported on a kind of not-for-profit basis.[27] At the end of a decade of work with Father Busa, writing specifically about the Dead Sea Scrolls project, Tasman claimed that they had "combined the modern machine with ancient spiritual writings" in order "to further our understanding of our basic theological heritage"[28]—a description of the work as humanities computing, using the kind of language still often heard in our own time about the value of the digital humanities. At around the same time, Tasman tentatively predicted the emergence of humanities computing: "The use of the latest data-processing tools developed primarily for science and commerce may prove a significant factor in facilitating future literary and scholarly studies."[29] Specifically, the work he had been doing with Father Busa in "language engineering" in retrospect looks like part of the emergent field of information retrieval, and of the mechanized production of indexes and abstracts from a corpus of "lectures and articles," for example, based on natural language processing. But Tasman places this in a broad context: "The impact of machine analysis will soon be felt in law, medicine, library science, chemical and oil industries, scientific and engineering research, and wherever the increasing volume of data makes its fingertip availability imperative."[30]

The "humanistic" experiment in furthering the understanding of "basic theological heritage" is in the end justified by the "impact" of its methodology on scientific and other fields (although those include, for example, library science).

This undoubtedly reflects the ongoing calculations by IBM about its present and future markets, the manifest and potential value to the company of supporting special projects like Father Busa's. IBM's websites and company histories tell the story of Tasman and Busa's experiments as leading to formalized linguistic data processing and contributing to the development of information retrieval and natural language processing in later IBM research, as in the current Text Analysis and Language Engineering Group, of the Knowledge Management Technology Department of the Thomas J. Watson Research Center of IBM Research, which applies techniques of natural language processing (NLP) to large document collections. This way of citing the pioneering work of Tasman and Busa tells us something in general about how the work was viewed early on and why it may have garnered support, once it became clear what Busa had in mind and Tasman had helped to formulate what could actually be done with the machines.

Tasman suggested in 1967 that Father Busa didn't fully grasp the ramifications of the project and all it entailed (and required) when he first arrived at 590.[31] He meant, especially, the wider implications for information science and data processing in general. The evidence from the early years supports this, since Busa, like many specialists at the time, repeatedly stressed the labor-saving and time-saving benefits of mechanization, how it could free scholars by automating otherwise tedious and impossibly time-consuming tasks. But in less than a decade, by the late 1950s, both Busa and Tasman came to describe the work as "literary data processing," and Busa called for a "new philology" using computers, both terms implying a more transformative role for computers in humanities research. Some of these new possibilities were surely suggested by exposure to the SSEC and other machines of its kind, at IBM and elsewhere, the ambitious architectures, theoretical rationales, and aspirations of which helped to shape ideas of what computing might do. As Busa himself said—while remembering something as seeming trivial as his browsing through technical books on the shelves of the IBM library—"all new ideas arise out of a *milieu* when ripe."[32]

The interests of the humanities scholar who was seeking support for his work in 1949 were one thing. The interests of the CEO who provided the support were another. What's often called the "collaboration" between the two was actually a matter of negotiating at the border where those interests overlapped. No doubt a bias in favor of scientific applications—of applied science and engineering "solutions" useful to the government, military, or large industrial clients—determined the distribution of resources and support. Still, it's significant that, while Father Busa was not able to use the SSEC itself, he was given essentially a scaled-down version of the same kind of deal as the scientific clients of the SSEC: free access first to punched-card equipment and then to a combination of that equipment with the processing power of the IBM 705. As he said in the first meeting with Watson, his Jesuit superiors had given him "time, encouragement, their blessings and much holy water, but unfortunately no money," so he could "recompense IBM in any way except financially."[33]

There were other ways in which the company was recompensed for its support, including public relations, and Busa's continuing to help advertise that support for many years.

Despite its scientific commissions, the SSEC was always an investment in the reputation and public image of IBM. The whirring tape drives and arrays of lights defining the space of the glassed-in showroom, operators and programmers walking around and working inside it, New Yorkers walking by on 57th Street, stopping at the windows to watch: the representational value of the SSEC between 1948–1952 was as enormous as the machine itself. The team was "constantly besieged by photographers," and "[t]he policy was to allow any normal request"[34]—and requests were frequent, from newspapers, newsreel teams, and magazines. According to IBM, prior to the dedication of the SSEC 279 domestic newspapers in 247 cities and 25 magazines, mostly industry or technical at first, reported the story; it was also on major radio and TV broadcast networks.[35] Popular broadcaster Arthur Godfrey reported on WCBS New York that "The IBM here in New York has come up with something new, a giant calculator that can add, subtract, multiply, divide and even do square roots and cube roots."[36] He then repeats claims about the "memory" of the SSEC that may have arisen in support of the argument that it was, technically speaking, a stored-program computer: "What's more, it has a memory. The results of problems it solves can be stored in its mechanical memory and then be fed back into a problem a week or a thousandth of a second later." Finally, Godfrey calls it a "robot brain" and jokes, "That's the way I always love my mathematics, to have some machine do it."

Even a fashion magazine shot a layout ("figure on a big future") with models leaning into and gazing at the machinery.[37] The images are oddly like all those photographs of Betsy Stewart posing at the controls of the machine (a version of which appeared on the covers of both *Electronics* magazine and *Radio Craft* for May 1948). Of course sex was used to sell computers, as well as clothing. But the fashion models remind us of how eroticized the images of computers and actual women operators often were at the time. It may be that the machines were also deliberately feminized by association in such images, made less threatening to imagined potential (male) customers and (statistically, probably female) operators. Both kinds of images, official PR shots with operators and on the fashion pages, inadvertently reveal the central (though subservient) role many women were in fact playing in developing and running the new technology—although not as many or as readily, perhaps, as had done during the war. The copy for the fashion spread, with chic irony, describes the machine's technical specifications as well as what the models are wearing. In fact, however attractively dressed, the models are in clothes one might imagine in an office, and the images attempt to represent an idea of working women, posed as if they were using the machines, not *only* using them for an exotic backdrop. In the end, despite themselves, the fashion images imply an access to and familiarity with the big machines by women, based on the real presence of the many actual women who were working in offices and labs in 1948, but whose presence would be reflected unevenly for decades to follow, as women's involvement in computing would rise and fall.[38]

Take for example Lillian Hausman, who was working at Columbia 1946–1947, just before the SSEC, and whom Herb Grosch described admiringly (if somewhat paternalistically) as "a superb operator—after all, she was the senior full-time scientific punched card expert in the whole world—but she knew a lot of astronomy. In fact, she probably could have done my part of the job, too."[39] She wired the plugboards to program the punched-card machines, as well as running the cards through them. Or consider Aetna Womble, who was hired by the new Watson Lab at Columbia. According to her obituary, "In 1947, she was the third woman to graduate from the Duke University School of Engineering, with an electrical engineering degree; after which she worked for IBM on their premier machine, at the time, the S.S.E.C. (Selective Sequence Electronic Calculator)."[40] Along with Betsy Stewart and a handful of other women, Womble participated in the public dedication of the SSEC in 1948, although, as was generally the case with the women working on the machine, she's not shown in any of the publicity photographs.

It's important to remember that there were women everywhere in early computing, in one capacity or another, from wartime "computers" using calculating machines, to plugboard "programmers," to keypunch operators, to system operators and some software programmers, once that became a possibility. A few powerful examples of operator-turned-programmers are better known, such as Grace Hopper, who worked with Howard Aiken on the Harvard Mark I and helped to develop COBOL (among other achievements), or, perhaps even more famously, the six women who formed the wartime operator team for the ENIAC at the Moore School of the University of Pennsylvania: Kay McNulty Mauchly Antonelli, Jean Jennings Bartik, Frances Synder Holberton, Marlyn Wescoff Melzer, Frances Bilas Spence, and Ruth Lichterman Teitelbaum. But there was also Sister Mary Kenneth Keller, BVM, a nun who may have been the first American woman to earn a PhD in Computer Science (at the University of Wisconsin, Madison, 1965), who helped to develop the BASIC programming language and founded the School of Computer Science at Clarke College in Iowa.[41] Like other American companies, IBM hired large numbers of women during the war, due to the labor shortage. But the company (again, like others) asked many of them to leave their jobs after the war to make way for the returning male veterans.[42] In fact, one woman who worked at IBM's Watson Lab at Columbia, Eleanor Kolchin, was hired at the end of the war in 1946 as a programmer and says that "[a]t that time, IBM fired you if you got married," as part of the company's policy on giving hiring preferences to veterans.[43] In 1951, however, IBM changed its internal rule and declared that a "female employee will not be required to resign from the company upon marriage."[44]

Women hired by IBM in the 1940s were likely to be directed to jobs as keypunch operators, large numbers of whom the company trained with IBM-specific skills in order to reinforce its control of the market for its machines.[45] These were lower-paid entry-level jobs, gendered as most clerical office work was. But as early as the 1940s, IBM also hired women as customer service representatives, in part because "IBM leaders realized that many potential customers were afraid of their machines and unsure how to use them to the utmost." They needed "instruction and reassurance" when the machines gave them trouble.

> Thus IBM officials decided that rather than selling the machines and then leaving the buyers to cope with them on their own, they would lease them and provide long-term service contracts guaranteeing that a knowledgable, calm, tactful employee would be available on short notice when problems arose. For such jobs, bright, "personable" young women, recent graduates in mathematics from good colleges, from which they were specially recruited, seemed to fit the bill. As early as 1943, IBM hired hundreds of women for these jobs....[46]

Despite the sexism we see behind even this kind of opportunity, an increasing number of women entered computer-science degree programs as these became available and took computer-based jobs in the later twentieth century. But their numbers declined precipitously in the early twenty-first century—"women in computing" has never been a simple story of progress. One explanation may be that when "programming" became markedly less physical and clerical in the 1950s and 1960s, and was regularly automated using stored-program machines and software proper, more men moved to take these newly professionalized, higher-paying jobs, in a process of direct displacement.[47]

I'll have more to say in Chapter 4 about the young women who performed most of the labor in Father Busa's own center. For now, I just want to call attention to the role played by women in the later 1940s when it came to the public face of computing in general, the mixture of expertise and technical mastery that was so often on display, whether intentionally or not, and even in cases of stereotypically sexualized exploitation of the idea of the feminine.

Even stranger than the fashion shoot was the use of the SSEC in a 1952 film, *Walk East on Beacon*, which told the story of a top-secret government project running secret calculations on a "new high-speed calculator"—a part played by the SSEC, filmed on location in its own showroom, with some IBMers, including Betsy Stewart and Wayne Brooke, hired as extras.[48] The resulting film noir is an FBI procedural and a lurid piece of Cold War propaganda, based directly on an article by J. Edgar Hoover himself about the recent Rosenberg spy case (the trial was held in March 1951), published in the mass-market *Reader's Digest*, May 1952.[49] The credits for the film include thanks to the FBI for its assistance. Like similar FBI-assisted films of those years, *Walk East on Beacon* contained plenty of gee-whiz forensic technology, what Hoover's voice over calls "scientific techniques of crime-detection" and surveillance, from microfilm to hidden cameras—including a hidden live TV camera. The script emphasizes the intensive "research" of FBI agents and their scientific techniques for exploiting "data." Hoover says in *Reader's Digest* that the Bureau had "mobilized every resource known to us" for the case. So it's all the more striking when, in the fictionalized account, those resources don't include access to large-scale computing, yet, nothing beyond the punched-card machines it was using in real life at the time to process its famous files. A similar film-noir procedural from 1948, *The Street with No Name*, shows FBI agents researching a national fingerprint database in punched-card form. At one point the camera zooms in and lingers on the image of a black metal sorting machine as the cards are rapidly processed into vertical slots. By the time of the 1952 film, the SSEC stood in for a new generation of academic-industry-government computers, from Princeton's IAS to the ASCC and the ENIAC, and in fact the SSEC itself was getting some government contract work in real life, including that commission for calculations for the "Hippo" bomb project at Los Alamos. Soon enough, of course, intelligence agencies would become the quintessential users of the data-processing capabilities of such systems. At one point in *Walk East on Beacon*, a smiling government-contracted scientist tells an FBI investigator to drop by and visit the computer lab sometime, but then another scientist laughingly warns: "if he's granted an audience, the calculator won't stand for any trifling questions!"

In one key scene, you can clearly see the IBM logo below the panel of flashing indicator lights. The film was a piece of corporate promotion, as well as political propaganda. From its initial rollout, the SSEC was represented as a miraculous electronic brain that could answer difficult and complex questions, as in one image, dated December 16, 1950, and published in *The Saturday Evening Post*, captioned "Oracle on 57th Street" (Figure 2.3). IBM headquarters, with a cut-away SSEC showroom, becomes a plinth or temple for the colossal oracle, a feminized allegory of the machine's genius. The idea of a computer as a feminized magical oracle was commonplace at the time. In *Walk East on Beacon*, the fictional scientist refers to the computer as his "Princess," and in England's Bletchley Park, where Alan Turing led the codebreakers during the war, the Bombe machines were referred to as "the Oracle," and were said to be "like some eastern Goddess who was destined to become the oracle of Bletchley."[50] In context, we can see that the general idea of large-scale computers as exotic, feminized oracles, and in particular IBM's SSEC as the Oracle on 57th Street, may have been an unconscious idealization of actual women like Betsy Stewart and the legion of female operators she represented. Like the hiring of women as customer service representatives, it may also have been an effort to feminize and thus render less threatening, more personable, the new colossal machines.

FIGURE 2.3   Advertisement, "Oracle on 57th Street," *Saturday Evening Post*,
December 16, 1950 (author's copy).

In the ad's image, the Oracle is reading printout and feeding it down to the tiny
humans below, including, apparently, some non-specialist passersby. The cartoon is
actually a print ad for Shell Oil, which, we're told in the copy, has "collaborated
with IBM engineers" (in researching lubricants). So it's also a bit of cross-marketing
of IBM as what in later decades it would call itself: "the solutions company":
"Calculating machines" are "the question-answering 'oracles' of business," the ad
says. In fact, in 1948–1949, and for some time thereafter, the questions posed to
machines of this kind would have had to be in the form of mathematical calculations, not natural language queries—perhaps the real meaning behind the line
about the imaginary version of the SSEC in *Walk East on Beacon*, that it "won't
stand for any trifling questions!"

Evgeny Morozov has pointed to the instrumentalist market-creating assumptions about computing which define everything in society—even the messiness of democratic politics—as "problems" for technology to "solve."[51] In the multi-platform media campaigns around the SSEC we glimpse a moment when the idea of "business solutions" and the ideology of techno-solutionism were just being formed, at the intersection of relationships between government, business, and science. But the idea of seeking solutions in mid-century science, while it may be based in general on a kind of positivism, arose from more specific social contexts, and it's important that we understand those contexts. The idea of technology as problem solving arises in part out of laboratory and workshop culture, in which mechanics or engineers tinker and tweak in order to discover how to fix a broken component, for example. On the one hand this culture is related to that of the military Seabees, the "can do" philosophy and even ironic claims to do the impossible. On the other hand, however, it's part of experimental scientific culture in general, the intellectual's love of problems to solve for their own sake. It's the reason chess and crossword puzzles were associated with cryptanalysis and, eventually, with computing during the war. What's being "solved," in such cases, isn't necessarily some profound, fundamental human problem, or even an everyday inconvenience rendered as if it *were* a profound human problem, as in much Silicon Valley hype, but a delimited intellectual puzzle—like finding a neat solution to an equation, crossword, cipher, or riddle. It's an illusion that such problem solving is disinterested and neutral. Business and government alike marketed this ethos as part of what their machines could do. But such promises remained in tension with its more pragmatic and often ironic origins among the researchers themselves, like an inside joke of the trade, both bragging and debunking: "The impossible takes a little longer." No *engineer* would have been likely to pronounce that "impossible" in entirely unironic tones. The utterances of classical oracles were themselves in the form of opaque riddles, remember. They required deciphering and were subject to dispute. So calling the computer an oracle may contain inadvertent (and perhaps anxious) contradictions, a half-conscious acknowledgement of the serious limitations of its "solutions," the esoteric nature of its operations, and the necessity for human specialists, coders and decoders, to interpret and make something—something productive and profitable—of the solutions it provides. Even in disciplines with scientific aspirations (such as mid-century linguistics), humanities research has typically foregrounded those kinds of tensions and the need for interpretation, especially given its dependence on natural-language historical and archival materials, which require cultural frameworks for interpreting them as data.

The SSEC also inspired another movie computer from the 1950s, the fictional EMARAC in *Desk Set* (1957), starring Spencer Tracy and Katherine Hepburn.[52] The giant computer in this film, with iconic spinning tape drives and panels of blinking lights—and punched-card input—is installed in a TV studio reference library by a kind of Taylorite efficiency expert played by Tracy. The machine's name is a play on ENIAC, and it's eventually nicknamed "Emmy." It appears at first to threaten the jobs of the librarians, all female and supervised by the Hepburn character, pointedly named Bunny Watson (after the IBM family), who has a high IQ and a prodigious memory, and "connects many things with many things." In other worlds, with some technical training, she's actually the perfect operator-as-collaborator for the big machine. When she makes her entrance, she's just come from IBM, where she's seen a demonstration of the "new electronic brain," as she reports with some concern. In the end, a harpy-like female operator brought in by the consultant is sent packing and the plucky reference librarian bonds with the machine—after she first sabotages it and then Tracy's character repairs it using one of her hairpins. It's a kind of beauty-and-the-beast plot, but a serious aim of the movie is to reassure viewers, as the characters are reassured at the happy ending, that computers are meant to assist human experts, not replace them, a common theme in the 1950s, when in fact layoffs were a real consequence of the new automation. Even the film admits that the payroll and accounting departments were downsized after a similar machine was brought in. It proves how limited it is by generating false pink slips and "firing" the whole company. That machine, Tracy's character says, was different, "just a calculator." The film implies that computers are evolving along friendlier, more collaborative lines in their relations with human users. In fact, in 1957, customers for automaton might have used large-scale calculators, but they were much more likely to still be using suites of punched-card accounting machines. The opening credits, which scroll by printed on continuous paper in an IBM machine, thank IBM for its "cooperation and assistance." From IBM's perspective, *Desk Set* was another act of product placement as public relations. Its existence implied the need for such reassurances in the late 1950s, a need that would only grow in the 1960s, with the beginnings of a backlash against computers and the military–industrial complex that gave rise to them and which they supported.

The historical value of the SSEC is bound up with the image of computing it represented—no small thing culturally. With the SSEC Thomas J. Watson, Sr., "took the computer out of the lab and sold it to the public,"[53] a strategy the company (and others) would continue to follow. The campaign around the SSEC as what is now called a marquee system bears a striking resemblance to other IBM campaigns, including, for example, IBM researchers' using scanning tunneling microscope technology in 1989 to build the company logo from individual atoms; and "the world's smallest stop-motion movie" (according to *The Guinness Book of World Records*), *A Boy and His Atom*, an animated short made in 2013 by manipulating single atoms, frame by frame.[54] The film shows a stick-figure boy playing with a single atom as if it were a bouncing ball, and concludes by spelling out—what else?—"THINK" and "IBM" at atomic scale. On one level, this sort of campaign is obviously a publicity stunt, but it's also a serious demonstration of advanced scientific and industrial research at IBM (the company holds a record number of patents). *A Boy and His Atom* was made available on YouTube, but behind it lay the development of "the world's smallest magnetic memory bit, made of just 12 atoms," as the company website points out. More recently, in related work, IBM Research used a tiny "chisel"—a sharp silicon tip 10,000 times smaller than a sharpened pencil—to remove material and sculpt objects.[55] Although it can be used to prototype microcircuits, for example, in order to "demonstrate the tool and to stimulate the enthusiasm for nanotechnology for a new generation of scientists," IBM used it to create something with more immediate publicity value: the world's smallest magazine cover, an actual design for *National Geographic Kids*, 11 × 14 micrometers (2,000 of the covers would fit on a single grain of salt). The SSEC's was a similar sort of campaign, starting with the dedication event, at which Wallace Eckert's calculations for the lunar ephemeris made a splash. At once reassuringly playful and technically impressive, demos of this kind serve multiple purposes. They sell IBM as an advanced technology company, and they represent the idea of actual and theoretical future uses of its technologies among a broader public. Interestingly, they often take the form of applying the attention-getting technology to the creation of artistic and cultural products—versions of print magazine cover designs and animated movies—what we might call the domain of the popular humanities, broadly defined.

Perhaps the biggest recent publicity campaign of this kind at IBM, based at a new headquarters on Astor Place in New York City, was for Watson, a system named for the CEO with whom Father Busa met in 1949. Its most famous public application was winning the quiz show *Jeopardy!* in 2011, which it did without being connected to the Internet, applying machine learning based on a very fast processor and its own massive database. It answered questions—or, rather, according to the rules of the game, it responded to answers with appropriate questions ("What is . . . ?"). In historical context, it's worth noting that Watson's kind of cognitive computing is ultimately descended from the kind of work Busa and Tasman helped to inaugurate, the processing of language instead of numbers. Watson could not have been possible without Busa's eventual focus on treating a text-base in the way a database would later be treated—as a store to be mined, analyzed, rearranged algorithmically, in order to reveal patterns or raise new questions. At mid-century, the SSEC was (literally) the poster child for the kind of aspirations that eventually led to Watson. Busa was unable to use the SSEC, but he and Tasman did use the 705 a few years later, going from punched-card machines and the IBM Cardtype, to the IBM 1401, the IBM 1410, and the IBM 7090 by the late 1960s; as IBM machines improved the capabilities of their tape-drive systems, Busa's research "progressed," as Tasman said.[56] The SSEC was dedicated to science. But the smaller scale, less publicized "humanistic" work with punched-card machinery by Roberto Busa and Paul Tasman, the first phase of which was undertaken roughly during the SSEC's lifespan (1949–1952), marked an adjacent path, a small swerve that would eventually connect to the trajectory of some central aspirations for computing—not to mention to a key strain in humanities computing and what later became known as the digital humanities.

The SSEC was officially dedicated on Wednesday, January 28, 1948, on the second of two days of combined ceremony and demonstrations for the press and the scientific and business communities, by invitation from IBM's Department of Pure Science. Proceedings had begun on Tuesday the 27th with a luncheon that included scientists, business and academic leaders, developers of the machine, and IBM executives. The attendance and seating list shows about 200 invitees, including the Watson family. The famous scientist and father of programmed-computer architecture, John von Neumann, was there, sitting at a table with mathematician Oswald Veblen, IBM's Wallace Eckert, and others. Howard Aiken of the rival ASCC at Harvard is on the list, as is John Mauchly, developer (with Presper Eckert) of the ENIAC. The Provost of Columbia attended. Trustee of Columbia Thomas J. Watson, Sr. made a speech in which he introduced "the latest development in the field of higher calculating devices," before introducing the chief developer, Professor Wallace Eckert.[57] A copy of the speech in the IBM Archives contains penciled edits that may be by Watson himself. Even in the typed draft, the word "Electronic" in the full name of the SSEC is underscored as if for verbal emphasis, a graphic reminder of the importance of the shift to the use of vacuum tubes that IBM saw as one of the machine's important competitive features. Watson says that the war interrupted the company's "regular" program of "development," but that this resumed with the peace, "with an emphasis on the application of electronics," mentioning the completion in 1946 of "the first electronic calculator for commercial use."

The luncheon speech begins and ends with a common theme for Mr. Watson, Sr., the role of humans in discovery and achievement. The so-called machine age, he says, is actually the "greatest MAN AGE" ever. Addressing "leaders in pure and applied science" in the audience, he asserts that, "we sometimes hear the expression—Mechanical Brain. There is no such thing."

> The calculator which we are dedicating today has come about as the result of scientific thinking and the highest type of engineering skill. Now that we have it, it will only be useful in the hands of scientists, who will use it as a small tool to relieve them of a certain amount of physical and mental effort in solving their problems and furthering the development of scientific research for the benefit of humanity.

Later in the text of the speech, Watson, or whoever made the penciled edits, changed the sentence reading "The United States' economic development will be measured by the results of our scientific development" to "The United States' economic development will be measured by the achievements of its scientists," emphasizing human actors, evidently to counter what he thought of as popular misconceptions about the growing autonomy of "calculating machines." He closes by thanking by name the top developers behind the SSEC, pointedly including representatives from both sides of the divide between pure and applied science.

For the formal dedication ceremony the next day, the CEO began a shorter speech with, "As we stand within the structure of the new Electronic Calculator," and then Frank Hamilton presented the lunar calculations that were already running on the machine, using an easel, followed by Rex Seeber, who explained that both data and instructions are fed into the machine on "standard IBM punched cards, with the use of standard equipment," holding up one of the cards to show the audience. He then went on to explain the operation of the machine, component by component: punches, readers, tapes, tubes, relay memory, light panels, output printers, and cables beneath the raised floor. "Those of you who are above the steps will now realize that you are really within the machine, with the basic units around you in a U, the important cables below you, air ducts for the air conditioning in the ceiling overhead." The week before, Mr. Watson Sr. had reportedly inspected the showroom and approved, except, he said, for the large pillars standing in the middle of the room. Those should be removed, he declared, supposedly failing to understand that they were load-bearing columns for the 20-story building above them. The engineering staff found the story highly amusing for years thereafter. In fact, like everything else surrounding the story of the SSEC, it illustrates the constraints imposed by physical infrastructure of all kinds on the computing designs of the day. Even the logical architecture, including whether the machine could store its instructions and modify them on the fly, was a direct function of what was available and constructible under imposed deadlines and budgets: surplus vacuum tubes designed for radio, punched card-stock tapes, the room with pillars in place that had been a women's shoe store, its windows open to the view of 57th Street shoppers as the machine inside, which defined the space of the room rebuilt around it, ran its calculations in an ongoing four-year demo. The large-scale SSEC marked IBM's public pivot into high-speed electronics (though it hedged its bets in a hybrid system that also used electromechanical parts for core functions, those relay switches). When asked in 1967 whether the shift from electromechanical to electronic equipment at IBM and elsewhere, marked by the SSEC, meant that "the tail began wagging the dog," and whether he had to "change [his] outlook to adjust to this new equipment," Wallace Eckert replied, "Oh yes."[58]

> But anybody who is a professional computer, this is just second nature to him. He always looks at what his tools are and he wants to find out what it does well and he's always conscious of economic balances and the law of diminishing returns, as he pursues a particular idea.[59]

For the dedication ceremony, new brochures were printed (in sepia instead of in four colors, as the first batch had been) with an image of the showroom in which the columns had been airbrushed out. The image *sans* columns appeared on a card (with the dimensions of an iconic punched card), on the flipside of which was printed a bulleted list of facts about the SSEC, each bullet a printed image of a punched-card hole, covering things such as memory capacity, punched-tape memory entry, reading speed of the tape-rendering units, and overall speed—the last pointedly given as "250 times as fast as the IBM Automatic Sequence Controlled Calculator," the Harvard Mark I. The events of January 27–28 were jointly hosted, as it were, by the Columbia contingent and 590 Madison, designed to ensure IBM full credit, intellectual as well as engineering, for the new machine, with the general public as well within the scientific and business communities.

On the morning of the dedication, which included "a demonstration and technical session," the machine developed a bug, and while a luncheon was going on in the Club Room on the second floor, the engineers were busy "sweating blood" in the first-floor showroom where the SSEC was waiting for its debut.[60] But once the guests arrived to stand around "inside" the calculator, the machine ran through the "moon problem"—the lunar-position equations—without a hitch. The averted crisis was memorialized for years at annual celebration dinners held by the development staff (offsite, away from 590 and at nearby Midtown bars, since IBM had a no-alcohol policy at the time[61]). Toasts were made and comic songs were sung. These latter were drinking songs and party entertainments, but also inside jokes, parodies of the well-known company songs IBMers had sung at events since early in the century, rallying the sales force (e.g., "Ever Onward, IBM"), or declaring loyalty to the company and its leaders: Thomas J. Watson, Sr. figured in many of them by name.[62] Parodies of these kinds will show up later in Thomas Pynchon's influential 1965 novel, *The Crying of Lot 49*, in the songs of the fictional Yoyodyne Corporation: "High above the L.A. freeways, / And the traffic's whine, / Stands the well-known Galactronics / Branch of Yoyodyne. / To the end, we swear undying / Loyalty to you. . . ."[63] The SSEC parodies, written by engineers and scientists, served other purposes than the company songs, such as venting tensions between the technical staff and what were already being thought of as "the suits" (Herb Grosch believed he was the first IBM employee to wear a beard and a sports jacket).

One of the songs first sung at the second anniversary party for the SSEC in January 1950 (to the tune of "Heigh-Ho, Heigh-Ho") was about the bug: "It's broke, it's broke / Is what the girls all croak. . . . The circuits are a joke / We positively can't fix it / It's broke, it's broke."[64] This lament gives way abruptly in the final chorus to:

> It's fixed, it's fixed
> Is what we gladly say
> Just as the gals put on their coats
> It's fixed, it's fixed, it's fixed
> …
> The time is five-oh-six
> You positively can't go now
> It's fixed, it's fixed.

Other songs for the same occasion joked about the filming of *Walk East on Beacon* and suggests the movie was a distraction to keep the coders happy in the face of unrealistic demands from the client:

> Oh, I've been working on the
> International Business Machines Sel. Seq. Electro. Calculator
> All the live long day
> I've been working on the
> International Business Machines Sel. Seq. Electro. Calculator
> Just to gather up my pay.
>
> . . . .
>
> The problems that they bring us
> Are filled with calculus
> That will drive us nuts someday someday
> But for compensation
> We have movies on location
> And a chance to be a star someday someday

Another (to the tune of "Casey Jones") made fun of the film's fictional "secret calculations" (called the "Cornell Integrations" and the "Princeton variables"):

> Put in your cards and set up your tapes
> Press the button and let's make haste
> For the F.B.I. we will force it through
> And I'll watch the tubes so they don't turn blue.

The fragility (the engineers called it "unreliability") of the radio-technology vacuum tubes is implicitly compared in the final chorus to that of old jalopies, "a Stanley Steamer and a Model T." The general irreverence toward the machine and the company contrasts with the sententiousness of the official speeches, plaques, and press releases. If nothing else, the parodies give us an after-hours glimpse of the coders' and engineers' pragmatic sense of the material limitations of the supposedly magical, oracular machines they were being asked to build and on which they were supposed to solve profound problems. Sometimes they give us more than a glimpse:

> We've got a lovely little computer
> There it is a-standing like a king
> Big tubes, little tubes, some that work as they should
> Give it a test, then a long rest, that's what the old Muscat said.
> We've got a lovely little computer

Every problem you give us will make us rich
There stands my boss, to whom I'm a total loss
Singing roll or bowl a ball a penny a pitch.

In context, the "old Muscat" would seem to be Rex Seeber. But the "boss" and the "suits" in general, the "demonstrators" running the demo, are treated in the satirical song as carnival barkers, the observers from the press and among the invited experts as "customers" in the carnival tradition:

We've got a lovely bunch of demonstrators
There they are a-pointing as they go
Big lies, white lies, that's the stuff they hand
But we know the son-of-a-gun ain't worth a tinker's damn.
We've got a lovely bunch of demonstrators
And they try to hard to make it good
Here comes a jerk, give him all its worth
Singing roll or bowl a ball a penny a pitch — etc.

The satire should resonate with anyone who attended a tech demo in the decades that followed, during which programmers were called on to run scripted and sometimes "canned" versions of the latest amazing technology. In the joke the "lies" are, most of all, about the perfection of the machine, and especially its unquestioned ability to solve difficult problems.

In fact, the SSEC did run those serious astronomical calculations at the demo, despite the limitations of the machine, including those 12,000 fragile vacuum tubes. It was said that the lunar calculations run that day were used twenty years later by the Apollo program. The real lesson of that connection may be that the Apollo program itself used the same model as the SSEC project, its combination of taking on a difficult, seemingly impossible problem and solving it with applied science based on adventurous pure research, and of generating popular support for the work with high if vague aspirations about expanding the reach of humanity, goals that might be called—were called at the time—"humanistic," but which were at bottom about pressing the values of the humanities into service of the state and of commerce. Reading that plaque on the wall of the SSEC showroom, it's not difficult to imagine how IBM might well have welcomed the collaboration, however limited, with the Jesuit priest working on a medieval philosophical corpus. As Paul Tasman said of expanding the method to the Dead Sea Scrolls, the work "combined the modern machine with ancient spiritual writings to further our understanding of our basic theological heritage"—he might have added philosophical, literary, historical, and artistic heritage.

The history of the SSEC helps us to understand the background to such claims, and it complicates the picture of that idealized collaboration. At the same time that he was loaning out his machine to make what amounted to a Cold

War propaganda film, and using it to contribute calculations to the hydrogen bomb project as well as the lunar ephemeris (along with other commercial and scientific problems), Thomas J. Watson, Sr. also looked for educational and social applications, partly in the tradition of corporate philanthropy, but also because he really was interested in finding "humanistic" applications, thereby having the universal value of his equipment demonstrated by being used in "novel" ways that were "socially useful." To put it bluntly: these demonstrations served to associate IBM with the values of the humanities. It's a useful reminder of how humanities computing can serve the purposes of computing as much as it serves the purposes of humanities research, how research in natural language data mining, for example, might seem useful to both industry and government, as well as scholarship. IBM's website claims today that "IBMers have been using cultural projects to stretch the boundaries of technology for generations. In the process, they have made it possible for scholars, museums, libraries and governments to make their work accessible—and newly understandable—to people all over the world."[65] The order of operations, and the order of intentions, in that formulation, what comes first and what comes "in the process," would likely be reversed by many humanities-computing and digital-humanities scholars, some of whose work is included in the site's description of the preservation and access of cultural heritage. On that same web page, IBM cites as a key example Busa and Tasman's work on the Dead Sea Scrolls in the 1950s.

This history-to-come is already implied in the story of the big SSEC demo of January 27–28, 1948, which in effect continued in the 57th Street showroom, in one form or another, for four more years after that and was still going strong (and still being noticed on the street and in the press) when Father Busa arrived at the building in the fall of 1949. The next chapter shifts attention from the splashy SSEC demo of 1948 to Father Busa's and Paul Tasman's more modest—but not altogether different—demo of 1952, held at the same location at IBM headquarters. This was the first major public demonstration of a technical methodology for "literary data processing," which fed into one strand of what became known as humanities computing and, in our own time, an influential stream of the digital humanities.

Notes

1 Photographs #32, #34, #38. Busa Archive. (#32 and #34 are available at the website for this book.)
2 A. Wayne Brooke, "SSEC, The First Electronic Computer," unpublished typescript, in A. Wayne Brooke Papers, MC 00268, Special Collections Research Center, North Carolina State University Libraries, Raleigh, NC (Box 1, Folder 8), 2-3. In 1949, one year after the SSEC debuted, two contenders appeared in England, EDSAC at Cambridge and Baby at Manchester. The machines at Bletchley Park used by wartime codebreakers, the Colossi, were operational by 1944. The debate over priority for programmable and stored-program machines in the U.S. usually focuses on the

IBM ASCC, also known as the Harvard Mark I (1944), John Mauchly's and J. Presper Eckert's ENIAC (1946), and EDVAC (operating in 1951 but documented in detail by John von Neumann in 1945). The ENIAC is probably most commonly considered the first general purpose computer, but the SSEC, which debuted two years later, was designed from the start for a wider range of government and industry applications, not as a purpose-built laboratory machine.

3 Brooke, "SSEC, The First Electronic Computer," 2–2.

4 Wallace Eckert interview by Lawrence Saphire for IBM Oral History of Computing Technology (Interview TC-1, July 11, 1967), A. Wayne Brooke Papers, NCSU (Box 1, Folder 15), 8. Cited courtesy of International Business Machines Corporation.

5 Eckert interview by Lawrence Saphire, 7.

6 Transcript of Ken Clark interview by Lawrence Saphire for Oral History of Computer Technology (Interview TC-6, August 8, 1967), in A. Wayne Brooke Papers, NCSU (Box 1, Folder 18), 22. Cited courtesy of International Business Machines Corporation.

7 James W. Cortada, *Before the Computer: IBM, NCR, Burroughs, and Remington Rand and the Industry They Created, 1865–1956* (Princeton: Princeton University Press, 2000), 44.

8 Cortada, *Before the Computer*, 45–46.

9 Cortada, *Before the Computer*, 45.

10 "Never Stumped," *The New Yorker* (March 4, 1950), 20–21.

11 Herbert R. J. Grosch, *Computer: Bit Slices from a Life* (Lancaster, PA: Third Millennium Press, 1991; 3rd Ed., 2003), accessed online at Columbia University Computing History website, ed. Frank da Cruz, http://www.columbia.edu/cu/computinghistory/computer.html#[-8-].

12 My account of personnel and institutional arrangements for the Watson Laboratory in is based on Grosch, *Computer*, Chapter 1, as well as the Columbia University Computing History website, ed. Frank da Cruz, http://www.columbia.edu/cu/computinghistory/.

13 Grosch, *Computer*, 73–74.

14 Grosch, *Computer*, 7.

15 A. Wayne Brooke, unpublished typescript, A. Wayne Brooke Papers, NCSU, Appendix A. Cited courtesy of International Business Machines Corporation.

16 See Thomas Haigh and Mark Priestley. "Innovators Assemble: Ada Lovelace, Walter Isaacson, and the Superheroines of Computing," *Communications of the ACM* 58.9 (September 2015), 20–27. DOI: 10.1145/2804228. In our own time, as the authors say, even the well-motivated "quest for 'girls who code' is erasing the history of women who operate . . . ."

17 "Never Stumped," *New Yorker* (March 4, 1950), 20–21.

18 George Dyson, *Turing's Cathedral: The Origins of the Digital Universe* (New York: Pantheon Books, 2012), Kindle edition, loc. 4309.

19 A. Wayne Brooke, unpublished typescript, A. Wayne Brooke Papers, NCSU, 11.

20 Eckert interview by Lawrence Saphire, 30.

21 Harry Reed quoted in George Dyson, *Turing's Cathedral*, loc. 1685.

22 Norbert Wiener, *Cybernetics: Or Control and Communication in the Animal and the Machine* (Cambridge, MA: MIT Press, 1948).

23 N. Katherine Hayles, "Cybernetics," in W. J. T. Mitchell, and M. B. N. Hansen, eds., *Critical Terms for Media Studies* (Chicago: University of Chicago Press, 2010), 144–56.

24 Norbert Wiener, *Cybernetics*; N. Katherine Hayles, *Electronic Literature: New Horizons for the Literary* (Notre Dame, IN: Notre Dame University Press, 2008), 45, 48.

25 Jussi Parikka, *What Is Media Archaeology?* (Cambridge, UK: Polity, 2012), 3.

26 Eckert interview by Lawrence Saphire, 9

27 Paul Tasman interview by Lawrence Saphire for IBM Oral History of Computer Technology (Interview TC-99, August 14, 1968), 10. IBM Archives, courtesy of International Business Machines Corporation.

28 Paul Tasman, *Indexing the Dead Sea Scrolls, by Electronic Literary Data Processing Methods* (New York: IBM World Trade Corporation, 1958), 12.

29 Paul Tasman, "Literary Data Processing," *IBM Journal of Research and Development* 1.3 (1957), 249–56 (249).

30 Tasman, *Indexing the Dead Sea Scrolls, by Electronic Literary Data Processing Methods*, 12.

31 Tasman interview by Lawrence Saphire, 15–16.

32 Roberto Busa, "The Annals of Humanities Computing: The *Index Thomisticus*," *Computers and the Humanities* 14.2 (1980), 84.

33 Busa, "The Annals of Humanities Computing: The *Index Thomisticus*," 84.

34 A. Wayne Brooke, unpublished typescript, A. Wayne Brooke Papers, NCSU, 11.

35 IBM internal document on SSEC publicity, IBM Archives, courtesy of International Business Machines Corporation.

36 IBM internal document on SSEC publicity, "Sample News Reports," 2, IBM Archives, courtesy of International Business Machines Corporation.

37 Fashion-spread clipping: "Count on a Bright Future," A. Wayne Brooke Papers, MC 00268, Special Collections Research Center, North Carolina State University Libraries, Raleigh, NC (Box 2, folder 39). On British computer industry marketing exploiting the image of women operators (which closely resembles that in the U.S.), see Marie Hicks, "Only the Clothes Changed: Women Operators in British Computing and Advertising, 1950–1970," *IEEE Annals of the History of Computing* 32.2 (October-December 2010), 2–14, http://www.mariehicks.net/writing/Hicks_Only_the_Clothes_Changed_Annals_32_4_Final.pdf.

38 For a more recent assessment, see "Solving the Equation: The Variables for Women's Success in Engineering and Computing," American Association of University Women report (2015), http://www.aauw.org/research/solving-the-equation/.

39 Grosch, *Computer*, 81.

40 Aetna Katherine Womble-Dowst Obituary, http://www.obitsforlife.com/obituary/186609/Womble-Dowst-Aetna.php.

41 See Denise Gürer, "Women in Computing History," *ACM SIGCSE Bulletin* 34.2 (ACM Press, 2002), 116-120; W. Barkley Fritz, "The Women of ENIAC," *IEEE Annals of the History of Computing* 18.3 (1996), 13–28. On Sister Mary Kenneth Keller, see Wikipedia: http://en.wikipedia.org/wiki/Mary_Kenneth_Keller.

42 Grosch, *Computer*, 102; Janet Abbate, *Recoding Gender: Women's Changing Participation in Computing* (Cambridge, MA and London: MIT Press, 2012), 18-19.

43 Bianca Boskar, "The Face of a 'Computer' from 1946," *Huffington Post*, February 1, 2013, http://www.huffingtonpost.com/2013/02/01/watson-scientific-computing-lab_n_2592670.html?ncid=txtlnkushpmg00000043.

44 Rebecca J. Rosen, "The Internal Memo That Allowed IBM's Female Employees to Get Married," *The Atlantic*, February 4, 2013, http://www.theatlantic.com/technology/archive/2013/02/the-internal-memo-that-allowed-ibms-female-employees-to-get-married/272832/.

45 See Robert Sobel, *IBM: Colossus In Transition* (New York: Bantam Books, 1983), 81.

46 Margaret W. Rossiter, *Women Scientists in America Before Affirmative Action 1940–1972* (Baltimore and London: Johns Hopkins University Press, 1995), 269.

47 Wendy Hui Kyong Chun, "On Software, or The Persistence of Visual Knowledge," *Grey Room* 18 (Winter 2005), 26–51, http://www.brown.edu/Departments/MCM/people/chun/papers/software.pdf.

48 A. Wayne Brooke, unpublished typescript, 12. Brooke reports the IBMers were paid "at 'bit-part' rates." He made $10 for his brief non-speaking role.

49 J. Edgar Hoover, "The Crime of the Century: The Case of the A-Bomb Spies," *Reader's Digest* 58.349 (May 1951), 149–68.

50 Andrew Hodges, *Alan Turing: The Enigma* (Princeton: Princeton University Press, 2014), Kindle edition, 240.

51 Evgeny Morozov, *To Save Everything, Click Here: The Folly of Technological Solutionism* (New York: Public Affairs, 2013).

52 Kevin Maney, *The Maverick and His Machine: Thomas J. Watson, Sr. and the Making of IBM* (Hoboken, NJ: John Wiley & Sons, Inc., 2003), Kindle edition, loc. 3698. *Desk Set* (film), director, Walter Lang, Twentieth-Century Fox, 1957. Although the film appeared in 1957, it was based on a stage play by William Marchant in 1955, much closer to the heyday of the SSEC. In the Marchant script the name is spelled EMMARAC ("Electronic Magnetic Memory And Research Arithmetical Caculator").

53 Maney, *The Maverick and His Machine*, Kindle edition, loc. 3698.

54 "A Boy and His Atom: The World's Smallest Movie," IBM Research website, http://www.research.ibm.com/articles/madewithatoms.shtml#fbid=vQLsyjC5w6s.

55 "World's Smallest Magazine Cover," IBM Research website, http://www.research.ibm.com/articles/smallestcover.html#fbid=vQLsyjC5w6s.

56 Tasman interview by Lawrence Saphire, 18.

57 Thomas J. Watson, Sr., typescripts of speeches for SSEC dedication, January 27–28, 1948, IBM Archives, courtesy International Business Machines Corporation.

58 Eckert interview by Lawrence Saphire, 28.

59 Eckert interview by Lawrence Saphire, 28.

60 A. Wayne Brooke, unpublished typescript, A. Wayne Brooke Papers, 10.

61 Grosch, *Computer*, 97.

62 Lee Hutchinson, "Tripping through IBM's astonishingly insane 1937 corporate songbook," *Ars Technica*, August 29, 2014, http://arstechnica.com/business/2014/08/tripping-through-ibms-astonishingly-insane-1937-corporate-songbook/.

63 Thomas Pynchon, *The Crying of Lot 49* (1966; New York: Harper & Row, 1990), 83.

64 The parodies quoted here and below are from typescripts, probably by A. Wayne Brooke, in the A. Wayne Brooke Papers, NCSU (Box. 2, Folder 29).

65 IBM 100 Icons of Progress, http://www-03.ibm.com/ibm/history/ibm100/us/en/icons/preservation/.

3

THE MOTHER OF ALL HUMANITIES COMPUTING DEMOS

The First Public Demo of Busa's and Tasman's Punched-Card Method of "Literary Data Processing," June 27, 1952

On June 27, 1952, at IBM World Headquarters at 590 Madison Avenue in New York, Rex Seeber, of the Department of Pure Science, gave one of his final presentations on the large-scale calculator, the SSEC, a machine he had helped to build. The SSEC was just about to be decommissioned. As we saw in Chapter 2, this machine, the "Oracle on 57th Street," had occupied the ground-floor showroom for almost four years and was soon to be disassembled and removed. IBM had announced in April that it was in the process of building a new large-scale electronic machine, the "Defense Calculator," or IBM 701, which would be twenty-five times faster than the SSEC.[1] That codename during development was more a matter of patriotic branding than an indication of exclusive purpose. It may even have had something to do with offsetting the negative publicity over the antitrust proceedings brought against IBM in January 1952 by the Department of Justice, by calling attention to the company's national strategic importance. The 701 would soon be installed in the IBM showroom, inaugurating a line of computers manufactured for government, scientific, and business users. In the meantime, in summer 1952 the SSEC was on display for a few final weeks. One photograph from the June 27 event shows Rex Seeber standing on the steps to the raised floor of the custom-designed room, facing back toward a group of men standing together under an oversized "THINK" sign.[2] The interdisciplinary group included several priests in Roman collars, among them Father Victor Yanitelli, an instructor in Modern Languages at Fordham University. In addition there was Meriwether Stuart, Professor of Latin at Hunter College, and Henry Silver, Staff Adviser on Scholarly Publications for the American Council of Learned Societies. Silver had been with Columbia University Press and was responsible at the ACLS for advising scholarly publishers on "new processes and methods to make the scholar-author conscious of the economic and mechanical problems involved in the publishing of his product."[3]

Although he's not visible in this photograph, Father Roberto Busa was also there that day. In fact he was back in New York in order to co-host the day's events with Paul Tasman. Seeber's presentation of the SSEC was really just a supplemental attraction, although, as I suggested in Chapter 2, it was a highly significant one in terms of what the SSEC symbolized about the shift to electronic computing and what Busa could have learned from it about the potential for electronic data processing. The group had actually come to the IBM Hall of Products that day for a demonstration of a very different technology—more old-fashioned and less flashy than the SSEC but sharing in the spotlight it still generated—punched-card accounting machinery. This kind of office machinery was still in widespread use at the time, especially in cities like New York where business information was concentrated. But there was something new, something unusual about the event that day. The point was to demonstrate Busa's and Tasman's method of repurposing those punched-card machines in order to process natural language, a method for analyzing so-called "literary" texts by treating them as sources of linguistic data.

Between his first visit to IBM in 1949, hat in hand, and this triumphant return in 1952 as co-presenter at a formal demonstration, Father Busa had taken the *Index Thomisticus* from general proposal to funded project. How he did that—what happened in 1950–1952 as he traveled back and forth between Europe and the U.S., coordinating with IBM and a worldwide network mostly of his own making—is the subject of this chapter. Two and a half years' activity culminated in the demonstration at 590 Madison Avenue. It was the climax of the start-up period of what would turn out to be a multi-decade research project, and a watershed moment in work that would come to be seen by many as the origin of humanities computing.

In the chapter title I refer to the June 27 event as "the mother of all humanities computing demos," an allusion to Douglas Engelbart's famous live demo, December 9, 1968, at San Francisco's Civic Center for a meeting of the Joint Computer Conference. There Engelbart showed what he called the NLS (or oN-Line System), a collection of prototypes for controlling, organizing, and communicating with networked computers that would become standard in the Internet era: the mouse, the kind of intuitive text editing a mouse afforded, screen conventions such as files and windows, hyperlinks, collaborative shared text, even live video conferencing. The system was, as they say (always in retrospect), ahead of its time, and so was the public presentation, which deployed multiple media and elaborate technical connections. Engelbart sat at a terminal wearing a headset microphone and explained the projected images on a large screen—a format that still dominates technology demos and TED Talks today (though speakers now often stand). The audience was reportedly impressed. The presentation's ironic name, taken from Saddam Hussein's blustering name for the first Gulf War, "the mother of all battles," came later, in Steven Levy's retrospective account published in 1994, because Levy thought he recognized in the demo a harbinger of computing in the 1990s: "It was the mother of all demos."[4]

Over the three decades since, the technology demo has become a conventional, recognizable genre of its own. A developer shows an unfinished version of a hardware or software product (or combination of both) as a proof of concept and, often, as an early bit of marketing. In a formal presentation at least a working prototype is shown. Although it's expected that the new technology isn't finished, and therefore that the demonstration is more or less "canned" for the occasion, the idea is to get a sense of how the device will work when it is finished. Usually, it's put through a limited set of tasks with the understanding that more functionality will be available upon release. Everyone's familiar with Apple Computer events starring the late Steve Jobs, for example, but this genre goes back decades before, to engineering demonstrations within companies and, less often, for the public. Engelbart's was not the first such demo, but it was overwhelming in its showmanship, ambitious scope, and the key audience it reached—hence the nickname.

Father Busa wrote to Douglas Engelbart at Stanford at least once, in 1970, just two years after Engelbart's big demo, requesting a copy of the influential paper "Augmenting the Human Intellect," and saying that he would like to be able to quote it in his own upcoming presentations. He enclosed a list of his publications.[5] I don't know whether Engelbart sent his paper or whether he read Busa's work in turn, but the letter provides intriguing evidence of Father Busa's ongoing interest in systems engineering and human–computer interface (HCI) design. Looking back, you could say that his own 1952 demo, although not widely known in itself, has become for humanities computing and digital humanities what Engelbart's 1968 demo became for online computing. It marks a shift in the way a key technology was understood, a source of specific methods and assumptions that would attract other practitioners and form what later came to seem the mainstream of the field. In the case of Busa's and Tasman's demo, it turned out to be the general concepts of how to use punched-card machinery to treat language as data to be processed, even more than the particulars of their methods, that influenced practice over the long term. But just as in Engelbart's case, the public event itself, the fact of the demo and the form it took—its audience and reception, considered in historical context—is just as meaningful as the content of what was presented that day.

My comparison to Engelbart is partly ironic, of course (and doubly ironic, at that, since it inherits the irony of Levy's hyperbole). Only in retrospect did Tasman's and Busa's modest gathering seem historically important, and it's still known mostly among practitioners in humanities computing and digital humanities. Even many of those who are aware of Father Busa's work on the *Index Thomisticus* have never heard the story of the demo. Unlike Engelbart's huge conference audience, Busa's June 1952 demo addressed a relatively small group, perhaps around twenty, along with some IBM operators and staff members, who participated at various stages. First a luncheon was held a few blocks away at the Sherry Netherland Hotel. Back at IBM for the demo, the invited audience stood clustered around the machines in IBM's walnut-paneled Hall of Products, walking in a group from one punched-card machine to another as the demonstration proceeded (see Figure 3.1). Tasman did most of the hands-on explaining, it would appear. At one stop, he held up a strip of the punched paper tape that fed into the Tape Card Punch from a reel mounted on the console, and showed how its encoded data was transferred to a deck of cards for further processing. These Tape Card Punch machines, with converters running in both directions, tape-to-card or card-to-tape, descended from versions created in 1941 by adding electromechanical relays and tape readers to punched-card machines. They had been used heavily by the military during the war, then installed commercially in the postwar period for customers such as railroad companies, RCA, Bethlehem Steel, Western Electric, Vanity Fair, and Merrill Lynch.[6]

At other stations along the progress of the peripatetic event, Tasman showed IBM accounting machines of the kind that he and Busa had been using, including a gang punch, a 407 Tabulator, and the new Cardatype Accounting Machine, which

FIGURE 3.1 Demo of the methods of literary data processing at IBM World Headquarters, June 27, 1952; Paul Tasman reading from *Varia Specimina Concordantiarum* to Francis Cardinal Spellman, while Roberto Busa and Thomas J. Watson, Jr, look on. Participants include Victor Yannitelli, S.J., L.P. Pennell, J.W. Perry (Busa Archive #10).

was mentioned both in the published *Varia Specima Concordantiarum* (1951) and in Tasman's oral history interview (1968) as being crucial to the project. (In fact, copies of the *Varia Specimina* were shown to guests and read from by Tasman during the event.) The IBM Cardatype was essentially a punched-card reader integrated with an electric typewriter, which could produce up to four different formatted documents from any single action on the part of an operator, and could run pre-punched cards while also allowing for manual interpolation of the data. The significance of this kind of machine for a project based on natural language and leading to the formatted, printed output of indexes in multiple iterations may be difficult for us to grasp, in our own era of ubiquitous word-processing, desktop-publishing software, and inexpensive personal printers in every office and middle-class home. Especially in the first decade, Father Busa repeatedly mentioned the problem of "listing" and then printing the results of the punched-card work in human-readable form, and he treated the shift to an offset system for the printing of pages as an important final stage in the overall process.

In one photograph, Tasman addresses the demo group as a whole in the windowed entryway of the building on 57th Street, perhaps making an introduction; key figures sit in chairs in a circle—anchored by Cardinal Spellman, T. J. Watson, Jr. (newly named IBM's President), J. G. Phillips (Vice-Chairman), and L. P. Pennell, Treasurer and Director of IBM's World Trade Corporation, along with academics (several of them priests)—with others standing around behind them (including Father Busa). From the camera's position we can see through the large windows in the background to cars on the street outside, a sign for the Chase Savings Bank across the street, and even one passerby on the sidewalk looking back through the window towards the camera inside. One is immediately struck by the gendered nature of the event, though it was typical of corporate functions at the time, of course, and was typical of the technology industry in particular: almost all are men in suits, who stand or sit amidst the accounting machines, arranged around the showroom floor. Several anonymous women sit at the controls of the machines (one woman stands near the back), no doubt IBM operators and programmers there as technical support for the demo, waiting to be called on. Father Busa's captions and identifications for the photographs in the Archive sometimes list, among the names of those depicted, an anonymous "computer"—the job description of a human operator with accounting or mathematical skills, whose job it was to actually run the machines.

Recent work by Melissa Terras and Julianne Nyhan has begun to identify some of the women operators involved in the production of Father Busa's *Index Thomisticus*, as we'll see in Chapter 4. But many photographs in the Busa Archive, as in the IBM Archives, remain haunted by images of unidentified women working at the punched-card machines, sometimes, as in the case I've been discussing, just out of frame or looking down at their controls instead of up at the (male) public speaker or at the camera. As I've said, this gendered division was typical for the time, during the transitional phase from plugboard setup, sometimes called programming, to software programming proper.[7] Some of the pictured women probably prepared the machines in the first place, configuring them by arranging the plugboards, and others actually punched the data onto the cards, or ran the cards through sorters. IBM actively recruited women in the postwar period for such work. A brochure from 1947, with the revealing title, *My Fair Ladies*, illustrated with photographs of actual IBM employees, is a good example of this effort—but also of the sexist assumptions that still channeled most women into clerical operations rather than high-level jobs.[8] There were a few exceptions, such as Jean E. Sammet, who had an MA in mathematics and developed the FORMAC language in 1962 while working for IBM, and who became a manager and the first female president of the Association for Computing Machinery in the 1970s.[9] Ruth Leach Amonette is another particularly interesting example.[10] She became the first female executive and Vice President at IBM in 1943 at the age of 27, after being "discovered" on the job, demoing typewriters at the 1939 World's Fair in San Francisco (the Golden Gate International Expo). After training, she was placed in charge of women's programs during the war and was responsible for women's education at IBM, establishing some of the training programs that surely helped to inspire Father Busa's own training school in Italy, as we'll see in the next chapter.

The majority of women recruited by IBM in the 1940s and 1950s were directed to jobs as operators—that ambiguous position between mere clerical laborer and skilled configurer of the complicated office machinery. In the photographs taken at IBM for Father Busa's and Paul Tasman's June 1952 demo, the women at the machines remain (so far) unidentified, but their presence serves as a vivid reminder of the gendered nature of the machine-human architecture of computing at the time, despite some new opportunities for some women in the emerging field.

The wider contexts for the 1952 demo—the activities of the roughly two years that led up to it and the institutional and social contexts surrounding it—are as important for understanding its significance as are the technology and specific techniques presented that day. After that first meeting with Thomas J. Watson, Sr. in November 1949 and being assigned to Paul Tasman of the IBM World Trade Corporation, Father Busa lost no time. By early spring 1950 he was back in Milan, continuing experiments at IBM headquarters there that he and Tasman had begun in New York. He made a second visit back across the Atlantic by ship later that year. It's worth remembering that only a few years before, it would have been impossible for the priest to travel back and forth between Italy and the U.S. in this way. At the peak of the conflict, oceangoing ships, including passenger liners, sometimes sailed in zigzag routes, with protective convoys, or were painted like warships, in order to evade U-boat attacks. (Meanwhile, IBM machines, along with encryption engines and prototype computers, were being used by the Allies, most famously at Bletchley Park, to crack Axis codes and track the patterns of attacks.) Just to cite one example of the change in ocean transportation after the war: the August 8, 1948 issue of *LIFE* magazine contained a notice about the *Isle de France*, a refitted Merchant Marine ship that had just "arrived in New York on her first voyage since her wartime service as an Allied transport."[11] The next year, still only 4–5 years after the end of the war, Father Busa began his own transatlantic odyssey—a kind of intercontinental commute—making annual trips to IBM and other locations in the U.S. and returning to Italy each time to an increasingly sophisticated infrastructure for his research there, meanwhile presenting his work at international conferences and expos. All of this he continued for years. A shipping manifest shows that on April 1, 1952, for example, he sailed from Cherbourg to New York on the Queen Elizabeth, arriving on April 6th and giving his address as the Jesuit residence at Fordham University, 501 E. Fordham Road in the Bronx, New York (now Kohlmann Hall and still a Jesuit residence as I write); on April 8, 1954, he made the crossing via the same route, this time on the Queen Mary, arriving April 13th. But back in 1952, for his return trip to Italy, Father Busa had to sail on a merchant vessel, which spent ten days at anchor in Newport News waiting for a load of coal, then set sail on July 13th, landing in the commercial port at Naples on August 8th.[12] These would have been a remarkable series of journeys for any academic researcher at the time. Frequent Atlantic crossings were a crucial feature of the infrastructure of Father Busa's work in its first decade, and really until the punching of cards was completed in 1967. A practical concern over infrastructure was the essential reason he relocated the project for a time to America (in Boulder, Colorado) in 1969–1971. In 1958, a brief newspaper story in New York dramatized Father Busa's latest arrival in New York, painting a verbal picture of the priest's disembarking from an ocean liner at Pier 84 on the Hudson River at 44th Street, where the port was much more crowded and active than it is today, with hundreds of passenger ships and freighters arriving and departing in the harbor daily and coming in and out along the piers; Busa is described as carrying a batch of punched cards he had brought from Italy—in this case containing data on the Dead Sea Scrolls—that "later will be fed into a special '705' data-processing IBM machine, which will analyze the words and try to make sense of them."[13] Several photographs in the Busa Archive show him onboard passenger ships, and two from September 10, 1956, show him in his coat, briefcase in hand, apparently arriving at the foot of a covered gangplank, being met by Paul Tasman of IBM, the two men shaking hands and smiling.[14]

Often in those early years Father Busa sent many letters to New York and elsewhere in America in anticipation of his spring journeys to the west, beginning with the first inquiries to Fordham about accommodations. By spring 1950, for example, Father Busa had for months already been involved in an intensive letter-writing campaign in preparation for what would be his first return trip to America after the initial meeting at IBM. For the most part, he wrote to many potential supporters, asking them to write to IBM in his behalf. Father Busa understood that the work would require long-term and evolving institutional and technical support. It would be almost two decades before all the data entry for the *Index Thomisticus* was completed. And the evidence suggests that IBM's support remained uncertain during 1950–1951. The company seems at first to have committed only to a series of trials, experiments designed with Tasman's help and run mostly at IBM Italia in Milan, to test possible methods for the kind of index work Busa had in mind. The letters Busa solicited were meant to secure the long-term commitment to the project of building the complete index to the entire corpus of St. Thomas; later this expanded to include other projects. Any major academic research project, especially interdisciplinary work, depends on the cultivation of a professional social network of potential collaborators, supporters, and peer reviewers. Especially for humanities research, Busa had little choice but to cultivate the network himself. At the time, this meant writing many letters.

In soliciting the references, Father Busa started within his own Jesuit order. In New York he thought to contact Father Robert I. Gannon, S.J., who had recently retired as President of Fordham University to a Jesuit community on Staten Island. (As we saw in Chapter 1, Father Busa wrote to Gannon's successor, Lawrence McGinley, S.J., in 1949 before making his first trip to Canada and the U.S.) It may have been at this point that Gannon interceded and arranged for New York's Cardinal Spellman to contact IBM to vouch for Father Busa and his work.[15] Francis Cardinal Spellman was a prominent if controversial figure, an anticommunist crusader and conservative cultural monitor, who corresponded with J. Edgar Hoover for years and became involved in a very public debate with Eleanor Roosevelt over aid to parochial schools in the summer of 1949, just as Father Busa was arriving in North America. At any rate, as Archbishop of New York (and a graduate of Fordham), he was an obvious choice of authority figure who could speak to the CEO of IBM on behalf of the Jesuit and his philological research project on St. Thomas. The recommendation seems to have been provided at the end of 1949 or early in 1950, and Cardinal Spellman attended Father Busa's demo in June 1952, as we've seen.[16]

At about the same time that he was securing the Cardinal's reference, Father Busa wrote to a list of American and Canadian academics to ask them for letters of recommendation, mostly to be sent directly to IBM. The very fact of this letter-writing campaign suggests how tentative IBM's support must have been in those first months or years, and even at key junctures thereafter. In effect, Busa was gathering expert testimony in support of a kind of grant proposal to IBM—or a renewal of a grant begun in 1949–1950. Most of the letters, therefore, were from his academic peers, including those in adjacent disciplines who might have an interest, nonetheless, in the kind of philological work he was pursuing. The result was a sort of advanced peer review of the proposed project, its methodology, and Busa's scholarly qualifications. A February 11, 1950 letter from the eminent classicist and Aristotelian, Werner Jaeger of Harvard, begins by recalling with pleasure Father Busa's visit during the previous fall, and sends "as promised"—clearly Father Busa had already requested these—"a few lines with my opinion about your project."[17] As he admits, Jaeger doesn't quite understand the role of mechanization in this new kind of concordance, and he is cautiously equivocal when it comes to predicting the success of the work, the probability of Father Busa's achieving his goal.

> An index generalis to all the works of St. Thomas Aquinas would be a tremendous task, but judging by the example of the index Aristotelicus which was done by Bonitz a long time ago and is still the foundation of all Aristotelian studies, I feel that such a work would be a blessing for all Thomists in the world, since no one is able to comprise in his memory or personal notes the whole of Thomas's work. It would of course be difficult to select and train an efficient staff for this undertaking, but how that could be done is not the question with which I am concerned in this letter, and it transcends my competence anyway.
>
> So this is all I can say, but I think it is what you wanted to hear from me, and you are free to make use of my opinion in your attempt at realizing your idea.

Jaeger's letter makes clear the risks taken by Father Busa and the effect of those risks on his campaign for support. The restriction of expectations for the *Index* to what will be useful and helpful to scholarship avoids making any more sweeping claims for its impact. A "blessing" for all Thomists, but still a "tremendous task" and one for whom it would be "difficult to select and train an efficient staff." Not exactly a ringing endorsement, but probably a sufficient contribution to the effort of convincing IBM that professionals considered the goal worthwhile and the method potentially useful, at least.

Jaeger's letter of support from Harvard was matched by one from Columbia, jointly signed by Paul Oskar Kristeller (philosopher and scholar of Renaissance humanism) and Ernest A. Moody (philosopher and Medievalist). It's another rather perfunctory recommendation, again hedged in various ways and addressed "To whom it may concern," but overall it's more positive than Jaeger's. The two scholars are "glad to state" that the planned index seems "a worth while enterprise that promises to provide a most useful instrument of study and research in Thomas and medieval studies," and that Father Busa "approaches his difficult task with the proper scholarly method." They defer to "the opinion of several colleagues who know him and who are able to judge his work," that he's "well qualified" and is likely to complete the task as planned. Once again, in a follow-up note from Kristeller to Busa (in Italian), the scholar admits that he and Moody don't fully grasp the technical aspects of the project, but they are in favor of it, nonetheless; and Kristeller incidentally thanks Father Busa for the list of publications he sent, which he has forwarded to the Columbia library.[18] It's interesting that both Jaeger and Kristeller were Europeans, like many of their generation of scholars, displaced by the war. As classicists, both were familiar with textual problems, and the work of both could be seen as within the tradition of historical language studies, philology broadly conceived (which is the way Father Busa conceived of it). In other words, they were good choices for referees.

In the years that followed, Father Busa would learn to direct the requested letters to the very top of IBM, and he would come to garner more specific and more effusive recommendations. Some of his contacts in the U.S. would become international colleagues to whom he would return for references from year to year. One letter from Howard Comfort in 1956 expresses gratitude for the "suggestion" that the referee "send a note to Mr. Watson" and encloses a copy of the note for Father Busa's own information and approval.[19] By then, Comfort was a colleague and a friend. Father Busa had met him in the U.S. in 1949 and kept him up to date on the work, for which Comfort expressed his full support. On May 16, 1952, another "hearty endorsement of the work" was to be sent to Thomas Watson (probably Mr. Watson, Jr., since he was the new President of the company) by Charles R.D. Miller, Secretary of the Medieval Academy of America and Editor of *Speculum,* a journal in which Father Busa had recently published an announcement about the project.[20] It went beyond the writer's personal opinion, speaking for his scholarly organization as a whole: "It is the belief of the Mediaeval Academy that improved methods for preparing concordances and word lists are highly important to humanistic and spiritual studies. The Mediaeval Academy is interested in seeing these new methods further developed and perfected along the lines of Father Busa's present experiments." The closing line to Mr. Watson, Jr. reveals the obvious practical purpose of Father Busa's letter-writing campaigns in these early years, and suggests how far the project remained on a tentative, renewable basis for some time: "It is our hope that you will be moved to go ahead along the lines suggested by Father Busa," Miller concludes.

In early 1950, Busa's contacts were newer and less well-established. Still, of the surviving requests for letters of this kind, only a couple seem to have produced negative results or refusals. The most interesting example is from Father David L. McGlow[?], S.J., of the Philosophy department of Loyola (Marymount) University in Los Angeles, forwarded to Busa from Loyola's Father Rector (so it may have been through the latter that Father Busa had solicited the response in the first place).[21] It's a rare example in the Archive of an opposing view of the value of the use of computing in humanities research—or, indeed, of overly "mechanical" approaches, even by hand, without using computers. Its author takes issue with the very idea of a *complete* concordance, one comprised of *every* word in the corpus, calling it "a sort of fetish of scholarship gone wild." The plan, he says, is insufficiently interpretive—a complaint that would continue to be brought against computing in the humanities for decades and, indeed, continues today to figure in critiques of the digital humanities. The planned *Index* represents "a drift in the direction of pure mechanical verbalism which would tend to deaden rather than revivify the thought of St. Thomas. (I think that he himself would have been horrified at the thought!)." In conclusion, Father McGlow admits he is no philologist, but says he believes that "philology overemphasized seems to have deadened much of modern scholarship."

For Father Busa, on the contrary, renewing philology was the whole point. A rigorous historical study of language, a study of its material, minute particulars, but with contextual interpretation as the ultimate end, was the form of scholarship to which his own work most often aspired. His definition of philology seems to have started with linguistic particulars—details of morphology, syntax, lexical roots—but also, in the broader humanistic tradition of great European scholars such as Eric Auerbach and Milman Parry, for example, with an eye to the effect of such knowledge on a humanistic understanding of cultural expression.[22] Indeed, Busa saw the study of language as a way to reveal intended (and in the case of St. Thomas, inspired) meanings. His own PhD thesis revolved around one such particular, the word representing the concept of interiority in the work of St. Thomas—as the subtitle says—as a route to an "interpretation of the metaphysics of presence" in his works.[23] But in the process of researching it, Busa pursued ever more granular understandings of the lexical terminology, the actual words. This took him into increasingly rigorous mechanical processes for breaking down those words, treating the vast corpus of St. Thomas as a kind of exploded-view diagram from which each word has been atomized, extracted, marked up, and connected to related words elsewhere in the corpus. The mechanics of the process began with handwriting on paper index cards, but they were no less mechanical for that. As Stephen Ramsay has argued (2011), they were arguably *algorithmic* in the etymological sense of the term, the mathematical sense that goes back to the word's medieval origins, meaning a set of rules or steps in a procedure for solving a problem. That problem for Father Busa was ultimately a deeper understanding of St. Thomas's text, one that transcended the immediate semantic content of any given work. What the exasperated Father McGlow failed to grasp is that Father Busa's algorithmic process of exploding and re-sorting the words, all the words, was deeply old-fashioned in theoretical terms—especially when we remember this was the era that saw an increased influence in academic criticism of structuralism and, following that, poststructuralism. The metaphysics of presence, which was essentially the topic of Busa's thesis on the works of St. Thomas, would in later decades become the primary target of the practice known as deconstruction. For Busa, mechanization was to serve hermeneutics. He aimed to interpret, to reveal meaningful patterns, different dimensions of the language. It's just that some dimensions were too extensive (while their evidence was too minute) to be grasped by the unassisted eye and mind of the reader across an oeuvre of over ten million words. Philosophical and theological questions drove his linguistic research, and this led him to develop the complex process of literary data analysis. Looked at another way, in the Jesuit tradition, Father Busa sought the divine presence in all things; IBM's punched-card machinery was at first only a means to this ultimate end. As we'll see, however, it developed a kind of theoretical momentum of its own.

That thesis by Busa on St. Thomas was actually published in 1949, as his quest for machinery was just getting underway. So his research took a decidedly methodological turn that year. The letter writing and social networking of 1950–1951 coincided with two new publications: an announcement in *Speculum* in July 1950 and the *Varia Specimina Concordantiarum* pamphlet—Father Busa often referred to it as a book, and indeed it added up to approximately 180 pages—in August 1951. Given their later-recognized importance as landmarks in the history of humanities computing and the digital humanities, as scholarly publications go, these are noticeably quirky, unconventional in both form and circumstance. One is just an announcement of intent; the other is a kind of self-published methodological rationale with sample data (the resulting indexes, which take up more than half the book).

The *Varia Specimina Concordantiarum* was published in parallel English and Italian texts and the English is sometimes awkwardly murky, as Father Busa himself later acknowledged.[24] It contains a lengthy description of the methodology followed by the actual concrete results—various indexes and concordances produced from the texts of the *Hymns* of St. Thomas. The slightly earlier *Speculum* piece appeared in the Announcements section, which included calls for donations to a memorial fund for graduate students, for example, a notice of a new committee at the British Academy to oversee the compilation of a prosopography (a list of persons and their networked relations) of the later Roman Empire, and a note about the new Medieval Studies program at St. Louis University. Busa's announcement may have been written for him by the editor or someone else. It takes up less than a full page, but it serves as a kind of declaration of intent, a stake in the ground and a call for input and suggestions, the kind of thing one might expect to find in *Notes & Queries*. And it gives a sense of how Busa conceived of the project at its inception.

> The Rev. Robert [sic] Busa, Professor of Metaphysics in the Aloisianum, the Faculty of Philosophy of the Society of Jesus, in Gallarate, near Milan, Italy, proposes an *index verborum* of all the works of St Thomas Aquinas. He has presented the reasons for this work before the International Congress of Philosophy held at Barcelona in October 1948, and in his book: *La terminologia tomistica dell'interiorita Saggi di metodo per un'interpretazione della metafisica della presenza* (Gallarate, 1949). The work envisaged is not to be a lexicon, giving the meaning of all the words, but would make available to scholars the basic material of such a work and of studies introductory to the compilation of a lexicon.[25]

The project will involve two parts, the announcement says, (a) a general card file of all the words, and (b) "indices and concordances to be drawn from such a file." Then, a seemingly odd claim: that "[t]he cost of this work will be underwritten by Italian industrialists." This probably refers to the members of what became the Italian committee, made up of members of the Crespi-Ferrario family of textile manufacturers, whose son Father Busa had accompanied to the U.S. in 1949, and others, and headed by Archbishop Montini of Milan (the future Pope Paul VI), which would eventually oversee the school and the Center for Literary Data Analysis (CAAL) at Gallarate, an institution I'll say more about in Chapter 4. The note in *Speculum* suggests that the committee was already planned, if not fully in place. More immediately, funding and material support was to come from IBM. Although we might presume it was already forthcoming from IBM by 1950, based on Father Busa's later account and since Paul Tasman had begun working with Father Busa on preliminary experiments, Busa's references to the company remain tellingly tentative at this point. After calling for opinions on the advisability and usefulness of such a project, the announcement ends with a call for "any information … about such mechanical devices as would serve to achieve the greatest possible accuracy, with a maximum economy of human labor. (Father Busa has been in contact with IBM in New York, the RCA laboratories in Princeton, the Library of Congress and the Library of the Department of Agriculture, in Washington.)." That awkward third-person may indicate that someone in the U.S.—perhaps the Editor of *Speculum* himself, since we know he was shortly thereafter in correspondence with Father Busa—helped to write or translate the piece. Paul Tasman says that Father Busa's English was still weak when he arrived at IBM in late 1949, though he quickly became fluent. More important, in spring or early summer 1950, when the note must have been drafted, the precise technologies to be used were still an open question, and the role that IBM would play seems far from settled.

Father Busa departed from Cherbourg on the Queen Elizabeth on April 1, 1952, and arrived in New York on April 5th. Following the pattern of 1950, in early 1952 he was furiously writing letters in anticipation of the summer and the upcoming demonstration at IBM headquarters. Once again, as in 1950, he asked referees to send letters to IBM and even seems to have suggested their contents in some cases. Both Father Busa and Paul Tasman sent copies of the *Varia Specimina Concordantiarum* to potential supporters, and the pamphlet would have been both a prompt and a source of particulars for the letter writers. One March 19, 1952 letter from Howard Comfort, Cultural Relations Officer for the U.S. Foreign Service in Switzerland, thanks Father Busa for sending the *Varia Specimina Concordantiarum*, calling it an indication of an "important marriage of scholarship and modern mechanization," and suggests that Busa's work had made good progress since the two had first met (presumably in 1949, when he had helped Busa join the American Philological Association).[26] The letter closes with best wishes for Father Busa's "forthcoming trip to the United States." Although I've been citing letters, it's important to remember that, once he was in New York, some of Father Busa's networking probably took place on the telephone, in person, and, even before his arrival, he communicated by "wire"—a few telegrams in the Archive attest to this—and there are also lists of names and addresses of contacts in New York with phone numbers added in pencil. He traveled a good deal in the U.S., going to Boston for the annual meeting of the Medieval Academy of

America, for example. It was after this visit that the Secretary of the Academy and Editor of *Speculum* wrote to IBM with the "hearty endorsement" of the Academy as a whole. Father Busa not only solicited letters of endorsement, just as he had done in early 1950, he supplied "talking points" for at least one of his correspondents, a fellow Jesuit.[27]

All the letter writing and other networking in the spring led up to the June 27 formal demonstration. Attendance was by invitation, and the backgrounds of the invitees reflected Father Busa's own overlapping alliances as a Jesuit scholar of classical language and literature with an interest in computing technology. The guests included IBMers, representatives of the Catholic hierarchy, academics from various fields, classicists in particular, and representatives of scholarly organizations, as we've seen, such as the American Council of Learned Societies, and the Modern Language Association. On June 24 Father Busa sent a telegram to Professor Meriwether Stuart, a classicist at Hunter College and the Secretary of the American Philological Association (which, again, Busa had made a point of joining in 1949):

DEMONSTRATION OF MECHANIZED LINGUISTIC ANALYSIS PROJECT ARRANGED FOR TENTHIRTY FRIDAY MORNING JUNE 27TH STOP HIS EMINENCE FRANCIS CARDINAL SPELLMAN WILL BE PRESENT STOP WOULD APPRECIATE YOUR PRESENCE AT IBM 590 MADISON AVENUE HALL OF PRODUCTS NEW YORK STOP PLEASE CONFIRM FATHER BUSA CARE IBM WORLD TRADE NEW YORK BUSA.

The same telegram was sent to multiple contacts in the New York area, and Busa kept lists of the invited. Note that the telegram reveals one pragmatic reason for Cardinal Spellman's invitation—Father Busa clearly saw him as a local dignitary who could draw other attendees.

The telegram refers to the demonstration of the "project," but, given the unfamiliarity of the methods involved, the event inevitably had to focus first on the demonstration of the technology itself—how the punched cards were to be prepared and processed, and how each machine worked at various stages. Like more recent tech demos, this was simultaneously about gaining publicity— and in this case for IBM as well as for the project itself—and about sharing the intellectual results of the research and exposing them to peer review. One series of photographs shows Paul Tasman standing in front of a punched-card machine next to Cardinal Spellman and Father Busa, T. J. Watson Jr. looking on, and an attentive group gathered around. In one image, Tasman holds a deck of punched cards. In another, he appears to be reading to the Cardinal from a copy of the *Varia Specima Concordantiarum*.

The published work and the demo were integrated parts of the research in progress in the labs in the U.S. and in Italy, many iterations of cards being processed through the machines, and the work was extended to conferences where Father Busa explained the methodology to international audiences. Like the demo, the *Varia Specimina Concordantiarum* spotlighted the methodology—in part because it was still emerging, still taking shape. The published explanation served as its own kind of demo, taking the reader step by step through the process before reaching the test-bed results at the back of the pamphlet. The introduction defines key terms and surveys existing concordance projects, particularly the *Thesaurus Linguae Latinae* (TLL) in Germany, consisting of 10 million cards but making use of the kind of contracted copying over many years by many workers that Busa's mechanization was meant to supplant. Concordances had long been central to classical philology, but Busa saw a need for a more efficient method of producing them, given "the exhausting amount of work entailed and the sheer materiality of a great portion of it."[28] That interesting phrase—"sheer materiality"—is a translation from the Italian of "*della greve materialita*"—the *heavy* materiality, referring to the burdensome and mechanical nature of much of the work.

> This latter strikes everyone, even the least expert, and it is sometimes taken as a reason for despising such work and bestowing compassion upon those who "waste" energy which might have been utilised better elsewhere; but only those who have had a hand, or at least an eye, in this sort of work will realise that it is not a matter of purely material labour.[29]

On the contrary, such work requires "intelligence . . . training . . . caution and rigour," Busa says (18).[30] The "most material" stages involved in compiling a concordance are then listed: transcription, multiplication, lemmatization, sorting and alphabetizing, and "typographical composition of the pages" to be printed.[31] Again he cites two well-known German projects (the TLL and *Mittleateinisches Wortenbuch*) as examples of "a kind of mechanization" for the multiplication stage, but which involves contracting the "services" of copying bureaus, which use a variety of still labor-intensive methods, including electric typewriters.[32]

   In this context Busa tells of his own search for a "more comprehensive" system of mechanizing the material labor of concordance building, and how this led to testing the Rapid Selector, for example, and deciding to use "electric accounting machines."[33] Then the essay performs the difficult task of describing the suite of machines Tasman and Busa had used, and each logical task they performed with the punched cards (a process I summarized in Chapter 1). Busa mentions the prospect of "new model IBM machines" just on the horizon, which will allow for better printed output, and summarizes the efficiencies of automation: "when one glimpses at the unimagined possibility of carrying out, for example, in four years a work which would have required otherwise half a century . . . ."[34] The experiments began with the text of the third canto of Dante's *Inferno*, not one presumes because it depicts the arrival at the mouth of Hell (and calls for abandoning all hope), but because its poetic lines were suited to the format of the punched cards, and the canto is brief enough to process in whole. After that, Busa and Tasman processed four hymns of St. Thomas, the texts of which they punched and ran through the machines six different ways, with the clear implication that the words of the text, once encoded on the cards, could be analyzed in any number of ways. As Busa says, these six experimental indexes "were compiled in a few hours by means of IBM machines," and the possibilities are left open-ended. It is, as he says, meant to be an "alluring" example of what might be possible.

Just before the demo, in March 1952, Father Busa published another short essay (in German) explaining the research in progress, "*Mechanisierung der philologischen Analyse*" (the "mechanization of philological analysis").[35] It covers much of the same ground as the *Varia Specimina Concordantiarum*, although without as much framing context about the history of indexes. However, the German essay is illustrated with four black-and-white images of the IBM machines. These appear to have come from IBM manuals or brochures, and they help give specific material forms and names to Busa's punched-card machines (one imagines the details of the technology might have mattered more to readers of *Documentation News*, where the article was published, than to the educated general public at the time).

Busa and Tasman were able to show such machines in action at the demo, handling punched cards and sending some through the machines, allowing invitees to inspect the machinery and cards up close. At least one copy of a printed poster was produced, perhaps for the occasion, showing a flow chart of the procedure. This may have been co-drafted by Paul Tasman himself—it's labeled "Mechanized Linguistic Analysis Project" and dated "6-17-1952, New York, IBM World Trade Sales Engineering, PT-[?256]."[36] For key boxes in the diagram (connected by directional lines), the draftsman has sketched 3D decks of punched cards. The structure is somewhat more detailed than the simplified explanations in Tasman's and Busa's publications at the time. At the necessary step, double dotted lines mark a stop-work in the procedure for human intervention ("SCHOLAR WRITES ENTRY WORD LIST"). Although I'm only aware of this one copy (so it may have been a one-off), it's possible a version of the engineering flow chart was handed out or posted at the demo, where the detailed diagram could have explained the abstract logic behind the physical steps the visitors were to witness.

Father Busa's status as a pioneer of computing in the humanities is tied up with his focus on natural language, literary, philosophical, and religious texts. The centrality of textual analysis to the digital humanities has been challenged in the past decade, sometimes from the perspective of film and media studies, for example, or of disciplines that focus on maps or historical artifacts, or from the perspective of a broader materiality, research centered on physical objects, mechanical and electronic making and tinkering. This new materiality challenges idealist notions of the digital, in an era when, as I've argued elsewhere, new forms of digital humanities have emerged in response to what William Gibson has called the "eversion" of cyberspace.[37] All of this adds up to a shift away from the exclusive emphasis in mainstream digital humanities on text markup and encoding, the production of digital scholarly editions, and the digitization of paper-based archives—in other words a shift away from taking as a given the centrality of Busa's tradition of linguistic computing.

It's somewhat less controversial to assert the centrality of textual analysis to the longer tradition of humanities computing (into the 1990s, say). But if we look in detail at the mother of all demos, the supposed origin of the text-centric tradition in humanities computing, we see that it was always already stubbornly physical in extra-textual ways, dependent on the sometimes anachronistic materiality of paper flow charts, metal accounting machines in the IBM showroom, and the punched-card system with its crucial paper components, generating piles of chad as waste. We're also vividly reminded of the hands-on, engineering-style approach taken (of necessity) by researchers and operators alike, despite the traditional textual content under study (e.g., Dante and Aquinas). The work was very different from the kind of alienated batch processing one might expect in the so-called mainframe era.

It may surprise those who have accepted a simplistic narrative in which personal computers defeated giant mainframe systems and opened up computing to tinkerers, to hands-on human creativity, not to mention those who see a capaciously multimedia and materialist digital humanities as recently succeeding a traditional text-bound humanities computing, but the late 1940s and early 1950s actually saw a messy, often kludgy approach to what was only just starting to be thought of as "computing" itself, a human-limited, break-and-fix, hands-on style, even at the highest levels of corporate and government machinery. And all the more was this the case when it came to nascent humanities computing. Father Busa's demo reflects this messy material approach and this culture of computing. The emphasis on repeated testing, hand-drawn flow charts, experimental punching and handling of punched cards, on the spot, as part of the process, and indeed on discovering and demonstrating the precise nature of the materiality of the technology involved at every turn—in all of these ways, rather than just in its focus on classical texts, the demo of 1952 established certain practices of humanities computing for the half century to follow, practices that have become even more important for today's digital humanities.

It's also true, on the other hand, that Busa's machines were owned by the largest of large corporations. Paul Tasman's presence is a reminder of the corporate supervision the work received. A demo is one thing; day-to-day freedom to experiment is another. The story of the demo also reveals the ways in which corporate interests shaped the research which the corporation supported. On the simplest level (at the bottom line), the demo was held in the Midtown Hall of Products—a showroom for IBM's wares, past and present, from time clocks to typewriters, accounting machines to advanced electomechanical calculators. The choice of location was surely a practical way for Tasman and Busa to have easy access to a full suite of punched-card data-processing machines in one convenient location that would also impress the guests. But the location for the event also offered a kind of targeted marketing to the non-scientific academic community, and, secondarily, to those who would learn about the event through the press, just as with the SSEC's scientific calculations run at *its* previous demo. The collaboration between Busa and IBM illustrates the way in which corporate interests can be strengthened through even modest investments in cultural heritage and preservation, through support for educational and "humanistic" research, or novel applications that are beneficial to society at large, then leveraged by public relations to show how the company is solving the problems of mankind and extending the reach of "the mind of man" (while also extending its own corporate interests). And, as I've said, IBM's interests in 1949–1952 surely included shoring up postwar diplomatic relations with the Vatican, Italy, and Europe as a whole just at the advent of its World Trade Corporation.

As we'll see in the chapters that follow, after the initial trial period in the early 1950s, IBM continued to invest in Father Busa's research for decades, including (mostly through IBM Italia) providing rent-free equipment and support for his operator training school and Literary Data Processing Center in Gallarate. But it's clear that Busa felt the need periodically to make new requests, to renew interest within the company, and sometimes to move the work to locations where equipment was available—to keep his project adjacent to the technical and monetary opportunities. Even the repeated retelling of the story over the decades by the priest about his meeting with the CEO can be seen as a contribution to his efforts at fundraising and maintaining IBM's support. At the end of the first decade of his work, in a letter of October 30, 1960, to Arthur K. Watson of IBM, after discussing machinery and an upcoming conference in Tübingen, Father Busa closed by reporting that the work of the Center (CAAL) continued "at full speed," and then posed a question: "Do you think will God praise this co-operation of a high businessman with a priest? I guess yes, for in the Bible He said that the business can, if we want, lead people to find Him each day."[38] A copy of the letter was sent to Paul Tasman with a typed note attached (probably written by an assistant to Mr. Watson) that joked, "Mr. Tasman, As a Bible student I wonder where Father Busa finds such a statement??? Kay M." I leave the biblical question to the theologians, but the very fact that Busa posed the question (then answered it so quickly) indicates that he recognized in 1960 that it was debatable and might be controversial, the cooperation and alliance between the businessman and the priest, the technology corporation and the academic (and Jesuit) research project. The wider historical contexts of the start of that alliance back in 1949, culminating in the demo of 1952, remind us of the compromises and potential complicities that came with corporate and state funding for Busa's academic research, not just in the macroeconomic sense that the *Index Thomisticus* benefitted from its very small portion of the company's profits, but in the sense that Busa's intellectual work was made to stand adjacent to IBM's global commercial endeavors, including its military and Cold War defense contracts, which increased significantly in the years following atomic bomb tests by the Soviet Union (1949–1951), the start of the Korean War (1950), the test of a hydrogen bomb by the U.S. (November 1, 1952), and, for example, the development of the SAGE (Semi-Automatic Ground Environment) computerized air defense system starting in the mid-1950s, based in part on the architecture first used in the IBM 701 Defense Calculator.

Humanities research programs that deliberately operate across the boundary of the "two cultures"—as digital-humanities projects do—are perhaps especially vulnerable to such complicities. At mid-century, such questions formed the historical backdrop against which the American National Endowment for the Humanities was established in 1965, out of legislation emphasizing that "The encouragement and support of national progress and scholarship in the humanities and the arts, while primarily a matter for private and local initiative, are also appropriate matters of concern to the Federal Government."[39] The legislation frames the need for such support in terms of a kind of dialectical relation between the humanities and the sciences, between culture and technology:

> (3) An advanced civilization must not limit its efforts to science and technology alone, but must give full value and support to the other great branches of scholarly and cultural activity in order to achieve a better understanding of the past, a better analysis of the present, and a better view of the future.

> (4) Democracy demands wisdom and vision in its citizens. It must therefore foster and support a form of education, and access to the arts and the humanities, designed to make people of all backgrounds and wherever located masters of their technology and not its unthinking servants.[40]

Almost four decades later, a dedicated Office of Digital Humanities was created at the NEH. But the founding legislation already contained within it the idea that the humanities in a democratic society offers a valuable critical perspective on developments in science and technology—an alternative to "unthinking" capitulation to concentrated power. The initial decade of Father Busa's work predated the founding of the NEH, but it took place in the postwar context that demonstrated the need for that kind of government intervention in the ongoing relationship between academic research and the interests of corporations and the technologies they develop.

After numerous presentations and demonstrations at international conferences during the 1950s, in September 1958, Father Busa gave a public presentation to a very large international crowd in the IBM Pavilion at the World's Fair in Brussels, Expo 58. This was the first major world's fair since the end of the war and it was weighted with the symbolism of postwar alliances and Cold War conflicts. In the 1950s, the Cold War "replaced empire as an international motor force behind" world expos of this kind.[41] This helps to explain Expo 58's mid-century futuristic theme, with the giant Atomium at the center of the fairgrounds, a metallic building over 300 feet high and shaped like an iron crystal cell, with nine spherical rooms representing atoms, connected by tubular walkways. It was a monument to science and engineering, of course, but "also part of an ongoing policy among Western governments to depict atomic power as something capable of promoting peace as well as war."[42] The Cold War is even the context within which to understand the announced theme of the fair as a whole: "a new humanism," which the organizers tied directly to finding "peaceful uses of nuclear energy and to building better international relations."[43]

In keeping with this theme, IBM's Pavilion and its participation in the American Pavilion at the fair promoted the positive uses of computing, *its* humanistic applications—for the expansion of knowledge, for example, and for better living and enhanced leisure time; everyone was already aware that computers were crucial to the national defense. The IBM Pavilion, located in the Commerce section of the fairgrounds, had the company's logo spelled in giant letters across its metal and glass facade. It was designed by Eliot Noyes, the new consultant in charge of all of design for IBM. The exhibits inside were designed by Eames Office, also consulting for IBM under Noyes, along with Paul Rand (who created the famous IBM logo that persists today). A special screening room showed a 10-minute animated film made by Charles and Ray Eames, *The Information Machine: Creative Man and the Data Processor.* I'll have more to say about the film and the Expo in the next chapter.

All of this was part of the context in which Father Busa performed this second major demo of the 1950s, six years after the triumphal first one at 590 Madison Avenue. The pavilion also featured an IBM 305 RAMAC computer (Random Access Method of Accounting and Control), with its magnetic storage system of 50 disks stacked vertically like a space-age tower inside the sleek grey cabinet, programmed for the fair to answer questions about world history in ten languages.[44] (The RAMAC also used a magnetic drum and magnetic core, as well as punched cards for input and output. It was advertised as storing on its disk system five million characters, as much as 64,000 IBM punched cards.[45]) The IBM Pavilion reportedly attracted nearly 100,000 visitors in its first six weeks.[46] Many of them would have seen the demonstrations of Father Busa's work in Literary Data Processing. Among the photographs in the Busa Archives are two sets of apparently duplicate images, shot from two different angles, in which Father Busa is seen giving a presentation on a large raised dais.[47] In one image he's showing a poster and explaining the *Index Thomisticus.* In another he's holding a microphone and addressing a large crowd (Figure 3.2). The IBM logo on the machines is prominently visible in one set of photos but has been blocked out with blank white rectangles in the duplicate copies. I don't know why or at what point the logos were erased in the photos (but not erased in the historical record of the Archive). It may have been for legal reasons: depending on the publicity purposes to which the images were to be put, it may have seemed desirable to avoid claims of advertising or sponsorship, for example (Expo 58 was also the occasion of coverage about Busa's work on a local TV program, and this may have had something

FIGURE 3.2 Roberto Busa demonstrates literary data processing at the IBM Pavilion, World's Fair (Expo 58), September 3, 1958, Brussels (Busa Archive #127).

to do with the masking, as well). There may be no particular significance to the retouched logos in the photographs. But it just so happens to call attention to the omnipresent company name everywhere else in so many of the other iconic photos of Father Busa over the years. Along with all the mentions of IBM in the written accounts of his research, such images amounted to a default branding, as it were, of Busa's research agenda for more than half a century by the technical, financial, and intellectual alliance he forged in New York in 1949.

Not that he had much choice of a supporting organization if he wanted to use punched-card equipment at the time. There were a few other companies building large-scale calculating machines, prominent among them Remington Rand. In fact, a kind of adjacent index project, on the Revised Standard Version text of the bible, was going on in the 1950s, led by the Reverend John W. Ellison, using Rand's UNIVAC (Universal Automatic Computer), which used magnetic tape as its primary storage medium. That machine had been introduced in 1952 (just after Busa's mother of all humanities computing demos). It was widely reported on in the press and famously used by the CBS television network to predict the outcome of the 1952 election through statistical analysis. When, early in the evening, the "marvelous electronic brain" named Eisenhower as the likely winner over Stevenson, the programmers assumed there must have been some error and went silent. Only after the unexpected results came in was it revealed that the

UNIVAC had got it right in the first place. Thomas Watson, Jr. recalled that the UNIVAC was so popular at the time that it symbolized "the computer" for many in the general public, just as the SSEC had done for a brief time; when IBM's first real commercially available computer came out just afterwards, it was sometimes referred to as "IBM's UNIVAC."[48] Ellison's bible concordance was published in 1957, when Father Busa was still working on the *Index Thomisticus* but also, by then, the Dead Sea Scrolls project, which is the subject of Chapter 5. When Father Busa heard of Ellison's work, he quickly got in touch. He later claimed that Ellison's example spurred his own use of magnetic tape for processing (starting with the IBM 705).

> One day I learned from the newspapers that an Episcopalian minister, Rev. John W. Ellison, who was preparing a concordance of the Revised Version of the Bible (he published it in traditional ways in 1957), had used Remington magnetic tapes, which at that time were not plastic but iron. I went to shake hands with him and said: "You are a great ally of mine!" Immediately after I went to IBM: "See what Remington is doing?" Since that time the processing of the IT has been done mainly by computers and punched card equipment was used only peripherally.[49]

That last statement is something of an exaggeration. Punched-card machines continued to be used quite centrally by CAAL throughout the 1960s, even if much of the processing for the *Index Thomisticus* had been shifted to tape. But the connection to Ellison was significant, and was based on a true intellectual collaboration, especially during the years Busa and CAAL were focused on the Dead Sea Scrolls. The Busa Archive contains an entire folder devoted to Ellison, with documents dating from an initial inquiry in May 1956 to correspondence between the two scholars during the fall of that year.[50] They shared details of their respective methods, Busa made some inquiries to Remington Rand, and a brochure from that company is even preserved which features material on the UNIVAC and an article on Ellison's concordance.

Another adjacent possibility: in this case, parallel lines that did not meet. Father Busa continued to work more or less exclusively with IBM equipment. Seen from another point of view, Busa's decision to use punched-card equipment through the agreement with IBM afforded him an unprecedented arrangement for a humanities scholar at the time. In effect he gained access to a regularly updated variety of information processing machines free of charge, or nearly so, both in Italy and in the U.S., at IBM headquarters in New York (and later, in Colorado). Just as important, he gained a high-level collaborator and consultant in Paul Tasman, someone who was deeply interested in the problems of language processing and who also published and gave presentations on the results of their efforts, a true interdisciplinary co-researcher. In a few short years Busa and Tasman established a structure for transatlantic collaboration, and building on that Busa founded a training school of his own on the IBM model, a center for Literary Data Analysis in Italy, with the machinery and support provided by the world's dominant provider of punched-card machines (and punched cards themselves). Retaining his access to IBM facilities in New York, Father Busa first established what he called his own "department" at IBM Italia in Milan, a kind of interim step to creating the CAAL center at Gallarate. The *Index Thomisticus,* and Father Busa's research in general, was branded as IBM-sponsored; in exchange, he gained a kind of advanced laboratory on two continents, with material support unprecedented at the time in the humanities (and at a level still rare today). This strand of humanities computing emerged and then developed at the intersection of international corporate interests and the goals of humanistic scholarship.

Once again, it's important to stress that Father Busa's work is not the only origin of humanities computing, much less of digital humanities. The closer you look, the more dispersed and distributed appear the emergences of the varied practices later called by those names. But Busa's work with IBM was a key contributing force in the historical emergence of humanities computing, not least because of the complicated institutional and social relationships that enabled the work at such a scale, across boundaries not just of academic disciplines but of competing academic and business interests, the interests of the corporation and the Church, intellectual pursuits and accounting techniques, philology and punched cards, the humanities and technology. In this sense, it's hard to disagree with the observation of Thomas Nelson Winter that "Father Busa knew the nature of the task and knew what he was looking for."[51] This was not just a matter of technical knowledge. More than one source suggests that Busa really didn't know very much about punched-card technology itself when he began discussions with IBM (though he soon learned). What Winter means is that he had a logical and intellectual grasp of the overall task of the *Index.* What this chapter has shown is that he also quickly gained a commanding grasp of the institutional and social networks that would serve that end. As Father Busa himself described it later, "I had to solve problems which no longer exist today. Without assistance and in addition to finding financial support, I had to develop and test a method which had no predecessor and had to use a technology which developed progressively."[52] Another observer noted in 1961 "the manner in which, thanks to his psychological insight," Father Busa "knows how to win over people and institutions and to impress them favourably [with] himself and his work"—and that this made up for limitations when it came to "material expedients" for the work.[53] He learned in practice about the flexibilities of the system that he and Tasman had designed, about the kinds of linguistic research that mechanization might make possible. In the same way, he learned in practice about the interdisciplinary possibilities opened up by new institutional arrangements, possibilities that went well beyond the initial need to make an index.

Looking back later from his vantage at the end of the century, Father Busa saw his arrangement with IBM as marking the emergence of linguistic computing, at least, which branched out from that point into its own history, as something distinct from numerical and scientific computing. Writing poetically, we might even say evangelically, he describes the beginning of this history in 1949 as a "spark … which has developed into a blaze of activity that now covers the entire life of the world."[54] The priest understood this as the workings of "the spiritual world," as he said, the historical events as "signs of the hand of Providence." His language deliberately echoes the charge famously attributed to the founder of the Jesuit order, St. Ignatius: "Go forth and set the world on fire." Even from a more secular and skeptical perspective, however, from the perspective of human history and its complications, it's possible to appreciate the remarkable influence of what he and Tasman demonstrated in June 1952. It did indeed lead to a kind of "blaze of activity" in literary and linguistic computing, and humanities computing in general. The scope has not been as universal as Father Busa believed it would be, but it's significant that he saw the arena of this new activity, of humanities computing, as "the entire life of the world," a formulation which we can take as referring to the various artifacts of culture with which humanities computing might engage. In the next chapter we'll look at the founding of the first Literary Data Processing Center (arguably the first full-fledged humanities computing center) in Gallarate, Italy, which Busa saw as the key node in what he hoped would become a worldwide network of scholarship, one center among many centers of activity. It didn't happen exactly as he imagined it, but the model of intensively focused research nodes linked at different scales and across institutional structures remains an influential ideal for interdisciplinary work of this kind today.

Notes

1   Thomas J. Watson, Jr. and Peter Petre, *Father, Son & Co.: My Life at IBM and Beyond* (New York: Bantam Books, 1990), Kindle edition, loc. 3420.
2   Photograph of Rex Seeber (#13). Busa Archives. My descriptions of the 1952 demo draw on a group of ten photographs in the Archives (#07– #16), with Father Busa's own captions and identifications (some of these photos are available on the website for this book http://priestandpunchedcards.tumblr.com).
3   *The President's report to the Board of Regents, 1948–49* (Ann Arbor, MI: University of Michigan Libraries, 1948), 356.
4   Steven Levy, *Insanely Great: The Life and Times of Macintosh, the Computer That Changed Everything* (New York: Penguin, 1994), 42.
5   Douglas C. Engelbart, "Augmenting the Human Intellect: A Conceptual Framework" (Washington, D.C.: Air Force Office of Scientific Research, 1962), http://dougengelbart.org/pubs/papers/scanned-original/1962-augment-3906-Augmenting-Human-Intellect-a-Conceptual-Framework.pdf; letter from Roberto Busa to Douglas Engelbart (addressed to "Dog Engelbard"), March 3, 1970, Busa Archive (Rel. Cult. USA 1 1952).
6   IBM website, https://www-03.ibm.com/ibm/history/exhibits/vintage/vintage_4506VV4003.html.

7   See Wendy Hui Kyong Chun, "On Software, or The Persistence of Visual Knowledge," *Grey Room* 18 (Winter 2005), 26–51, http://www.brown.edu/Departments/MCM/people/chun/papers/software.pdf.

8   The brochure, *My Fair Ladies* (IBM, 1957), is discussed in Janet Abbate, *Recoding Gender: Women's Changing Participation in Computing* (Cambridge, MA and London: MIT Press, 2012), 65–66.

9   "Jean E. Sammet," Wikipedia, https://en.wikipedia.org/wiki/Jean_E._Sammet.

10 "Ruth Leach Amonette," Wikipedia, https://en.wikipedia.org/wiki/Ruth_Leach_Amonette. Both Jean Sammet (see footnote 9) and Ruth Leach Ammonette are briefly discussed in Margaret W. Rossiter, *Women Scientists in America Before Affirmative Action, 1940–1972* (Baltimore and London: Johns Hopkins University Press, 1995), 269–70.

11 "The 'Isle de France,'" *LIFE,* August 8, 1948, 38.

12 Roberto Busa, unpublished autobiographical manuscript. Cited with the kind permission of Marco Passarotti, CIRCSE.

13 "IBM to Tackle Dead Sea Scrolls Riddle," *New York World Telegram and Sun,* January 8, 1958. Busa Archive (Stampa Estera 1710). The story about Busa's arriving with punched cards at the pier may have been an embellishment by the reporter, though it's not out of the question, given his regular crossings and limited funds for shipping.

14 Photographs of Roberto Busa being greeted by Paul Tasman, apparently on a pier, labeled (by Busa) "New York, September 10, 1956" (#29, #30), Busa Archive. (#29 is available on the website for this book. http://priestandpunchedcards.tumblr.com.)

15 Roberto Busa, "The Annals of Humanities Computing," *Computers and the Humanities* 14.2 (1980), 83–90 (84).

16 I'm not aware of any surviving letter of recommendation, but Busa's accounts repeatedly mention the referral or "presentation," perhaps in the sense of formal introduction by a mutual third party. Francis Cardinal Spellman was present at later events, starting with the demo of 1952. It's worth remembering that the contact may have been made by telephone. As I noted in Chapter 1, one account says that Fordham University's recently retired president, Robert I. Gannon, S.J., first contacted Cardinal Spellman in behalf of Father Busa.

17 Letter from Vernor Jaeger to Roberto Busa, February 11, 1950. Busa Archive (Gall. Rel. Cult. 1940, USA tab).

18 Letter from Paul Oskar Kristeller to Roberto Busa, March 12, 1950. Busa Archive (Gall. Rel. Cult. 1940, USA tab).

19 Letter from Howard Comfort to Roberto Busa, October 10, 1956. Busa Archive (Gall. Rel. Cult. 1940, USA tab).

20 Letter from Charles R. D. Miller to Thomas Watson, May 16, 1952. Busa Archive (Gall. Rel. Cult. 1940, USA tab).

21 Letter from Father David L. McGlow[? the signature is unclear], S.J., n.d. Busa Archive. (Gall. Rel. Cult. 1940, USA tab). The word "Fr. Rector" is handwritten in the salutation, on stationery from the Department of Philosophy.

22 Later on, Father Busa repeatedly called for a "new philology," as discussed in Chapter 5.

23 Roberto Busa, *La Teminologia Tomistica dell' Interiorita. Saggi di metodoper una interpretazione della metafisica della presenza* (Bocca: Milan, 1949).

24 Letter from Roberto Busa to Robert D. Eagleson, July 4, 1966. Busa Archive (Rel. Cult. 1944, misc.): "The English translation of the introduction to the Varia Specimina is . . . hilarious: it has been done by a British lady, but only after publication I had been informed that there is much to laugh about: my knowledge of English was not sufficient as to realize it by myself."

25 Busa, Roberto, S.J. "Announcements: Complete Index Verborum of Works of St. Thomas," *Speculum* 25.3 (July 1950): 424–26.

26 Letter from Howard Comfort to Roberto Busa, March 19, 1952, Busa Archive (Gall. Rel. Cult. 1940, USA tab).

27 See memorandum to Fr. Conway, S.J., (dated by hand) June 2, 1952, about a letter for T. J. Watson, Sr., Busa Archive (Gall. Rel. Cult. 1940, USA tab).

28 Busa, Roberto, S.J. *Sancti Thomae Aquinatis Hymnorum Ritualium Varia Specimina Concordantiarum: A First Example of Word Index Automatically Compiled and Printed by IBM Punched Card Machines*, ("Archivum Philosophicum Aloisianum. A cura della Facultaà di Filosofia dell'Istituto Aloisianum S.J. Serie II. N. 7. Fratelli Bocca: Milan, 1951)," 18.

29 Busa, *Varia Specimina Concordantiarum*, 18.

30 Busa, *Varia Specimina Concordantiarum*, 18.

31 Busa, *Varia Specimina Concordantiarum*, 20.

32 Busa, *Varia Specimina Concordantiarum*, 20.

33 Busa, *Varia Specimina Concordantiarum*, 22.

34 Busa, *Varia Specimina Concordantiarum*, 34.

35 Roberto Busa, "*Mechanisierung der philologischen Analyse*," in *Nachrichten für Dokumentation* 3.1 (March 1952), 14–19. In Marco Passarotti, Ciula, A., and Nyhan, J., eds., *One Origin of Digital Humanities: Fr. Roberto Busa, S.J. in his own words* (Forthcoming, Springer Verlag), trans. Philip Barras.

36 Flow chart, Busa Archive. Unaccessioned papers, received March 2015.

37 Steven E. Jones, *The Emergence of the Digital Humanities* (New York: Routledge, 2014). http://priestandpunchedcards.tumblr.com.

38 Copy of letter from Roberto Busa to Arthur K. ("Dick") Watson, October 30, 1960 (personal copy), forwarded to Paul Tasman with a note attached from Kay M. Quoted by permission of Professor Jordan Nash.

39 National Foundation on the Arts and the Humanities Act of 1965 (P.L. 89-209), http://www.neh.gov/about/history/national-foundation-arts-and-humanities-act-1965-pl-89-209.

40 National Foundation on the Arts and the Humanities Act of 1965 (P.L. 89–209).

41 Paul Greenhalgh, *Fair World: A History of World's Fairs and Expositions from London to Shanghai, 1851–2010* (Winterbourne, UK: Papadakis, 2011), 68.

42 Greenhalgh, *Fair World*, 228.

43 Robert W. Rydell, *World of Fairs: The Century of Progress Expositions* (Chicago and London: University of Chicago Press, 1993), 193–94.

44 "Chronological History of IBM: 1950s," IBM Archives website, https://www-03.ibm .com/ibm/history/history/decade_1950.html.

45 See the ca. 1956 promotional video on the RAMAC in Jentery Sayers, "Making the Perfect Record," *American Literature* 85.4 (December 2013), http://dx.doi .org/10.1215/00029831-2370230; promotional material, SCALAR: http://scalar.usc .edu/maker/record/ibm-305-ramac-promotional-material-ca-1956?path= mediapath.

46 "A History of Progress: 1890s to 2001," IBM Archives website, https://www-03.ibm .com/ibm/history/interactive/ibm_history.pdf.

47 Photographs #133 and #134, #127 and #136. Busa Archive (#134 is available on the website for this book).

48 Watson, Jr. and Petre, *Father, Son & Co.*, loc. 3768–72.

49 Busa, "The Annals of Humanities Computing," 85.

50 John W. Ellison materials, Busa Archive (Gall. Rel. Cult. 1940, Rev. Ellison folder).

51 Thomas Nelson Winter, "Robert Busa, S.J., and the Invention of the Machine-Generated Concordance," 9, UNL Digital Commons, http://digitalcommons.unl.edu/classicsfacpub/70/.

52 Busa, "The Annals of Humanities Computing," 87.

53 Félicien de Tollenaere, English typescript, draft for *Nieuwe wegen in de lexicologie* (Amsterdam, Noord-Hollandsche Uitg. Mij., 1963), 28. Busa Archive.

54 Roberto Busa, unpublished autobiographical manuscript. Cited with the kind permission of Marco Passarotti, CIRCSE.

4

CENTERS OF ACTIVITY

The Founding of CAAL, the First Literary Data Processing Center in Gallarate, Italy, 1954–1956

Although he sailed to America on the Queen Elizabeth in spring 1952, Father Busa had to return to Italy later that summer on a merchant ship, arriving at the busy commercial port of Naples on August 8. He passed through customs there with chests of donated clothing sent from American friends for families of Italian orphans in Italy, another small reminder of his clerical vocation, which of course continued along with his intellectual work, as well as of the situation of postwar Italy even seven years on. The customs officers made a show of laughing as they pulled lingerie out of the chests, saying, "Eh! Reverend, this is charity!" Telling the story years later, Father Busa said the officers acted "not out of malice, but to have fun with jokes (Naples)."[1]

Father Busa's travels throughout the 1950s make for a complicated international map, marked with almost annual transatlantic trips to and from America, but also short visits to European cities to present papers or demonstrate his work: Paris, Geneva, Leuven, Bruges, Brussels, Manchester, Oxford, London, Frankfurt, and Tübingen, just to make a partial list. In 1980 he said: "Since 1949, I have visited America 35 times. First, I needed to keep in touch with IBM technicians. My second purpose was to exchange ideas with people starting to make use of computers in scientific documentation, soon rebaptized as information retrieval and now as information science."[2] Continually in motion, it was as if he were building an expansive scholarly network by sheer physical motion, traveling from place to place to make the connections personally. On the map of his work, however, there were two key locations: New York City, where his visits to IBM were usually limited to a few months at a time and were often broken up by short trips out to other locations in America; and Milan, with the nearby town of Gallarate, about 40 kilometers away, his personal and professional home. Father

Busa's Italian base remained there, at the Jesuit Aloisianum College (named for St. Aloysius Gonzaga), where he was a member of the Faculty of Philosophy. This immediate locale remained relatively unscathed in a region of Italy that had been hard hit by the war. Reconstruction in and around Milan continued well into the decade that followed. Gallarate's economy had been based on the textile industry since the nineteenth century, which was still in the mid-twentieth century in the hands of local families. It was to the patronage of these families that Busa turned for his own initial travel expenses, as we've seen, and, more formally, for financial support and advice for the research center he wanted to build. Nearby Milan was a cosmopolitan, international center of commerce, finance, culture, and industry, and Father Busa primarily worked there at IBM headquarters for the first few years of the decade and he kept an office in Milan for a time in the 1960s. But Gallarate was home territory, where he was most influential and had access to the greatest number of resources. The fact that it was a close commute to and from Milan made it particularly convenient as the center was established and its research developed. The network of social and professional ties anchored in Gallarate made the project possible.

This chapter is about Roberto Busa's establishment of the first humanities computing center in Gallarate in 1956, the CAAL or *Centro per L'Automazione dell'Analisi Letteraria* (the last term often later rendered as *Linguistica*): the Center for the Automation of Literary (or Linguistic) Analysis. But the real topic is how this happened, through social networking built on material resources garnered from different kinds of institutions, by creating and then connecting multiple centers, labs, schools, and programs, with the support of business, the Church, government, and academics, in the process institutionalizing the general idea and specific methods of computing in the humanities. As a later observer rightly noted, Father Busa knew "how to win over people *and institutions*" (my emphasis).[3] To understand Father Busa's role as a founder or pioneer of humanities computing, we have to understand the institutions and organizations he won over. These matter as much as any specific technologies and methods he used. Indeed, as he well understood, the technology he used involved more than mere machinery—it extended to the social structures and cultures of these institutions.

His core institutional relationship remained with IBM. The 1950s were a period of sweeping modernization at the company. In 1954, Thomas J. Watson, Jr., who was now in charge, hired architect Eliot Noyes to update the design of the lobby and showroom of IBM headquarters at 590 Madison Avenue. Noyes, whose work was influenced by the austerity of the Bauhaus movement, later described with a kind of aesthetic revulsion the "design schizophrenia" he found in the Hall of Products:

> a sepulchral place, with oak-paneled walls and columns, a deeply coffered painted ceiling, a complex pattern of many types of marble on the floor, oriental rugs on the marble and various models of black IBM accounting

machines sitting uneasily on the oriental rugs. These accounting machines, I might add, often had cast iron cabriole legs in the manner, I believe, of Queen Anne furniture.[4]

Even the machines were awkward hybrids of old and new eras. And Thomas J. Watson, Jr. himself recalled that the public face of 590 Madison "projected a split personality."

> If you looked in the window on the Fifty-seventh Street side of the build-ing, you saw the Defense Calculator [the IBM 701]—a set of drab gray cab-inets in a large room with dark carpets and yellow drapes. But if you walked around the corner onto Madison Avenue and went in the main lobby, you found yourself back in the 1920s. Dad had it decorated to suit his taste, and it was like the first-class salon on an ocean liner. It had the Oriental rugs he loved and black marble pillars trimmed with gold leaf. Lining the walls were punch-card machines and time clocks on display, cordoned off by velvet ropes hooked to burnished brass posts.[5]

The ground floor of 590 contained contradictory worlds, styles alluding to the ocean liners from Europe on which Busa sailed, and the modernism of new large-scale machines that were rooms unto themselves, the future of computing in the mainframe era. Part of Noyes's commission, which led to an appointment as Consultant Director of Design for IBM, was to replace this musty showroom with a modern space, a Data Processing Center with white floors and one wall painted red, the better to focus on the new, room-sized IBM 702 Data Processing System.[6]

While this redesign was just beginning, from the end of April through July 1954, Father Busa was once again in New York. On April 28th, he wrote to the Rev. E.B. Bunn, S.J., President of Georgetown University, about the possibility of a visit there, telling him that he was in the midst of his fourth visit to the U.S. and was "living at Fordham, but working during the working hours at the IBM World Trade Headquarters."[7] His commute from the Bronx campus of Fordham down to Midtown Manhattan would likely have been on the Third Avenue "El"—the elevated train line, with a stop near Fordham's front gate, then in its final year of service. During the summer of 1954, his trip was probably extended by a little over a mile, since that was when IBM's World Trade Corporation moved out of 590 Madison Avenue and into separate headquarters at 807 United Nations Plaza on the East River. That summer, Arthur K. ("Dick") Watson took over as head of the new subsidiary organization, marking a newly globalized enterprise. It would quickly come to dominate overseas markets, "in many cases to an even greater extent than the mother company did in the United States,"[8] in the face of a pending antitrust suit by the Department of Justice. Father Busa signed his letter to Georgetown's president using both the Fordham address and the new World Trade Corporation address, a graphic reminder of his dual affiliation, and a reminder that his place at IBM itself was never entirely fixed, even while he was in New York City. During the early 1950s, when he was back in Italy he worked at the Milan headquarters of IBM, recently renamed IBM Italia. As he tells Father Bunn, his own work is international by default, since he is "working in the IBM bureaus both in Italy and here in New York to continue my experiments on linguistic analysis mechanized by punched card IBM system."

The main purpose of the letter, however, is to express Busa's interest in research going on at Georgetown in stylometrics—the study of characteristic linguistic styles, often in order to more accurately attribute texts to authors—and machine translation, which were both at that moment the focus of the university's Institute of Languages and Linguistics. His own experimental work isn't precisely in the same area, Busa admits, but it "overlaps" with such research, in that he's "looking to find a fast way to detect the mathematical structure of the language." As he knew, just a few months before, on January 7, 1954, IBM had held a well-publicized experimental demonstration of machine translation at 590 Madison Avenue. A team from Georgetown's Linguistics group had overseen the demo, programming an IBM 701 Defense Calculator to translate into English a group of Russian sentences, based on a limited set of syntax rules.[9] A "girl" who didn't understand Russian was deliberately chosen as the operator, so that she could mechanically punch the Russian sentences onto IBM cards for the input. Then the "electronic 'brain'" as the press release put it, "dashed off its English translations on an automatic printer at the breakneck speed of two and a half lines per second."

> This amazing instrument was interrupted in its 16-hour-a-day schedule of solving problems in nuclear physics, rocket trajectories, weather forecasting and other mathematical wizardry. Its attention was turned at brief intervals from these lightninglike numerical calculations to the altogether different consideration of logic in an entirely new and strange realm for giant electronic data processing machines: the study of human behavior—specifically, the human use of words.[10]

This widely reported demo led to new funding and major national and international support for machine-translation research—lasting until the notorious ALPAC (Automatic Language Processing Committee) report of 1966, which determined that not enough progress had taken place in this area to justify continued government funding.[11] This particular area of computational linguistics would only be revived in earnest with the advent of the Internet and new data-intensive methods for automatic translation employed by Google, for example.[12]

Father Busa's remark about detecting "the mathematical structure of the language" suggests how far the practical work of making concordances had taken him into the realm of a linguistics that applied information theory to natural language. The term "mathematical structure" implies that logical patterns, even perhaps deep(er) structures, might be discovered and analyzed using data-processing machines and computers. Busa's and Tasman's methods assumed the possibility of treating language as data, and of automating algorithmic, ordered procedures for doing so, based on quantifiable patterns by which language itself and verbal texts were organized. The broader shared problem that connected machine translation and Busa's work was the automation of natural language processing.

Within a decade of Father Busa's letter to Georgetown's president, by 1963, the IBM-Georgetown system of machine translation was installed at both the U.S. Atomic Energy Commission at Oak Ridge National Laboratory in Tennessee and the headquarters of Euratom (the European Atomic Energy Community, founded with a treaty of 1957) in Ispra, Italy, on the shore of Lake Maggiore about 30 kilometers northwest of Gallarate.[13] This location became closely linked to Father Busa's Center and training school at Gallarate, which was located about halfway between Ispra and Milan. As Julianne Nyhan and Melissa Terras (with the help of Marco Passarotti) discovered when they interviewed some of the operators who trained and worked with Father Busa, the women frequently refer to Euratom in Ispra and suggest that Busa "played an important role" in helping them get jobs there, an arrangement that "would have been mutually beneficial because the work they undertook there was directly related to Busa's interest in the emerging area of Automatic Language Processing."[14] These students were mostly young women—girls, really, some as young as 14—who learned through practical experience how to use IBM machines to process punched cards. To reiterate how quickly all of these connections came together: the training school was founded in 1956, only two years after Busa wrote to Father Bunn about machine translation; the Georgetown system for machine translation was installed at the research center at Euratom in the early 1960s; shortly thereafter, with the help of that connection and their training on punched-card machinery, some of the students did indeed get jobs at Euratom.

Father Busa visited the Euratom center as early as 1961. Photographs show him talking to a small group that included language researchers standing around the control panel of an IBM 7090 system.[15] The ties between Gallarate and Ispra were more than an accident of geographical adjacency: Busa later recalled that it was he who "connected" the Russian-to-English research project at Georgetown to the Computing Center of Euratom.[16] He seems to have been both the agent who made the connection and to have been himself the connection, to have served as the liaison and facilitator of the arrangement. In 1961 he pursued meetings with L.E. Dostert and Peter Toma, who worked for the Georgetown group through a government contract, arranged for Toma to visit Gallarate, and met with Dostert in Frankfurt on April 6–7, 1961; out of that meeting Busa drafted a two-page memo of agreement, outlining a formal collaboration between CAAL and the linguistics group, which led to the installation at CETIS (the *Centre Européen de Traitement de l'information Scientifique*) at Euratom, Ispra.[17] The agreement begins by stating the shared religious interests of Georgetown as a Jesuit university with CAAL, and names "as a common target the idea of an international service of free electronic processing of concordances," exactly the ideal expressed in a conference presentation by Busa in France the same year.[18] The agreement also reveals that "the lexical research as it has been developed in Gallarate, may appear to [be] . . . among the most urgent requirements for a mature practical mt. [machine translation], i.e. the detection of those semantic categories which are not morphological, nor syntactical nor structural."[19] At the time, the Pentagon had "financed various centers" in machine translation, Father Busa says elsewhere, even claiming that he "was involved in this" (the financing of centers, but probably referring specifically to Ispra); his "contributions," he then says, "were on an exchange basis."[20] But his involvement clearly went beyond mere diplomacy:

> I supplied them, from my laboratory in Gallarate, with Russian abstracts of biochemistry and biophysics in Cyrillic script on punched cards, a million words. These were translated with the Georgetown programs. The translation was sufficient for an expert on the subject to be able to evaluate the merits of a more accurate translation done by hand, i.e., by a person's brain.[21]

The experiments in machine translation required machine-readable Russian texts on Cold War–appropriate subjects; Father Busa supplied these, not full texts but abstracts, presumably produced at CAAL from the full texts using the punched-card machinery. The students at Busa's school actually performed the labor of punching on cards the million words, almost certainly without understanding the Russian language they were processing. (With such targeted training, it's not surprising that some were hired at Euratom when they left the school.) The abstracts on punched cards could then be processed by the Georgetown-Ispra machine translation system.

Perhaps in return for this punched-card processing of Russian texts, Father Busa's laboratory at Gallarate—by which he means the operation at CAAL and at the Aloisianum College—would appear to have received some funding from Euratom. At least, references by Busa suggest as much. The April 8, 1961 memo of agreement with Dostert mentions "contracts with Euratom" as among the signs that CAAL is ready to "be inserted into the world growing up of the information processing techniques." In the same year, as I mentioned above, Busa presented a brief paper in French in 1961 at a conference on the work of CAAL. One section of the presentation was entitled "The international services of the Center," and consisted of a list of what he hoped to do "[t]hanks to funding from Euratom."[22] Based on such funding, Father Busa imagines maintaining a kind of consortium, a list or map of related centers around the world; publishing a bulletin or newsletter to communicate and share work going on at these centers; beginning to establish standards for shared terminology, codes, and methods; and finally, what he calls the "dream of international centers" providing, free of charge, electronic forms of linguistic data, on punched cards or tape for individuals or other centers (Busa,

1961, 67).[23] It's a remarkably ambitious set of desiderata. But it will seem familiar to anyone who has worked in humanities computing or a digital humanities center. What Father Busa spells out here in ideal form is a program for establishing an emerging interdisciplinary field of linguistic or literary data analysis. Decades later, many discussions of digital humanities are still focused on similar institutional issues: infrastructure for scholarly communication; discussions of standards (such as the TEI, the Text Encoding Initiative markup standard, for example), tools, and methods; and, through organizations such as ACH, ALLC, EADH, ADHO, and Centernet, institutionalizing the general ideal (whatever the reality) of wide collaboration among individual centers.

Cold War defense helped to fund both atomic energy research and research into machine translation (in the same facility at Ispra in Lombardy), and through a process of exchanges, more directly perhaps than many have realized, that research helped to fund the first center for humanities computing 30 kilometers away in Gallarate. Like a good deal of academic research, humanities computing emerged historically at the intersection of industry and government. Among other things, this means that the pressing search for funding was always part of the constitution of this kind of interdisciplinary work. What Busa called the "dream" of providing free (or at least not-for-profit) processing of linguistic data was the motive behind these practical infrastructural arrangements, but the arrangements also helped to shape the dream. At any rate, funding by government and corporate sources was not an afterthought, or something limited to the sciences: it was part of the plan for this important phase of humanities computing and it shaped the research agenda in specific ways, including perhaps how some "pure" research questions were articulated, shared, and with whom they were shared.

Father Busa was always clear-eyed and openly pragmatic about these relationships. At the time he made the presentation in 1961, IBM Italia in Milan was still providing free technical support to CAAL, supplying an all-important paper punched cards, and, through a "system of yearly points"[24] (essentially free rent), making available data-processing machines "with a retail value of 1.500.000 Lire a month,"[25] as well as making financial contributions to keep the center running. In addition, CAAL depended on the financial support of several "Italian captain[s] of industry" (for the use of local facilities at mechanical and textile factories in Gallarate, for example), and, finally, "small allowances" from the Italian Ministries of Education and of Labor.[26]

At the same time, Father Busa placed the issue of funding in very broad contexts: the overarching history of the written word, in which he saw his work participating, as if the rise of electronic text led inevitably to demands (and opportunities) for research on multiple fronts.[27] Just as in the time of Gutenberg, he says, when printed books were produced "alongside manuscripts," so in his own time, in addition to print journals and books there were the beginnings of the "electronic book." This media history he uses to frame the fact that industry and defense "feel compelled to fund research for the automation of information retrieval and machine translation," and for these, his own kind of work, the "automation of lexical analysis, is an absolutely necessary preliminary phase."[28] In a different publication, from 1962, Father Busa explained this intellectual opportunism using a satirical parable about the bulldozer of "progress," a figure for "technology triumphant with its latest creation: automation."

> People shuddered, considering it a crude, hard bulldozer that goes roaring ahead, crushing and shredding flowers, amongst which, a delicate and gentle victim, is humanism. Tomorrow is already upon us. The future has already begun: the lava-flow is spreading out and burning the green sides of the mountain. Inside the monster's operations room are men, encapsulated amidst gauges, clocks, warning lights and dials. Perhaps at the start they were not even aware of the elegiac wailings and lamentations of the "humanists." In fact they are satisfied with working. They claim to offer a service of public utility, because they consider that without them industry and commerce would no longer be able to answer to man's needs.[29]

The target of this satirical verbal cartoon isn't only the juggernaut of insensitive mechanization: it's also, at least implicitly, the naive idea of progress itself, the notion that what's now sometimes called "creative destruction" is inevitable. Finally, the satire can also be read as targeting the naiveté of *merely* aesthetic or appreciative, dilettante humanities, typified by careful collectors of "the choicest flowers" of culture.

As we continue to read, we become suspicious that the parable is at least partly about Father Busa's own work with IBM over the previous decade.

> Then, however—not yet ten years ago—the men involved in automation began to make the boss lean out from his cabin in the tower of electronics and ask philologists and grammarians, who were busy in the fields selecting the choicest flowers, questions such as these: Please, how many verbs are there in Russian that are active and transitive, and how many that are active and intransitive? How many are there in English? What is the greatest number of initial and final letters that coincides with the greatest number of words? Which words or linguistic situations are found within a radius of *n*-words, only when and always when "faccia" means "face", and which others only and always when "faccia" is a form of the verb "fare" ("to do/make")? Again: Please, would you arrange all the words in the dictionary according to the various morphological and grammatical categories? (Busa 1962, 105)

The interest of those in power in technical linguistic questions was never selfless or unmotivated, as Father Busa well knows and as his anecdote shows. Nonetheless, in purely pragmatic terms, it offers profound opportunities to scholarship.

What happened was sensational: a machine made us realize that no humanist is in such command of his own language as to be able to answer such questions. A machine, the skivvy of banal commerce and drudging industry, has revealed that there is still too little humanism of the serious and systematic type. Economic facts today demand a qualitative increase of grammatical and lexical sciences as one of the necessary conditions of their vital development. Yet they also offer the possibility, and this is neither petty revenge nor small satisfaction. (Busa 1962, 105)

Undoubtedly, the parable of the bulldozer is meant to illustrate the virtues of literary data analysis, a computerized philology, over merely aesthetic literary appreciation. It's a call for greater rigor in the humanities, for more "serious and systematic" research. But it's also a blatant lesson in pragmatics, an exhortation to seize the opportunities provided by the contemporary climate for funding: "The activities of production, trade, and defense demand the automation of 'information retrieval,' which I would translate as an opportune tracing system of useful knowledge."

Consider again the overlapping alliances, the "useful" adjacent possibles and practical opportunities that were exploited by just this corner of Father Busa's wide-ranging network: his ties to IBM, created starting in 1949, allowed him to connect linguistic research at the Jesuit university, Georgetown—research funded in the first place and made possible through collaboration with IBM—with international research into machine translation at the European atomic energy center (Euratom), research driven in large part by U.S. Pentagon funding, the perceived needs of Cold War intelligence, *and* by Busa's desire to make his own center at Gallarate a node through which this connection was made, at the same time gaining funds for his own research, the building of the *Index Thomisticus* and, in the late 1950s, the processing of the Dead Sea Scrolls (as well as other smaller projects). More ambitiously, this network provided at least the opportunity to bring into interrelation a growing number of centers where linguistic data processing might be done. Almost as a byproduct, the whole thing provided a practical opportunity for employment for some of his students.

The "exchange basis" on which Father Busa says he made the Georgetown-Ispra connection should be understood as a kind of educational or diplomatic exchange, in which CAAL's students and its operating budget benefitted as a result of providing certain services. In fact, "exchange" also suggests the currency involved. Finally, metaphorically, Father Busa served as an "exchange" in the technological sense, a switch or node for traffic, as in a telephone exchange. At mid-century, manual exchanges were still common around the world, in which human operators manually made connections at large switchboards by changing the configuration of wired plugs—the same basic technology as in the plugboards, with crisscrossed cables, used to program punched-card machines. Father Busa was not just an operator; he made himself a kind of human switch, someone who routed the interchange and formed the link with his own itinerant activity, and in so doing, extending an international network. His larger vision was for a worldwide system of centers and the ties that would link them together for the exchange of information, resources, and services, a world network of collaborative centers in literary data processing. In the 1962 paper I quoted above, the parable of the bulldozer and the call for exploring opportunities is followed by concrete examples: CAAL's multiple projects, and Georgetown linguistics research being used in Frankfurt and at Euratom. All of this, Father Busa says, represents "a new lexicology and new linguistics . . . developing amongst the researchers into techniques for the treatment of information."[30] He concludes: these new approaches "are more systematic, more exhaustive, more widely useful, and, I am emboldened to say, more humanistic than the traditional ones in use up to now."[31]

The methods, if not the ultimate goals, of Father Busa's research program were bound to be shaped by the material alliances through which they emerged, with their possibilities of funding, in both government and industry. This had undoubtedly been the case with IBM during the first decade. Busa's 1961 presentation in France characterized the work of CAAL in terms of "'industrial accounting'" ("*Comptabilité industrielle*"—his quotation marks), that is, "techniques for the continual control of production, time, and costs."[32] Although we might at first assume that the source of this industrial model, this focus on mechanization of scholarly labor, was his collaborating organization, IBM, it's important to remember that Busa came to America in the first place in 1949 driven by the desire for labor-saving machinery. After all, a historical precursor to Taylorite or Fordist "scientific" methods of management can be found in the hierarchical organization of the Jesuit order itself and the traditional labor of medieval monastic life, including printing, a technology closely aligned with Jesuit schools and missions. Just as one example of the way in which Busa's work did not entirely depend on modern American corporate culture for his institutional models: his own Jesuit institution, the Aloisianum, hosted in 1946 the founding of a Center of Philosophical Studies, among the projects of which was the publication of a massive Philosophical Dictionary. It would continue for years as a center sponsoring scholarly publications, often collaborative reference works. This model for academic centers had its roots in the medieval European academy. There's no question that Father Busa was drawn to theories of efficient modern management as organized around mechanized accounting and data-analysis equipment (and, later, computers). He said as much. But his implementations were also always made in overlapping contexts that included historical models for colleges and schools connected to textual production in Jesuit Catholic culture, as well as the significant nineteenth-century history of industrialization in Northern Italy, specifically the history of the textile industry in Gallarate and its environs.

For its part, IBM's corporate needs led it to continue to support the Italian priest's work. In January 1956, the company signed a consent decree in response to a U.S. government antitrust suit that had been pending for four years.[33] The suit was designed to limit IBM's dominance of the market for punched-card tabulating and accounting machinery. Among other provisions, IBM was forced to sell as well as rent its equipment to customers, and it was required to provide services, parts, and support for the used equipment it sold. This reminds us that the focus of many historians of technology on large-scale machines that can be identified as "ancestors" of later computers, the SSEC, ASCC, ENIAC, UNIVAC, etc., tends to underemphasize the ongoing importance of quotidian, "normal" technological practice, such as the widespread use of technically "out-of-date," lower-cost office machinery, several generations of which remained in worldwide operation in commercial, academic, and government settings for decades after the war. It was 1962 before IBM's revenues from "electronic stored-program computer systems exceeded, for the first time, those for punched-card systems."[34] And yet, "despite [a] rapid rate of installation of computer systems, punched card equipment continued to be used for many more years. It was needed to satisfy the requirements of small organizations and for special purposes, and it also served as information input-output equipment for many computer systems."[35] The data-processing technology environment during the 1950s was characterized by this kind of overlapping of platforms and jostling by competing applications. His humanistic work was one example of the kind of "special purposes" which punched-card machines continued to serve, from IBM's perspective. It was not an anomaly in this regard; there were many such special customers for punched-card machinery, even after the emergence of electronic computing.

The constraints of the 1956 agreement would not be finally lifted for forty years. Thomas Watson, Jr. later wrote that settling the case in 1956 "was one of the best moves we ever made because it cleared the way for IBM to keep expanding at top speed."[36] At the very least, settling the suit called for new *kinds* of expansion. In May 1956, Thomas J. Watson, Sr. formalized the distribution of power to his two sons. Thomas J. Watson, Jr. became the chief executive of the U.S. company and Arthur K. ("Dick") Watson became chief executive of the World Trade Corporation. On June 19, 1956, Watson Sr. died. It's probably no coincidence that it was in that year of fundamental reorganization at IBM, characterized by a new emphasis on globalization and new arrangements for distributing its data-processing equipment, that Father Busa founded CAAL in Italy, given how dependent his own enterprise was on the availability of IBM equipment and material support, in both the U.S. and in Italy.

Father Busa's background and training led him in a direction that converged with IBM's interests. The history and culture of the Jesuits, like other orders in the Catholic Church, included a vocation for worldwide missions, and explicitly emphasized the readiness to travel anywhere they were needed.[37] More generally, the Jesuits' sense of their own culture, as well as the way they were perceived historically, was characterized by a deliberate engagement with the secular world.

The founder, St. Ignatius, the tradition said, had made a decisive turn outward, away from the otherworldly withdrawal of the cloistered life.[38]

When it comes to Jesuit intellectual culture, Siegfried Zielinski's media archaeology provides helpful historical context. He describes the designs and inventions of the Renaissance Jesuit polymath, Father Athanasius Kircher, S.J. (1602–1680), as growing out of a worldwide "network of clients and patrons."[39] Zielinzki says of Father Kircher that he was "obviously an extremely industrious and gifted communicator," but that historians have missed the importance of "an organization that one may justifiably term an excellently appointed and strategically operating media concern."[40] According to Zielinski, "Kircher was situated at the very heart of the power center of knowledge, and he made masterly use of its network . . . ."[41] Despite the distance of three centuries between the two Jesuits, these observations apply remarkably well to Father Busa, including the role played by a worldwide network when it comes to developing and making use of technologies:

> The operating method of the Societas Jesu in the seventeenth century can be described from a media-archaeological perspective as governed by two principles, which were also of decisive importance in Kircher's own work. These principles were the international network of a thoroughly hierarchical and centralistically structured system of religious faith, knowledge, and politics, combined with the development of advanced strategies for the mise-en-scène of their messages, including the invention and construction of the requisite devices and apparatus.[42]

These parallels between Kircher and Busa are no accident. They grow out of the two scholars' shared Jesuit culture, key features of which were transmitted across the centuries, including the very idea of building a radiating center of activity with worldwide ties within which to instrumentalize contemporary scientific devices, often adapted from their original purposes, for the good of the greater mission.

Collectively and historically, the Jesuit mission has often included the founding of schools. They were arguably "the first religious order to undertake as a primary and self-standing ministry the operation of full-fledged schools for any students, lay or clerical, who chose to come to them."[43] The curriculum of their colleges— which were comparable to modern secondary schools—was built like all Renaissance education on the humanities as found in classical texts and languages (the Jesuit colleges that became "universities" taught the higher subjects of theology and philosophy). The method of instruction in the colleges, as in humanistic study in general in earlier periods, was close textual analysis, taking texts apart, word for word, which, interestingly, in the sixteenth century would often be referred to as "anatomization"[44]—a term that connects in interesting ways to the idea of "atomizing" or dissolving the texts in computer-assisted indexing. It was in large part through running these colleges that the order established its reputation for engaging the community at large.[45] Historically, Jesuit culture rests on:

> an implicit theological assumption of the compatibility of Christianity with the best of secular culture, according to the axiom of St. Thomas Aquinas, the theologian the Constitutions prescribe for the order, that grace perfects nature. The Jesuit adoption of the axiom suggests, once again, the ongoing impact of Ignatius's "turn to the world" at Manresa.[46]

The educational mission included calling for priests to engage in the intellectual life of the sciences, letters, and humanities. This translated in the case of many Jesuit schools in the early modern era into the installation of printing presses (though there were always concerns about whether these were profit-making, and naturally most of what they printed was liturgical or religious).[47]

What Father Busa founded in 1956 was a vocational "training school for key-punch operators," technicians of automated accounting machinery. But its first reason for being was research—the production of the *Index Thomisticus* and related projects—with students working in effect as interns, learning on the job for two-year stints. The school may well have been based in part on an IBM model that he would have seen at work both in New York and, perhaps more immediately relevant, once he came back to Milan, where he worked in the early 1950s and even established something like a "department" of his own within the IBM location, just before starting his own center.

> In Italy I worked in IBM offices for a few years. In 1954 I started my own punching and verifying department; two years later I established my own processing department, but employing large computers always in IBM premises. That year [1956] I started a training school for keypunch operators.[48]

IBM had for years given aptitude tests for admission to its own training courses. The programs were a way to strengthen their dominance of the market: the trainees (usually young women) would learn only the IBM systems and would therefore graduate as specialists on IBM equipment, no matter where they ended up working.[49]

Busa likely would have learned something from this model during the roughly five years (approximately 1951–1956) that his work was based at IBM Italia. For example, like IBM, he recruited competitively. There was an aptitude and screening test, which was apparently even administered at IBM Italia, and it would appear that all of those who were admitted received scholarships funded by industry and modest government grants, then got rigorous training, sometimes wearing blindfolds, for example, to test their ability to touch-type.

> For all those admitted, the requirement was that it was their first job. After a month of testing, only one out of five was accepted for a program of four semesters, eight hours per day. The success was excellent: industries wanted to hire them before they had finished the program. Their training was in punching and verifying our texts. . . . This school continued until 1967, when I completed the punching of all my texts.[50]

The student operators wore white lab coats as they worked, which may look to our eyes like a "scientific" uniform but was also like the uniforms worn by workers in various industries at the time.

The whole process was organized according to the principles of modern scientific-industrial management as interpreted for the specific technologies of punched-card processing. Or was it according to the Italian textile factories in the facilities of which operations were sometimes housed? Or, lab coats notwithstanding, was it inspired by the much older models of convents and monastic communities or Jesuit colleges (like Busa's own Aloisianum)? Any school Busa started would likely have been influenced by some combination of these models. Mechanization was the point, yes, and Father Busa explicitly described the school as making use of modern industrial methods.[51] But industrial design seems to have been combined with local and ancient models of production and scholastic models of education. It was after all a school, and the school was institutionally located at *both* the Jesuit College of Philosophical Studies, the Aloisianum, and in the locations of former factories, still financed and donated by mechanical and textile companies. The curriculum included mandatory classes in English and Theology, along with training in keypunch techniques.[52] Most students were teenage girls, many sent directly from their secondary school in Gallarate, run by the Canossian Daughters of Charity, as the interviews by Nyhan, et al. say. (Fourteen was the age at which they completed primary education and when many girls in the region left school.)

The training school had a vocational focus, but it was also clearly established as a Jesuit Catholic institution. Photographs—and one short documentary film that I've seen—of the CAAL dedication ceremony on December 17, 1956, show a formal ribbon-cutting performed by a young girl, after which guests proceed into a "room reserved for the prodigious machine(s),"[53] on which Archbishop Montini invoked a benediction. (Montini was to become Pope Paul VI; he served as Honorary President of the Center's advisory committee.) Attendees included representatives from IBM, foremost among them Paul Tasman, and local industrialists (including Mrs. Lucia Crespi, the mother of the young man Busa had accompanied to America in 1949) who were underwriting the Center financially. The ceremony and iconology in the images highlight what may get lost in later written accounts of the school: it was a hybrid institution that combined features from the technical culture of IBM (both in New York and in Milan) with features from the local culture of Jesuit Catholic education in Gallarate. From

Father Busa's point of view, the dedication on December 17, 1956, would have seemed the culmination of ten years' preparation, from when he first decided to pursue the *Index Thomisticus*.[54] The result was that he now served as a connection between American technology and Italian industry, academic and religious culture.

The Busa Archive contains a brief typescript of a chapter for a book in progress during 1961–1962 by the Dutch linguist, Félicien de Tollenaere (1912–2009), telling the story of CAAL in detail (I've already cited it above).[55] The advantage of this brief draft is that it was composed very close to the time of the founding of CAAL and apparently in consultation with Father Busa. The potential disadvantage, of course, is closely related to that last: the risk of insularity. It seems to have been partly based on Busa's early publications, as we would expect, but also on additional conversations with him, and then to have been submitted to him for comments and final approval—even proofreading and correction (there are notes and queries attached with responses that would seem to be Busa's). Finally, like almost everything else in the Busa Archive, this profile of Father Busa's work by another scholar was collected and preserved by Father Busa himself. Nonetheless, the de Tollenaere typescript offers a number of useful concrete details about the organization of CAAL during the crucial years of 1956–1961.

For example, Father Busa recalled in 1980 in a general way that between 1962–1967 the Center consisted of "a team of more than 60 full-time participants."[56] According to de Tollenaere, although CAAL had been established as a Center for four years by then, it was still physically dispersed in 1961,[57] with "the staff, the material and the machines" distributed across three different locations in the town of Gallarate:[58] the Aloisianum college itself, up a hill at the end of a tree-lined drive, "where the philological work ([using] hands and brains)" took place, preparing—primarily marking up—the texts, and lemmatizing the punched cards; a "factory"—by which he must mean the large industrial shed-like space at via Galileo Ferraris, 2 in the center of Gallarate, financed and donated by local mechanical and textile firms—where the IBM machines were housed and used to punch and process the cards; and in "a cellar in another factory where the remaining machines and the administration [were]"—possibly the Cuccirelli company's nearby location, under the directorship of Dr. G. Decio, on via E. Ferrario (despite the similar name, a different street several blocks away), where operations seem to have been based in 1959–1960, along with the Aloisianum, before the Center moved into the factory.[59] The plan was already in place in spring or summer 1961 to consolidate these operations into a single large building, where there would also be storage for the growing file of punched cards. That single building was the factory space at via G. Ferraris, 2.

I visited the site of the factory in Gallarate on March 13, 2015, the building that had housed Father Busa's final lab in the city, on via Ferraris—still standing, though much altered since the 1960s. It was under scaffolding for major renovation, and the multiply peaked and skylit, "sawtooth"-style shed-roof had apparently been removed some time ago, but the arched windows and decorative L-brackets protruding from the walls under the eaves, details recognizable from archival photographs, were still there. (Later in 2015, it was demolished.) My guide that day was Danila Cairati, who had served as Father Busa's secretary during the final decade of his life. Based on conversations (via the intermediation of Marco Passarotti) with her and with Gisa Crosta, Busa's first secretary at CAAL in the 1960s, I learned that the lab on via Ferraris was financed by a Sr. Valentini (who owed a mechanics firm and whose location CAAL seems to have used temporarily early in 1961), but it was donated for use by the building's owner, the textile manufacturer, Sr. Dragone. So the large space is sometimes referred to in the Archive as "lab. v. Ferraris" (for its location) and sometimes as "lab. Valentini" (for its financial patron).

Photographs in the Busa Archive show large crates encasing IBM machines being moved into and installed in this open-plan factory space, with power cords dangling from the ceiling, slender metal columns, and those angled skylights placed to facilitate the textile work that had gone on there before. (One series of photographs shows Father Busa—in one case with Livia Canestraro standing nearby—inside the empty building with file drawers full of the punched cards, just unpacked and stacked on the floor.[60]) The original manufacturing lines were replaced by long rows of mostly young women operators in white lab coats, sitting at grey-metal punched-card machines on rugs over the cement floor, or off to the side, working at tables on printed texts or with decks of cards (see Figure 4.1). Father Busa had an office at one end of the building and a meeting area was set up with curved modern chairs, upholstered in orange and grey. The walls were eventually decorated with abstract line-drawings of shapes resembling puzzle pieces, their outlines enclosing characters from various languages and glyphs. I suspect that these were meant to invoke the Dead Sea Scrolls fragments that CAAL had been working with for several years by then, and perhaps the general idea of textual fragments or linguistic "puzzle pieces" as a symbol of the work of the Center. Father Busa's office area was dominated by a large, colorful stained-glass window, with a modernist image of the head of Christ, boxed in against the back wall. In some photographs you can see passages in Greek (one from Romans 11:36, for example) and Hebrew inscribed, possibly on blackboards, on either side of the window. It's hard not to see these scriptural passages as alternative workplace mottos, along with the symbolically decorated lab space in general, a kind of variation in a Jesuit key on the IBM showroom at 590 Madison Avenue. Yet another inauguration ceremony was held in the factory space in 1961, five years after the initial establishment of the Center, this time attended by Giovanni Cardinal Columbo as well as various industrialist underwriters, to dedicate this new and final location of CAAL in Gallarate.

The industrial model for CAAL's work is vividly illustrated by the location and layout. Instead of textiles, texts; instead of weaving and sewing, punching and

FIGURE 4.1 CAAL ("lab"), via G. Ferraris 2, Galllarate, Italy, June 29, 1967 (Busa Archive #613).

sorting of cards: the reality in this case poetically invokes the historical connection between mechanized looms, which had in the nineteenth century often been controlled by punched cards, and mechanized linguistic processing using decks of punched cards that were directly descended (via Hollerith's inventions) from those Jacquard-loom punched cards, versions of which had surely been used in Gallarate's historical textile manufacturing. And yet, the building was found, donated, and repurposed not from a poetic or historical impulse, but out of the most practical considerations of money and physical resources, not the least of which was proximity to the academic campus of the Aloisianum, just up the hill from this center of light-industrial activity.

For a time in the 1960s, Father Busa also kept an office in the historical center of Milan, at via Cerva 35, at least sometimes with a secretary, because Milan was "a vast center of science, traffic and public relations."[61] Another "center": Father Busa listed the location in Milan as his professional address when attending a 1961 conference on machine translation, for example.[62] At the beginning of the new decade in 1961 CAAL was undergoing consolidation. Only five years later, in 1967, the operation would move to Pisa for a brief period, before moving again to Boulder, Colorado in the U.S. All of these moves were driven by the need to establish the finances and production of the *Index Thomisticus* and related projects relatively independently, so that Father Busa would be freed up, would "only have the scientific leadership of the organization."[63] In fact, for the entire life of CAAL and the *Index* project, he was always to remain the primary person responsible for fundraising, financial management, and training. As we'll see in Chapter 5, all of this had taken a serious personal toll on him by late 1958–early 1959—surely one of the reasons a more rational and stable infrastructure, including a physical home for the Center, was so desirable in 1961.

In early 1961, the CAAL staff was divided into two sections: one "scholarly," consisting of academic researchers in philology and linguistics (including for example Dr. Antonio Zampolli, who would go on to found his own center in Pisa in 1967, one of the earliest in computational linguistics); and one "technical," consisting of 22 "assistants," 17 of them punched-card operators, presumably most of them the young women trainees in the school. They worked in two 4-hour shifts a day, punching and verifying the cards. Three special operators were selected from among their ranks, possibly to supervise the processing of the punched cards.[64] All of the technical assistants were by then working under the supervision of Livia Canestraro (later Tonelli), who had been among the earliest students in the training school, starting in 1953–1954 (she remained at the Center until 1963).[65] She tells an interesting story of Father Busa's attempting (presumably sometime in the 1960s) to replace her with a young man.

> Father Busa, I don't know if under Jesuit influence or so, he didn't—because I was in charge of the group—he tried to, to substitute me with, with a man. . . . more or less everyone—we also had men that had arrived later for the sorting and tabulating machines—even the men revolted because the men's course, the one on the sorting machines etcetera, would have then been in Milan. But I had, I had learned on my own.[66]

The other operators rebelled against the change, Canestraro says, because she was simply the better supervisor. She appreciates that Father Busa clearly esteemed her work, and insists that she "was never treated poorly" and notes that she had opportunities, rare at the time for a young woman, to travel, for example. But she says that the lack of a "real diploma" from the Center was a drawback, despite all her training and practical expertise, and, in the end, she "was interested in women's . . . being able to do the same tasks as men."[67] After leaving the Center she went on to work as an editor.

Canestraro was the exception at CAAL: a woman in a supervisory role. As Nyhan and Terras observe, there's no evidence that any other women at CAAL were able to hold "more senior roles that were acknowledged as such," let alone to cross over to the intellectual or "scholarly" side of the Center's organizational structure. This two-tiered structure, of technical workers and scholarly or intellectual supervisors, underlay the other divisions of labor at the Center. Aside from the gender divide, this is part of the problematic legacy of early humanities computing that today's digital humanities practitioners face as well, the danger of replicating the "two cultures" divide as described by C.P. Snow in 1959.[68]

The training school was both internship and production line for data processing of texts. Reflecting this language, indeed, stopping just short of trademarking it, in 1963 IBM displayed at 590 Madison Avenue a small showcase about Busa's work, labeled "IBM Literary Data Processing" (Figure 4.2). It included a large poster with side-by-side images: a scribe, labeled "Medieval Manuscript Writer," and a technician in a business suit at the control panel of an "Electronic Data Processing Machine" (the IBM 705 EDPM). Alongside that, another poster describes indexing "the world's great literary and religious works," emphasizing as usual the labor-saving and time-saving affordances of punched-card accounting

FIGURE 4.2   Literary Data Processing showcase display, IBM World Headquarters, New York, 1963 (Busa Archive #498).

machines and citing as the prime example "the first concordance to the entire works of St. Thomas Aquinas . . . 13 million words, or sixteen times as many as contained in the Bible," which is "now being compiled by the new IBM Literary Data Processing method. Work has also begun on an analysis and index of the Dead Sea Scrolls." On the left, a profile of St. Thomas, on the right, images of punched cards from the *Index Thomisticus,* and further to the right, an image of a sample page of the printed *Index.* The quantification of the work—"13 million words" and the emphasis on savings of time and labor ("here are a few of the 44 steps involved in mechanical indexing")—are typical of Father Busa's own characterizations of the project in terms of the efficiencies of industrial production, as we've seen. The simple fact of the display at IBM headquarters featuring his work, fourteen years after Father Busa's first meeting with the CEO (where he used a different kind of poster, about doing the impossible), underscores the distance he had traveled, literally and figuratively, during the 1950s. The visual and verbal rhetoric of the display, the way in which the company presented the work to the public, emphasized the timelessness and cultural weight that came with philological work of this kind, the aura of the sacred layered on the sublime power of the new technology, while also branding the method as IBM's.

The textual samples and technical explanations on the posters are framed by religious and cultural images, in particular the iconic image of the monk in the scriptorium paired with the operator in the machine room. It's already on the way to becoming a cliché, this juxtaposition of monk and programmer, manuscript table (or letterpress) and computer. It recalls similar representations of "media" across the ages, as "extensions of man," in the work of Marshall McLuhan (whose own *Understanding Media* appeared at around the same time, in 1964). Partly, it means to close the distance of 500 years, to suggest that human cultural inscription will continue in the computer age, not just supported but augmented by the new "thinking machines"—a corrective to popular anxieties which we've already seen IBM addressing at the time. But the images in the display also highlight the human and institutional basis of the technologies of textual production, whether in the fifteenth or the twentieth centuries.

The specific image chosen for the display of the scribe (or "Medieval manuscript writer") is actually a late fifteenth-century self-portrait by Jean Miélot (or Jehan), a French scribe, priest, and humanistic scholar who translated and edited ancient classical and sacred texts.[69] No mere copyist, in other words, he was a model humanistic scholar, a priest responsible for the library of his patron, the Duke of Burgundy. Someone at IBM probably chose the images for their visual symmetry—both show men sitting in chairs at specialized workstations with tools of their work arranged behind them—rather than as a reference to Jehan in particular. And it may well be that the image just signified "scribe" in a vague or superficial way. But the general idea of the scriptorium is complicated by particular histories like Jehan's, just as the general idea of humanities computing is complicated by a historical understanding of the particulars of Father

Busa's work. Although in this case it's an unknown IBMer and not Father Busa depicted with the IBM machine, the symmetry of the situation—two priests, five hundred years apart, working on similar texts but using different technologies—must have appealed to the designer of the display. Both medieval and modern textual practices are products of the social and institutional conditions that make possible available technologies. However unintended, the comparison of Jehan and Busa exposes the deep roots of Father Busa's "pioneering" role—as simultaneously an artisan of mechanized methods for textual processing and a learned scholar of secular and sacred texts, exploiting the latest available technology for culturally conservative ends, always working as it were adjacent to the library or archive, translating, transcribing, and reproducing ancient texts in new formats. Historically, scriptoria varied widely. But all scribal stations or scriptoria were settings for social-institutional technologies of memory and inscription, designed to preserve and transmit cultural heritage. This is what the display tries in its own way to invoke for visitors to the showroom.

That phrase used in the display to refer to the work of Paul Tasman and Roberto Busa, "literary data processing," is worth pausing over, coming as it did just after IBM had installed its own new Data Processing Center right there in the 590 showroom, featuring an IBM 702 computer, in the line of the 705 that Busa and Tasman would use to process the data punched onto cards in Italy. As I indicated above, CAAL's Italian name seems to have been rendered for a time mostly as *Centro per L'Automazione dell'Analisi* **Letteraria** rather than, as it was perhaps more often in later years, *Centro per L'Automazione dell'Analisi* **Linguistica** ("literary" rather than "linguistic" analysis). Letterhead stationery for CAAL over the years reflects this difference and perhaps indicates something of a shift from one to the other, literature to linguistics. However, the terms were always somewhat interchangeable, since the punched-card processing focused on linguistic features in the general sense, language found in texts of a generally "literary" nature (ranging from philosophical discourse to poetry). One document by Busa (it appears to be a report to the advisory committee for CAAL) includes a section headed "Literary or Linguistic Analysis," and summarizes such analysis as consisting of two phases or components: (1) "indexes and concordances of words," and (2) "any other statistical survey of literature, in the most comprehensive sense of this word"—but starting with basic elements of language such as "phonemes, morphemes, prefixes, suffixes, endings, roots," etc.[70] In sum, to conduct literary *or* linguistic analysis as Father Busa conceived of it was "to determine the categories under which a sequence of expressions of human thoughts can be grouped, classified and described; it is also to collect and list the elements of the expression under the appropriate categories" (Busa, CAAL report). In other words, despite the use of "literary," Busa always looked to texts for their language, usually at a level well below the semantic.

Paul Tasman's preferred terms of art for the work were "language engineering" as well as "literary data processing," as spelled out in his pamphlet on the Dead Sea

Scrolls, for example, where he defines the latter term simply as "the adaptation of Electronic data processing techniques to the analysis of literature."[71] In another paper published in 1957, he explains that "*Literary* data processing" is a recent extension of the concept of data processing ("handling numerical data to produce accounting and statistical results") "to include data-processing techniques adapted to the requirements of literary analysis," which he associates with indexing and the making of concordances—as in Busa's formulation, with more or less "statistical results" of the study of the language of literary texts.[72]

If the mixed kinds of ancient texts found in the non-biblical Dead Sea Scrolls can be classified as "literary and religious," then the term "literary" just seems to mean something like "texts of cultural heritage" or texts of a broadly humanistic kind, defined in opposition to scientific or technical documents. This is what Tasman seems to mean when he refers to CAAL as the "Literary Data Processing Center in Gallarate, Italy," with the "L" standing for "Letteraria." In his own publications from around the same time, Father Busa also seems at times to have favored "Letteraria"[73] and to have referred to CAAL as "our Literary Data Processing Center."[74] Besides official CAAL stationery from the early years, a document stamp with a circular seal also spelled out the name with "Letteraria." Although CAAL's initial experiments were on a canto of Dante and four hymns of St. Thomas, and some later work was done on Goethe, for example, and its core project was a collection of medieval philosophical and theological texts, and eventually the non-biblical Dead Sea Scrolls, as we've seen, CAAL also took on some scientific and engineering texts. Even when the "L" was read as "Linguistica," it was clearly language in expressive or informational texts, not language in the abstract that the Center aimed to study. That said, there remains a possible fault line between "literary" and "linguistic," however, and the initial choice of "literary" may represent more than only terminological convenience.

In part, this may have been a rhetorical gesture meant to shape public perception. The term "literary" implied that the technology of data processing itself had lyrical possibilities, an historical and expressive dimension that might inspire awe, something arising from the nature of the texts but also reflecting back upon computing by association. As we've seen, IBM also had an interest in emphasizing the humanities side of this work. In the stress on "literary," something may have been (perhaps deliberately) gained rather than lost in translation, as it were, between Gallarate and New York.

The idea that IBM may have vetted or even helped to create the term "*Literary* Data Processing" for reasons of public relations, to help humanize the image of computers, would be in keeping with other efforts at the time. In another collaboration meant to shape popular perceptions of computing, Charles and Ray Eames made a short (10-minute) animated film for the Eliot Noyes–designed IBM Pavilion at the World Expo 58 in Brussels (I mentioned the film briefly in Chapter 3). As we've seen, the theme of the Expo, held under the shadow of the Atomium, was "a new humanism," meant in part to quell increasing public anxiety about nuclear power.[75] In this spirit, the IBM Pavilion was dedicated to promoting the idea that computing could serve humanistic ends, could be a "creative" tool compatible with human invention and art, at a time when it was already firmly associated in the public imagination with impersonal bureaucracy and Cold War defense. *The Information Machine: Creative Man and the Data Processor* opens with a vignette about primitive "man" and "his limited ability to speculate," to predict the outcomes of his wishes and actions, because he couldn't process all the relevant factors (the pertinent data). But, the voiceover says, "there were men whose wishes . . . had a habit of coming true. These men—and women—were artists." They were "seldom bored with anything," it goes on, and were "constantly building up stores of information in active memory banks" for later use.

> When confronted with a specific need, they would call on these memory banks for information, which they would run through, sort out, and relate to the problem at hand. These men could speculate and predict. They were artists, artists in many fields: architecture, mechanics, medicine, science, politics, and the art of relating factors . . .

—that last "art of relating factors," given the accompanying cartoon image of Socrates, being a term for philosophy. The animated line drawings of these ancient "artists" show a male inventor of the wheel, a female planter of corn and a spinner of wool, and a universal artist-figure of indeterminate gender, blurring the lines of specialization between artist, engineer, agriculturalist, or craftsperson, using "artist" to mean "Creative Man," as in the title—or what in today's technology jargon would probably be called an "innovator."

The IBM Pavilion represented "Commerce" at the fair, but that didn't preclude nationalistic aims in its own displays. Just two years earlier, IBM had made a more blatantly propagandistic film produced by its Military Products Division, explaining and celebrating the technology behind the Air Force SAGE air defense system, *On Guard!* (1956).[76] A cold-open voiceover says, "Today we must be on guard in the sky when it comes to protecting our resources, the national resources that are so precious to us"—as images of missiles and fighter jets give way to children in a playground, followed by the IBM logo and the opening credits. Images of jets and a mushroom cloud are counterbalanced by logo-branded IBM buildings and machines in operation: "To protect the future of America, the defense techniques of tomorrow had to be discovered now. They were discovered: in electronics." The film touts the need for machinery—tapes, magnetic drives, a brand new visual "display scope," but also, inevitably still, punched cards—to take in "continuous streams of data" and use them vigilantly to monitor the skies and provide predictive analyses and guidance.

The Brussels Expo 58 was orchestrated by a committee of planners with direct input from the U.S. government, and it aimed to represent an ideology of market-based democratic freedom (embodied in a lifestyle of leisure and creative fulfillment), in direct opposition to the communist system of the Soviet Union.[77] Powerful technology was central to that message, as it remains at today's Expos, with slightly different ideological orientations. (As I was researching this book, Milan was preparing to host Expo 2015 with a theme of "green" and sustainable global technologies and agriculture. Protestors organized under the motto "NoExpo" to demonstrate against the fair's theme, which they saw as a cover for the interests of global capital, spraying "NoExpo" graffiti on the walls of government buildings in Milan.)[78] Sputnik had launched October 4, 1957, and American technology, including computing technology, had to appear fully advanced in response. Thomas J. Watson, Jr., when consulted, urged the planners of the American Pavilion to "emphasize productivity" and America's standard of living; Arthur Schlesinger, Jr. argued that the pavilion should "refute the argument that 'Communism is the only way to master and apply the technical revolution to human life'"; one proposed slogan for the American Pavilion was telling in its directness: "Technology a Friend not a Foe of Culture and Democracy."[79]

The Eames's film about computers contributed to the general effort at the fair to represent Western society as free and advanced, as offering fulfillment (and practical problem-solving power) for the creative individual.[80] Eames Studios was given an award for the film by the U.S. State Department and it would continue to maintain a relationship with the United States Information Agency.[81] In the film, "art" and creativity have been computerized in order to enhance the significance—the meaningfulness—of computers. The whole strategy anticipates marketing campaigns twenty-five years later by Apple aimed at associating their computers and other products with the aura of creativity, with those "artists" and visionaries who "think different," from scientists and political activists to computer engineers. Steve Jobs famously liked to say that the most interesting uses of computers took place at the "intersection of technology and the liberal arts," and Apple marketing under his leadership always emphasized popular arts and what we might call humanities applications, including desktop publishing, design, photography, and video and music production, framed in abstract terms of creativity, inspiration, self-fulfillment, even genius.

The Eames's film moves quickly into the "complications" of society in "the last century," with illustrations of technology and the need for "the science of numerical relationships" to "catch up" to the changes, using new "tools" to help people "handle" the rapidly "increasing amount of data," as "something has now emerged that might make even our most elegant theories workable"—as the images cycle from abacus beads to cogs to vacuum tubes and "the electronic calculator." Then we see a man in a white shirt and tie (the typical IBMer) at the control panel of a large computer. At that point the animated drawings give way to a sequence of filmed images of actual card punches and tape drives in operation. "This is information," the voiceover says. "The proper use of it can bring a new dignity to mankind."

Clearly, the opposite possibility was a serious concern—that is, that the onslaught of information that came with computing might reduce the dignity of humankind, that the bulldozer would crush the flowers of humanity. Deliberately tying computing to humanistic endeavors, and to creativity itself, was one way to address this fear. Besides the nationalist–ideological motivations this was a good sales strategy for a computer company. But it was more. Intellectuals and scholars, as well as developers and engineers, whether (relatively speaking) inside or outside the military–industrial complex, were at the time seriously grappling with the ambiguities surrounding computing. Willard McCarty has put it most succinctly: "There cannot be any doubt that like everyone else in Europe and North America, scholars of the incunabular period [of early humanities computing] were exposed to the strongly polarized views of the machine that saturated popular media."[82] Discussions of cybernetics, automation, and artificial intelligence had for years included consideration of philosophical and ethical questions, and it was widely recognized that human interactions with computers could take multiple forms, and in areas traditionally associated with humanistic pursuits and the arts. Still, it's worth noting that the examples of computing shown in the Eames film are almost all from practical business and industrial applications. (Architecture, unsurprisingly in a film made by architects, is the bridging discipline.) Only at the very end do we return to the general "promise that there will always be room for those smallest details, that have been the basis for man's most rewarding wishes" (accompanied by sentimental images of roses and a heart). The artist and "creative man" is in the film sublimated into economic and scientific achievements, but with a residue of humanistic meaning now attached to computing itself. The humanities provide a context for the image of computing that IBM wants to project, but specific uses of computing in actual forms of creativity associated with the humanities are only barely in evidence in the film.

This general effort to display the artistic or humanistic potential of computing may be one reason Father Busa's work with Paul Tasman was so deliberately configured as *literary* data processing. It's surely one reason the work of CAAL was featured at the 1958 IBM Pavilion in Brussels. Not quite as directly as in the case of the Watson Laboratory at Columbia, IBM thereby achieved a stake in the emerging field it was helping to name and configure. Literary data processing, like information retrieval and the elusive goal of machine translation, was part of natural language processing in general, one strain of which would in the 1960s lead into computational linguistics. In the process the literary aspect of the subfield would increasingly give way. But its inception involved leveraging the cultural capital of expression, and that focus on cultural expression survived in the emergent field of humanities computing, as two of IBM's own simultaneous publications from 1971 attest—on *Literary Data Processing* and an *Introduction to Computers in the Humanities*.[83]

The company sponsored the first conference in this new field in 1964, where Father Busa presented on the *Index Thomisticus*. Looking back in 2014, Joseph

Raben reported on the Humanist Discussion List online his belief that the conference had been created primarily to publicize Busa's work—though the *New York Times* was in attendance and also reported on Raben's own project of analyzing the texts of Shelley and Milton, for example.[84] Raben, who became editor of the first digital humanities journal, *Computers in the Humanities*, remembered that the conference featured a good deal of research on concordance building and that it marked an early recognition by "members of the avant garde" that

> by restructuring the texts they were concording into a new order—here, alphabetical, but potentially into many others—they were creating a perspective radically different from the linear organization into which the texts had originally been organized. A major benefit to the scholar of this new structure is the ability to examine all the occurrences of individual words out of their larger contexts but in association with other words almost immediately adjacent. Nascent in this effort was the root of what we now conceive as a text database.[85]

There was a general adoption of Hans Peter Luhn's KWIC (key word in context) program, developed at IBM and, according to Paul Tasman, influenced by Busa's work, even by literary scholars such as Stephen M. Parrish (who co-sponsored the conference and co-edited the proceedings) and others.

> In hindsight it is evident that the greater significance of these initiatives was twofold: first, they made clear that even in their primitive state in the 1960s, computers could perform functions beyond arithmetic and second, that another dimension of language study was available. From the beginning signaled by this small event would come a growing academic discipline covering such topics as corpus linguistics, machine translation, text analysis and literary databases.
>
> . . . .
>
> Texts could be read non-linearly, in a variety of dimensions, with the entire vocabulary alphabetized, with the most common words listed first, with the least common words listed first, or with all the words spelled backwards (so their endings could be associated), and in almost any other manner that a scholar's imagination could conjure.[86]

Raben says he came out of the conference with "a vision of a newer scholarship, based on a melding of the approaches that had served humanities scholars for generations with the newer ones generated by the computer scientists who were struggling at that time to understand their new tool, to enlarge its capacities."[87]

That IBM poster in the display case at 590 Madison on Literary Data Processing, featuring Busa and Tasman's work and Busa's center, CAAL, dates from one year before the conference Raben is describing. It reflected significant features of Busa's work in its mature stage, from the mid-1950s to the early to mid-1960s. By that time, the company's interest in this kind of work was more than just a matter of image management—though, in part, it remained that, as well. It signaled a serious interest among some of its scientists and engineers (Paul Tasman and Pete Luhn among them) in natural language applications for computing. In a more general way, it was part of a continuing effort to humanize the technology, in response to anxieties about what looked at the time like the possibility of strong Artificial Intelligence, and against the Cold War background of increased espionage and surveillance, weapon design, and control. On the one hand, there were atomic tests and the SAGE system; on the other hand, literary data processing, with the promise of machine translation and the need to humanize computing technology connecting the two, as it were. It's representable by a Venn diagram with multiple overlapping centers: as we'll see in the next chapter, the interests of philology, as Father Busa understood it, overlapped with the interests of computing at mid-century, and the early history of humanities computing began to be written in that overlapping space.

Think again about the juxtapositions of Expo 58 in Brussels: in the shadow of the colossal metallic Atomium with its interconnected spheres, inside the modernist IBM Pavilion, the 305 RAMAC computer, with its brand-new random-access magnetic-disk storage system in a grey metal and glass cabinet, answered questions for onlookers about world history in ten languages; the Eames's animated short celebrated the "artists" whose thinking led to computers for data-rich decision-making; and crowds gathered to listen to a philologist-priest talk about literary data analysis. Father Busa stood in front of machines and posters with a handheld microphone and presented his method for using IBM machines to generate concordances to thirteenth-century Latin philosophical texts, and to analyze the ancient texts contained in 2000-year-old scrolls. At least for that moment, the machines on the dais had effectively been appropriated and transformed into "international Busa machines," just as Thomas J. Watson, Sr.'s joke had foretold. But Busa's work had also been bound up in the heated milieu of mid-century computing.

It's tempting, here, to adapt the Thomistic theological paradox about a circle whose center is everywhere as a metaphor for the first humanities computing center and its multiple activities, but more mundane explanations are at hand. The center at Gallarate was heavily networked, ultimately on the model provided of the culture of the Society of Jesus itself but also drawing on examples from the burgeoning computer industry. It had a global reach, a function of its institutional and social connections, actual institutions—with material interests of their own—including other nascent centers from France and Germany to Jerusalem, and people: Roberto Busa and Paul Tasman of IBM; G. Vuccino and others at IBM Italia; and Antonio Zampolli, for example, who had worked with Busa and later moved to IBM in the late 1960s and established a center at Pisa; the Georgetown linguists and their colleagues at Euratom; and, always, performing and supervising the machine-aided labor that drove the experiments, Livia Canestraro and all the other young women (and a few young men) who were students and operators-in-training at CAAL in Italy and its extensions in Boulder and Venice. Arguably the first humanities computing center, CAAL was a precarious and ultimately temporary organization, anything but self-enclosed. It was a pragmatic institutional idea with a shifting and distributed material basis, ultimately a field of activity that could be centered in a former factory or in rooms at a computer company, and whose vectors radiated out to other centers of activity. It took this larger amorphous international organization, created through varied strategic alliances, pragmatic arrangements, and social connections, to sustain for more than four decades the research projects begun by Father Busa. Not unlike the Internet, which also began to emerge during CAAL's first decade, the work was distributed among many nodes connected by multiple pathways, potentially allowing for the travel of methods and machines, data on stacks of punched cards or reels of tape, funding, and energy, all conveyed in the end by persons—first (and, frequently, last) by Father Busa himself. The next chapter looks at an expansion of the work at CAAL to include the analysis of the then-recently discovered Dead Sea Scrolls, work that stretched the resources of Father Busa and the Center and in the end did not result in a published index, but which still offers a fascinating example of an emergent method, through a series of experiments in literary data processing as a form of computerized philology.

Notes

1 Roberto Busa, unpublished autobiographical manuscript. Cited by kind permission of Marco Passarotti, CIRCSE.
2 Busa, Roberto, S.J. "The Annals of Humanities Computing: The *Index Thomisticus*," *Computers and the Humanities* 14.2 (1980), 83-90 (86).
3 Félicien de Tollenaere, English typescript, draft for *Nieuwe wegen in de lexicologie* (Amsterdam, Noord-Hollandsche Uitg. Mij., 1963), 28. Busa Archive.
4 Eliot Noyes speech cited in Paul Atkinson, *Computer* (Objeckt) (London: Reaktion Books, 2010), Kindle edition, loc. 546-50.
5 Thomas J. Watson, Jr. and Peter Petre. *Father, Son & Co.: My Life at IBM and Beyond* (New York: Bantam Books, 1990), Kindle edition, loc. 4279-87.
6 John Harwood, *The Interface: IBM and the Transformation of Corporate Design, 1945–1976* (Minneapolis: University of Minnesota Press, 2011), 45-46; and Watson, Jr. and Petre, *Father, Son & Co.*, Kindle edition, loc. 4291.
7 Letter from Roberto Busa to Rev. E.B. Bunn, S.J., April 28, 1954. Busa Archive (Gall. Rel. Cult. 1940, USA tab).
8 Robert Sobel, *IBM: Colossus In Transition* (New York: Bantam Books, 1983), 137.

9   IBM Press Release, January 8, 1954, IBM Archives website, http://www-03.ibm
    .com/ibm/history/exhibits/701/701_translator.html.
10 IBM Press Release, January 8, 1954.
11 On machine translation from the perspective of the history of digital humanities, and
    on the pioneering work of the British scholar, Andrew Booth, in particular, see Edward
    Vanhoutte, "The Gates of Hell: History and Definition of Digital | Humanities |
    Computing," in *Defining Digital Humanities: A Reader*, Melissa Terras, Julianne Nyhan,
    and Edward Vanhoutte, eds. (Farnham, Surrey, UK: Ashgate, 2013), 123-24. Vanhoutte
    also mentions the demo at IBM and notes that for a time there was some over-
    lap between machine translation and the kind of literary data processing begun by
    Roberto Busa (126).
12 See John Hutchins, "ALPAC: The (in)famous report," *MT News International* 14 (June
    1996), 9-12. Available online at: http://www.hutchinsweb.me.uk/MTNI-14-1996
    .pdf. Hutchins notes that the "Euratom system was the Georgetown University system
    installed in 1963 at Ispra, Italy" (as I discuss below).
13 See Jonathan Slocum, "An Experiment in Machine Translation," ACL '80, *Proceedings
    of the 18th Annual Meeting on Association for Computational Linguistics* (1980), 163-64.
    DOI: 10.3115/981436.981487.
14 Julianne Nyhan and Melissa Terras (forthcoming) *Uncovering Hidden Histories of the
    Index Thomisticus: Busa's Female Punched Card Operators*. My accounts of the training
    school at Gallarate are dependent on these interviews with some of the women oper-
    ators, as well as on conversations and exchanges with the authors.
15 Photographs #415-#419. Busa Archive. These may mark the initial visits by
    Father Busa. They are labeled Ispra and Euratom, dated 1961, and include Y. Lecerf,
    and P. Braffort, who were working on machine translation at Euratom, as well as Peter
    Toma of Georgetown.
16 Roberto Busa, Foreword to Schreibman, et al., eds., *A Companion to Digital Humanities*
    (Oxford: Blackwell, 2004), xix. Available online at http://www.digitalhumanities.org/
    companion/.
17 Memo of a "Conversation between Fr. Busa and Mr. Dostert at Frankfurt/M- 6/7-4-
    1961," April 8, 1961, Busa Archive (Rel. Cult. 1944).
18 Memo of a "Conversation"; and Roberto Busa, "Les Travaux du Centro per
    L'Automazione Dell'Analisi Letteraria," in *Cahiers de Lexicologie* 26.1 (1961), 64-68
    (my translation).
19 Memo of a "Conversation."
20 Busa, Foreword to *Companion*.
21 Busa, Foreword to *Companion*, xix.
22 ("Grâce au financement de l'EURATOM") Busa, "Les Travaux du Centro per
    L'Automazione Dell'Analisi Letteraria," 67. The timing implied in that phrase, "Thanks
    to funding from Euratom," remains ambiguous. I have not found documentation of
    the funding itself. It remains possible that it was only requested and prospective rather
    than received.
23 Busa, "Les Travaux du Centro per L'Automazione Dell'Analisi Letteraria," 67.
24 Paul Tasman, interviewed by Lawrence Saphire for IBM Oral History of Computing,
    32. IBM Archives. Cited courtesy of International Business Machines Corporation.
25 de Tollenaere, English typescript, draft for *Nieuwe wegen in de lexicologie*, 7.
26 de Tollenaere, English typescript, draft for *Nieuwe wegen in de lexicologie*, 7.
27 Busa, "Les Travaux du Centro per L'Automazione Dell'Analisi Letteraria," 67.

28 Busa, "Les Travaux du Centro per L'Automazione Dell'Analisi Letteraria," 67.
29 Roberto Busa, "L'analisi linguistica nell'evoluzione mondiale dei mezzi d'informazione," in *Almanacco Letterario Bompiani 1962* (Milan: 1962), 103-9 (105); trans. Philip Barras in Marco Passarotti, A. Ciula, and Julianne Nyhan, *One origin of Digital Humanities: Fr. Roberto Busa S.J. in his own words* (Forthcoming, Springer Verlag).
30 Busa, "L'analisi linguistica nell'evoluzione mondiale dei mezzi d'informazione," 107.
31 Busa, "L'analisi linguistica nell'evoluzione mondiale dei mezzi d'informazione," 107.
32 Busa, "Les Travaux du Centro per L'Automazione Dell'Analisi Letteraria," 66.
33 Watson, Jr. and Petre, *Father, Son & Company,* Kindle edition, loc. 4452.
34 Emerson W. Pugh and Lars Heide, "STARS: Early Punched Card Equipment, 1880-1951," IEEE Global history Network, Engineering and Technology History Wiki, http://ethw.org/index.php?title=Early_Punched_Card_Equipment,_1880_-_1951&redirect=no.
35 Pugh and Heide, "STARS."
36 Watson, Jr. and Petre, *Father, Son & Company,* Kindle edition, loc. 4452.
37 John W. O'Malley, S.J., *The Jesuits: A History from Ignatius to the Present* (Lanham, MD and London: Rowman & Littlefield, 2014), Kindle edition, loc. 120.
38 O'Malley, *The Jesuits,* loc. 242.
39 Siegfried Zielinski, *Deep Time of the Media: Toward an Archaeology of Hearing and Seeing by Technical Means* (Cambridge, MA: The MIT Press, 2008), 101-157 (113).
40 Zielinski, *Deep Time of the Media,* 114.
41 Zielinski, *Deep Time of the Media,* 116.
42 Zielinski, *Deep Time of the Media,* 118.
43 O'Malley, *The Jesuits,* loc. 242.
44 John W. Donohue, *Jesuit Education: An Essay on the Foundations of Its Idea* (New York: Fordham University Press, 1963), 39.
45 O'Malley, *The Jesuits,* loc. 69.
46 O'Malley, *The Jesuits,* loc. 218.
47 O'Malley, *The Jesuits,* loc. 280.
48 Busa, "The Annals of Humanities Computing," 85.
49 Sobel, *IBM: Colossus In Transition,* 81.
50 Busa, "The Annals of Humanities Computing," 85.
51 Busa, "Les Travaux du Centro per L'Automazione Dell'Analisi Letteraria," 66 (my translation).
52 As reported in interviews in Julianne Nyhan and Melissa Terras (forthcoming), *Uncovering Hidden Histories of the Index Thomisticus.*
53 I'm quoting from the title-card captions in a short film of the dedication ceremony, by Antonio Bonicalzi, "Cerimonia inaugurale del 'Centro Per L'Automazione Dell'Analisi Letteraria' Aloisianum di Gallarate, 17 Dicembre 1956," unaccessioned DVD, Busa Archive (my translation).
54 As pointed out by Félicien de Tollenaere, typescript, 6.
55 In a letter of June 23, 1962 to Busa, de Tollenaere begins: "A year ago . . . you made me swear [an] oath, that I should not publish a single letter about the CAAL without your *imprimatur.*" He says that his wife helped to translate the attached draft into English (there are also a few pages in French) and asks Father Busa for his "remarks" and includes three explicit queries to Busa (which he answered). In a letter of January 2, 1964, de Tollenaere writes to Busa: "I hope you are not too much dissatisfied" with the published book. Busa Archive (Gall. Rel. Cult. Est. 1943)
56 Busa, "The Annals of Humanities Computing," 86.

57   de Tollenaere, English typescript, draft for *Nieuwe wegen in de lexicologie*, 6.

58   de Tollenaere, English typescript, draft for *Nieuwe wegen in de lexicologie*, 1.

59   de Tollenaere, English typescript, draft for *Nieuwe wegen in de lexicologie*, 2-3.

60   Photograph #429, Busa Archive (available on the website for this book http://priestandpunchedcards.tumblr.com).

61   de Tollenaere, English typescript, draft for *Nieuwe wegen in de lexicologie*, 6.

62   "International Conference on Machine Translation of Languages and Applied Language Analysis, National Physical Laboratory, Teddington, UK, 5-8 September 1961," Appendix, List of Delegates, http://www.mt-archive.info/NPL-1961-participants.pdf.

63   de Tollenaere, English typescript, draft for *Nieuwe wegen in de lexicologie*, 6.

64   de Tollenaere, English typescript, draft for *Nieuwe wegen in de lexicologie*, 8.

65   de Tollenaere, English typescript, draft for *Nieuwe wegen in de lexicologie*, 8; interview with Livia Canestraro, in Julianne Nyhan and Melissa Terras (forthcoming), *Uncovering Hidden Histories of the Index Thomisticus*.

66   Julianne Nyhan and Melissa Terras (forthcoming), *Uncovering Hidden Histories of the Index Thomisticus*. Besides the division between scholarly and technical work, Canestraro's remarks imply that there was a gendered division of labor even among the technicals, with keypunch machines operated by the women and sorters operated by the men.

67   Nyhan and Terras, *Uncovering Hidden Histories of the Index Thomisticus*.

68   C.P. Snow, *The Two Cultures: And a Second Look* (1959; Cambridge, U.K.: Cambridge University Press, 1979).

69   "Jean Miélot," Wikipedia, https://en.wikipedia.org/wiki/Jean_Miélot.

70   Roberto Busa, "Centro per L'automazione Dell'analisi Letteraria," Busa Archive. Unaccessioned papers received March 2015, 11 (pages numbered by hand).

71   Paul Tasman, *Indexing the Dead Sea Scrolls, by Electronic Literary Data Processing Methods* (New York: IBM World Trade Corporation, 1958), 1, 12; Paul Tasman, "Literary Data Processing," *IBM Journal of Research and and Development* (July 1957), 249-56.

72   Paul Tasman, "Literary Data Processing," 249.

73   For example, Busa, "Les Travaux du Centro per L'automanzione dell'Analisi Letteraria di Gallarate," 64-68; and "The Index of All Non-Biblical Dead Sea Scrolls Published Up To December 1957," *Revue de Qumrân* 1.5 (1959), 187-98.

74   See for example the letter from Roberto Busa to Rev. William Le Saint, S.J., March 16, 1957. Busa Archive (Gall. Rel. Cult. 1940, USA tab).

75   Robert W. Rydell, *World of Fairs: the Century of Progress Expositions* (Chicago and London: University of Chicago Press, 1993), 193-94.

76   *On Guard!* (film), IBM Military Products Division, 1956, https://www.youtube.com/watch?v=YPQMwmdkVVU.

77   Rydell, *World of Fairs*, 193-96.

78   James McKenzie, "Italy Hopes Expo 2015 Launch Will Lift Doubts, Avoid Trouble," Reuters, May 1, 2015, http://uk.reuters.com/article/2015/04/30/uk-italy-expo-idUKKBN0NL2UJ20150430.

79   Rydell, *World of Fairs*, 196, 198.

80   Rydell, *World of Fairs*, Chapter 7.

81   Hélène Lipstadt, "'Natural Overlap': Charles and Ray Eames and the Federal Government," in *The Work of Charles and Ray Eames: A Legacy of Invention* (New York: Harry Abrams, in cooperation with The Library of Congress, 1997), 151-77 (154).

82 Willard McCarty, "What does Turing have to do with Busa?," 1-14, http://www
    .mccarty.org.uk/essays/McCarty,%20Turing%20and%20Busa.pdf.
83 *Literary Data Processing* and *Introduction to Computers in the Humanist* (White Plains, NY:
    IBM, 1971).
84 Joseph Raben, "On early humanities computing," Humanist Discussion List
    archive 27.908 (March 20, 2014), http://lists.digitalhumanities.org/pipermail/
    humanist/2014-March/011834.html.
85 Raben, "On early humanities computing," Humanist Discussion List.
86 Raben, "On early humanities computing," Humanist Discussion List.
87 Raben, "On early humanities computing," Humanist Discussion List.

5

COMPUTING PHILOLOGY

The Dead Sea Scrolls Project, "A Quality Leap and New Dimensions," 1957–1959

> In 1947, an Arab boy searching a cave for a goat stumbled upon the first
> Dead Sea Scrolls. They were in tatters when scholars received them. Words,
> even whole sentences were missing.[1]

It's a familiar tale of archaeological discovery, one which by now has entered
popular culture, from TV documentaries to traveling exhibitions. This particular version of the Bedouin shepherd's accidental discovery in the desert cave is
from the opening of an IBM promotional ad printed in *Natural History* for 1965.
Alongside a picture of archaeological workers at the mouth of a cave its title
reads: "IBM computers help men find secrets in scrolls, history in the stars—and
answers to literary puzzles." And the text explains that "[s]cholars used an IBM
computer and 'crossword puzzle logic' to test thousands of combinations of words
until they found the best-fitting meanings." After invoking Babylonian clay tablets
and Stonehenge, the ad concludes with a section headed "Helping solve Literary
puzzles":

> There are many unanswered questions about world literary figures, from
> Yeats back to ancient Homer.
>   Using IBM computers, scholars are getting many new perspectives on
> the work of these men. Disputes about who wrote what are being settled.
> Literary indexes that once took tedious years to complete can now be fin-
> ished in weeks.
>   *Computers are helping man fill in blank pages of his past, to gain a new under-*
> *standing of that fascinating subject—himself.*[2]

Without mentioning him by name, the copy makes a nod to Father Busa and his work on index building, which was expanded in the 1950s to include the Dead Sea Scrolls. The theme—humanistic uses of computers—begins with the genius of great authors and ends in the italicized final paragraph about filling in blank pages in culture and history (*"that fascinating subject—himself"*; italics in original). As superficial as it may seem, the ad presents a view of humanities computing at the moment of its emergence. It's a corporate view, to be sure, one filtered through the lens of popular science and shaped by the company's own promotional agenda, but it's a revealing view nonetheless.

For one thing, note the metaphor of puzzle-solving: physically piecing together scattered fragments of parchment, jigsaw-style; but also, more specific to this case, filling in letters and words using statistical textual analysis, something like solving a crossword puzzle. "Solutions" in the humanities may not have immediate practical applications, the ad suggests, but they add to the store of collective self-knowledge. Humanities research is driven by curiosity, unanswered questions, the need to solve puzzles, a kind of intellectual activity with a kinship to crypt-analysis, for example, the running through of combinatorial possibilities and filling in blanks in order to sort fragmented artifacts into intelligible, interpretable texts. This kind of research promised to expedite mechanical tasks, but also resolve disputes of scholarship: on the one hand, texts are processed efficiently and humanity's most profound questions are addressed; on the other hand, internecine scholarly disputes about attribution or dating may be settled.

This confidence in a puzzle-solving humanities is tempered, however, by the suggestion that in some cases the best computers can do is to help researchers gain "many new perspectives" on authors and texts, in other words to pose, even proliferate, questions rather than solve them. That some among those "many new perspectives" might be challenging or critical ones, opening up a self-multiplying series of *ongoing* disputes, or that the understanding might be increasingly complex and difficult to reconcile with dominant ideas about human history and identity, aren't mentioned in the ad, of course, although such truths would have been taken for granted among many humanities researchers at the time. Ironically, in 1965 when the ad was published, the history of scholarship on the Dead Sea Scrolls itself stood as a stark counterexample to the idea of humanities scholarship as puzzle-solving or as a way of resolving professional conflicts. Quite the contrary. And in practice, the literary data analysis IBM promotes, here, was more like exploding or atomizing texts into ever-multiplying constituent particles, opening them up to various reconfigurations, rather than like fitting their pieces together efficiently into satisfying, coherent wholes. Although the fact remained at odds with some public claims for the power of computing, emergent literary data analysis often looked more like a process of puzzling than a way to solve puzzles once and for all.

By 1965, much of the troubled history of scholarship on the Dead Sea Scrolls was as well known as the story of the shepherd boy and his goat. The tens of thousands of fragments making up hundreds of documents that became known as the Dead Sea Scrolls were mostly written on papyrus and parchment, stored in clay jars in caves on the northwest shore of the Dead Sea, the best known from caves near Qumran in the Judean desert (then Jordan).[3] The moment of their discovery by Bedouin shepherds in 1947 (who promptly sold them to an antiquities dealer) was an especially troubled time in the region, just before the Arab-Israeli War of 1948 and the establishment of the state of Israel, and this greatly complicated the passage of the scrolls from the desert to the scholars who would study them. The limestone caves had to be in effect rediscovered, and excavations continued, with stoppages more than once over the next decade, with key finds in Qumran in 1952 and again in 1956, for example.

One story illustrates the difficulties involved just when it came to accessing the scrolls. In 1949, the year that Father Busa was making his first visit to IBM, the Syrian Archbishop Samuel took four scrolls to New Jersey for safekeeping. Five years later, in 1954, while Busa and Tasman's early punched-card experiments were taking place in Italy and New York, and plans were being executed to establish CAAL in Gallarate, Samuel placed an ad in the *Wall Street Journal* listing the four scrolls for sale. The scrolls were kept in the vault at the Waldorf Astoria Hotel and in July were sold through an intermediary and returned to Israel.[4] Father Busa was visiting IBM in New York around the time of the negotiations over the scrolls at the Waldorf about eight blocks away, though he could not have known this. The first decade of Busa's collaboration with IBM happened to coincide with the discovery, removal, early publication, and controversial early studies of the Dead Sea Scrolls. This coincidence presented an adjacent possibility which Busa and Tasman—with the encouragement of their respective institutions, IBM, CAAL, the Roman Catholic Church—moved to exploit. By the later 1950s, their literary data processing was as often associated with the scrolls as it was with the *Index Thomisticus*. To this day, when IBM websites and the IBM Archives mention Busa's and Tasman's work, they emphasize the indexing and textual reconstruction of the ancient Hebrew, Aramaic, and Nabatean texts of the scrolls as much as they do the medieval Latin texts of St. Thomas.

This emphasis is partly in response to the continuing popularity of the Dead Sea Scrolls themselves, their appeal to the public imagination as well as to scholarly researchers, to they extent that they can sell out traveling exhibitions, for example. But it's also because the application of literary data processing techniques to the Dead Sea Scrolls, in the event, marked for Busa and Tasman a potential departure from merely assistive or instrumental indexing, revealing (despite their stated intentions) how computers might be used to explore and amplify the otherwise hidden dimensions of a collection of texts. The scrolls' indexing had to confront the contingent material artifacts by which the verbal texts survived and were conveyed—even if these weren't the primary concern of literary data processing. The punched-card analysis had to take into account a kind of forensic, materialist, vividly *philological* view of the scrolls as both artifacts and texts. This chapter looks at Busa's and Tasman's work on the Dead Sea Scrolls as marking a kind of philological turn. Busa and Tasman consciously described the work as dealing with textual "facts" in an instrumental way, and even said it should be free of interpretation. And yet the process itself of working on the scrolls revealed new ways to reveal hard-to-grasp dimensions of the texts. It was precisely by embodying the contradictions exposed by the process—machine and human, "mechanism and meaning"[5]—that this experimental (and, on the face of it, dead-end) project by Busa and Tasman pointed toward a new, computerized, philology.

The most important fact about the scholarly treatment of the Dead Sea Scrolls in the first three decades after their discovery is the long delay in their publication. It's a sometimes sordid story, involving disputes over the cultural and religious identity of the discovered materials (whether they were more significant to early Christianity or first-century Rabbinic Judaism, for example), as well as professional disputes over who had the right to study, edit, publish, and control access to the materials—and it led to conspiracy theories about their suppression, as well as general impatience among members of the scholarly community. The scrolls were first turned over by the Jordanian government to an all-Christian team of scholars in Jerusalem under the direction of a Dominican priest. Once most of the scrolls and fragments were in the Palestine Archaeological Museum in Jerusalem (later renamed the Rockefeller Museum), a forensic process began, piecing fragments together in more or less jigsaw-puzzle fashion, just as the IBM ad later said, placing them between plates of glass, and photographing the materials in both visible and infrared light, all of this work taking place in a room called the scrollery. As soon as it became possible to do so, the scrolls were transcribed, and some limited portion of the texts were published. Very early on, but at least by summer 1957, a team of younger scholars—first Father Joseph Fitzmyer, S.J., then Rev. Raymond Brown, Willard Oxtoby, and later, Javier Teixidor—was tasked with making a tool for editorial scholarship, a handmade index-card concordance to all the non-biblical Hebrew and Aramaic texts (starting with those found in Cave 4 but including non-biblical materials from Caves 2-10).[6] Eventually, something like 25,000 3 × 5-inch index cards were made, one for each word, in a format that should by now sound familiar to readers of this book: a lemma-word in the upper left corner, reference numbers to the manuscript(s) where it can be found (name of document and column number) in the upper right corner, and the lemmatized form, in the context of surrounding words, in the middle of the card.[7] The bottom left corner of each card contained a number for the index card itself, for filing it in one of the large wooden drawers in the basement of the museum. This indexing was begun in 1957 and completed by 1960.

At around the same time, according to Paul Tasman's later recollection, "the Vatican saw fit to include" the Dead Sea Scrolls "as part of the project" that he and Father Busa "were already doing."[8] It's an intriguing way to put it. Tasman may mean only that Father Busa's superiors approved of the Dead Sea Scrolls work, as they would have had to do in any case; or he may be suggesting that a more active commission came from the Vatican. One article in the Catholic magazine, *The Universe*, January 4, 1957, similarly referred to Busa's work at CAAL in Gallarate: "Already the Vatican Library has announced its interest in using the centre's equipment for an analysis of some of its manuscripts of the Dead Sea Scrolls."[9] At any rate, Tasman and Busa went to work on texts that were already under the control of other scholars, that were in many cases already being published in transcriptions, which had appeared in 21 journals and 5 books. They were not starting with the unpublished primary materials themselves, which were still in the Jerusalem museum (though Father Busa says they always compared their texts to photostatic facsimiles of the original scrolls).[10] By 1956, they had brought in two area experts in Ancient Hebrew Philology, the American Protestant Millar Burrows, of Yale, and the Italian Jesuit, Pietro Boccaccio, S.J., of the Pontifical Biblical Institute of Rome.[11] (A photograph taken at Yale, September 24, 1956, shows Tasman and Busa with Burrows, consulting a chart with columns of Hebrew letters while standing in front of a map of the Middle East.)[12] By late 1957 Father Busa was fully engaged in the task, though he underestimated its difficulty. On November 26, 1957, he mentioned that the "indexing of the non-biblical Dead Sea Scrolls will be completed in N.Y., probably before the end of January, when myself I shall be there"; and on December 3, 1957, he wrote, "God willing, I shall be in N.Y. next January for processing with IBM 705 the indexing of the Dead Sea Scrolls (non-biblical texts only: 35,000 words approx.)."[13] The work on the *Index Thomisticus* continued during this time, as well, and it was only months before Busa was to present at the World Expo 58 in Brussels.

It was about this same time, summer 1958, that the first phase of what became known as the Preliminary Concordance to the Dead Sea Scrolls was quietly being completed by hand, for internal scholarly use, by the team working in Jerusalem, led by Joseph Fitzmyer, S.J. As we'll see, this onsite card-file concordance would come to public attention thirty years later, when it played a crucial role in the publication of some of the texts of the scrolls. I've seen no indication that Busa was aware of this concordance being prepared by hand on index cards in Jerusalem, work which continued until 1960.[14] But he reached out to Fitzmyer by late 1958, just after the younger Jesuit had left Jerusalem. Busa explained his own computerized project and asked Fitzmyer to help prepare some Aramaic and Nabatean texts for it. At that point, Busa's goal was to publish his own machine-generated index as soon as possible. The two Jesuits reached an agreement: Busa mailed printed texts and instructions by November 17, 1958, and Fitzmyer did the linguistic analysis (primarily lemmatization of Hebrew words) as requested. Fitzmyer wrote to inquire about the status of the project in March 1959. By his own account, he had already completed his work on his own handwritten Preliminary Concordance, with similar data fields on the cards (but for a different set of texts, as-yet unpublished ones—whereas Busa was indexing already published texts, scrolls that by December 1957 had appeared in journals and books).[15] Until the 1980s, the existence of that card-file Preliminary Concordance would have been unknown outside a fairly narrow circle of Dead Sea Scrolls scholars. (Of course, this doesn't absolutely rule out the possibility that it was known to Father Busa.)

If the two teams had known of one another's work at the time, neither would have seen the work as a duplication. Despite the obvious resemblances between the punched cards and the handwritten index cards and their contents, and the overlapping linguistic approaches, and even though both were technically making concordances, they were for different sets of Dead Sea Scrolls texts. Actually, the comparison of the two indexes helps to highlight what's most significant about the Busa and Tasman project. First, they used computing instead of handwritten cards to more efficiently build and print their concordance. Second, and more important, because those punched cards *were* made, they were able to experiment with a form of literary data processing, an open-ended, step-wise (algorithmic), and iterative process of dissolving and reconstituting the texts as linguistic data, a process that used both punched cards and magnetic tape to inscribe data in forms that could be rearranged and analyzed in any number of ways.

Although it wasn't the focus of their intentions, it's this latter process which truly sets Tasman's and Busa's work apart from the handwritten Preliminary Concordance. The more interesting comparison may be with what happened to the Preliminary Concordance over thirty years later—again, not by intent. In 1988, the then-head of the Dead Sea Scrolls editorial team, John Strugnell, made pages from photocopies of the Preliminary Concordance with the cards laid out in rows and columns.[16] Thirty copies of the whole were disseminated to various researchers around the world, including Ben Zion Wacholder at Hebrew Union College in Cincinnati. His graduate student at the time, Martin Abegg (who would go on to become a prominent Dead Sea Scrolls scholar), was writing his dissertation on one of the unpublished scrolls. This being the early era of personal computing, Abegg came up with the idea of using software to "invert" the concordance, working backwards to, as it were, reverse-engineer and reconstitute the text. He used the contextual material surrounding each word on its card, along with the reference numbers on the cards (when they were legible), and leveraged the computer's processing capabilities to stitch together, string by string, a complete text. Abegg worked on an Apple Macintosh SE, but more important, he used Apple's HyperCard software, an intuitively logical choice, since it was based on the metaphor of an index-card file but also offered simple database scripting, hyperlinking, and searching.

Professor Abegg told me in email that the Preliminary Concordance was often hard to read (he believes the original cards may have been written in blue ink), so only about a third of the index card numbers were legible to him in the photocopy.[17] For the first few documents, he started with surmises (that the word "war" would be in a text about warfare, for example) and followed the context words through the document as a whole (a familiar first step in cryptanalysis, incidentally), typing words into a word processor in order as he discovered them. "This proved more problematic with more fragmentary texts," Abegg says, since he often ended up "at the edge of a broken piece," a dead end, from which he had to begin the process all over again with a new guess at a probable word. Most of Fascicle 1, the first published booklet of a reconstituted text, was created in this bootstrap fashion. To speed things up, Abegg entered the entire Preliminary Concordance into the computer, word for word, using the FoxBase database software for the Mac. Then he ran a preliminary sort on the words by document name, column, fragment, and line number. After doing this work over the course of several months, he found that the word list was still out of order. So Abegg used a script in HyperCard to compare the strings on each card with others in the same line, and in that way reconstructed each line of the text. Afterwards he corrected indecipherable words and typos (which had been marked by the Concordance makers with an asterisk). After this first attempt to reconstitute a text, which resulted in Fascicle 1, Wacholder and Abegg were able to use "bootleg" photographs of the original scrolls, published in the *Biblical Archaeology Review* by Robert Eisenman (Fall 1991), to check their reconstructed texts.

Given the lack of publication and access to the Dead Sea Scrolls, Wacholder and Abegg decided to publish their reconstructed texts with the help of Hershel Shanks, Editor of the *Biblical Archaeological Review*, who had publicly lobbied for more open access. The texts appeared as a series of separate fascicles starting in 1991.[18] At around that same time, another full set of photographs was published, by the Huntington Library in San Marino, California. Some reviewers were skeptical about the accuracy and reliability of texts reconstituted from the Preliminary Concordance index cards, and some questioned the ethics of publishing the bootlegged texts.[19] A number of reports made much of the fact that a computer was involved, a detail that "caught the popular imagination—the latest technology applied to uncover the text of the ancient scrolls"; in keeping with the kinds of publicity we've seen around Father Busa's work, the Macintosh that Abegg used was dubbed "Rabbi Computer."[20] A *New York Times* headline September 5, 1991, exaggerated, "Computer Hacker Bootlegs Version of Dead Sea Scrolls," and *The Washington Post* September 5, 1991, announced that "Renegades" had brought to light the Dead Sea Scrolls: "Computer Used to Reconstruct Ancient Texts That Scholars Suppressed." (That last term is also an exaggeration; the delay of publication seems to have been as much a function of competition for scholarly turf as it was the result of any deliberate suppression.[21])

Martin Abegg was no hacker. He was just a PhD candidate with an interest in computers as well as textual philology. His Mac, with its relatively simple document-processing and database software, facilitated and sped up the reconstitution of the unpublished texts from images of index cards. The scholar who had begun the Preliminary Concordance, Joseph Fitzmyer, S.J., remarked in print when the bootlegged texts appeared, "that it was done with a computer is interesting. But one really did not need a computer to do it," since the cards were all numbered in order.[22] But this undervalued the computer's role, and the new perspectives it opened on the texts. The placement of each word in relation to other words in proper location would have been an extremely time-consuming and difficult task without the computer, essentially impossible for a lone graduate student. Abegg's achievement is like many other tasks—including desktop publishing, at the time—that were opened up to individual users (rather than specialists at large computing companies) by personal computers. The distance traveled to this PC era from Father Busa's punched-card machines in the 1950s was significant. That Abegg's reconstitution of the absent texts was accomplished at all opened up a sense of new possibilities for smaller-scale computerized textual analysis. It's significant that Abegg's own process was iterative and experimental in interesting ways.

As the public response to Abegg's work demonstrates, the very idea of combining computing and ancient philology was for many people exciting or disturbing (or both). This was 1991, when desktop computing was still relatively new and just before the World Wide Web, when "cyberspace" was frequently mystified, negatively as well as positively. We've seen similar exaggerations in response to Father Busa's work in press accounts of the "mechanical brain" or "robot" and about solving the most profound "puzzles" of mankind. In contrast to such popular metaphorical exaggerations, Busa and Abegg shared an interest in a more methodical kind of application for language analysis. This interest took a different form in each case (in the 1950s and the 1990s), though both cases are also different from more recent uses of computers to analyze and digitize the Dead Sea Scrolls—forensic study of DNA, for example, and the kind of high-definition imaging and spectral analysis that we now routinely associate with digitization of primary objects. Both Abegg, with his desktop Mac, and Busa, with his suite of punched-card machines and the IBM 705, "digitized" Dead Sea Scrolls texts, in the general sense that they translated words from the documents (transcribed into editions or onto index cards) into a form that accounting machines or computers could read and process. But like the work on the *Index Thomisticus*, the work on the Dead Sea Scrolls was not aimed at digitizing the archival objects in the simpler sense: it was not about better seeing the archival material objects (Busa worked with limited-resolution photocopies or no images at all; Abegg worked with no images at first and only later with photographs, used just to check his texts); it was not about providing wider access through electronic page images or transcriptions. The goal for Busa was to do something to the verbal texts, to dissolve and reconstitute them; Abegg wanted to reconstitute them from their already dissolved bits. But there's still a conceptual resemblance between the two projects. Over thirty years before Abegg fed the bits of text from the Preliminary Concordance into his Mac, Father Busa noted that it should be possible, theoretically, to reverse-engineer and reconstruct the "flow" of the original source text from the punched-card and tape "word records."[23]

Only Wacholder's and Abegg's lack of access to the original scrolls (or, more realistically, to images or reliable transcripts of them) led to the *need* for computer processing. In the event, Abegg's use of the computer resembled the acts of many classical philologists, who reconstruct missing texts from fragmentary or absent, merely postulated, material evidence. Busa and Tasman worked in the other direction. They started with recently completed texts, although these still had gaps in them, textual lacunae. These published editions had been made by other scholars working from the original witnesses, the scrolls themselves (and photographs of them).[24] Tasman and Busa then atomized those given texts: marked them up, broke them down or dissolved them, extracted individual words and other sigla (such as the four dots of the Tetragrammatron, representing in Hebrew texts the name of God), and noted the lacunae or gaps, then sorted and reconstituted the words as data, in order to study different possible arrangements, different possible dimensions of the texts. The immediate goal was sometimes to guess at a missing word; the ultimate goal was another set of lemmatized concordances. As with the *Index Thomisticus*, a cross-sectioned dimension was brought into view by following any given lemma and word family, newly perceivable, across the larger collection.

In the case of the Dead Sea Scrolls, the restoration of lost textual data—"filling in the gaps" as in a "crossword puzzle," but also potentially filling holes in the story of how the text got fragmented—was an added result of the process. Tasman and Busa calibrated and tested the system in advance, experimenting by deliberately leaving out words in the texts in order to see whether they could accurately be restored.[25] But starting with such fragmentary and hard-to-decipher texts, they had to do more than merely build a concordance—even the kind of complex, multifaceted concordance they were building for the works of St. Thomas. They had to focus at the same time on the artifacts (with mysterious cultural contexts) and their inscribed verbal texts (with their own multilayered cultural contexts). The tension between artifacts and the verbal texts the artifacts embodied made the Dead Sea Scrolls a challenging test-bed for computer-assisted study of cultural expression.

Writing about the *Index Thomisticus*, Stephen Ramsay has said that Father Busa's approach amounted to an early form of machine reading—but in a different sense than the machine translation research of the 1960s.[26] "The founding moment" of digital humanities, Ramsay notes, "was the creation of a radically transformed, reordered, disassembled, and reassembled version of one of the world's most influential philosophers."[27]

> Undertaking such transformations for the purpose of humanistic inquiry would eventually come to be called "text analysis," and in literary study, computational text analysis has been used to study problems related to style and authorship for nearly sixty years. As the field has matured, it has incorporated elements of some of the most advanced forms of technical endeavor, including natural language processing, statistical computing, corpus linguistics, data mining, and artificial intelligence. It is easily the most quantitative approach to the study of literature, arguably the oldest form of digital literary study, and, in the opinion of many, the most scientific form of literary investigation.[28]

This was not quite algorithmic *criticism,* in Ramsay's sense of consciously hermeneutic, semantic interpretation flowing from the machine processing of the text. Indeed, Busa and Tasman explicitly represented it on many occasions as merely assistive and preliminary to interpretation. In one instance, Paul Tasman stated flatly, even somewhat defensively, that the indexes in themselves "throw no new light on the Dead Sea Scrolls" but only give the scholar "a most valuable research tool for his work of textual criticism."[29] And, as Ramsay rightly points out, "Busa's own revolution was firmly rooted in the philological traditions to which modern criticism was largely a reaction."[30] In literary studies, the New Critics' formalism, based on a hermeneutics of close reading, was a reaction to the longer tradition of fact-assured historicist philology. The introduction of computing to literary studies at mid-century was often framed in ways that seemed a throwback to the positivism of the nineteenth century, presuming it to be more "scientific" (objective, fact-based) than hermeneutic reading practices. Automated text processing—like traditional textual editing and bibliography—was considered a useful preliminary procedure, a way to ground the work of critical reading.

Father Busa's theoretical orientation was indeed conservative, even based on what would later be called logocentric assumptions. He sought to recover authors' intentions, even their thoughts, as constituting the meaning of their texts (all in a framework of divine truth). And he believed these intentions could be revealed, gradually, through patient and meticulous linguistic analysis. In a 1990 essay he called for a "new philology," based on the possibilities opened up by computing, and when he was presented with the inaugural Busa Award in 1998, the citation echoed this call, celebrating Father Busa for helping to inspire the field, "both directly and through his extensive writings on textual computing and their potential to contribute to a New Philology."[31] But the 1990 essay on the new philology also clearly emphasized the limits of computing, which reveal themselves, Busa says, "exactly where philology is at its strongest: the interpretation of the whole from the whole," the "creative imagination" and "intuitive insight" into "value and meaning" that the human interpreter contributes.[32] For him, philology is ultimately a humanistic endeavor, one which precedes and constrains interpretation.

Sometimes, probably for rhetorical purposes, Father Busa insisted that philology required the higher faculties of human intelligence in order to stand against what he saw as exaggerated claims for computers and a strong form of artificial intelligence, just then beginning to emerge. One headline about his work in the French newspaper, *Detective,* April 15, 1957, is telling—"*Des robots savants vont étudier les manuscrits de la mer Morte*" ("robot scholars to study the Dead Sea Scrolls manuscripts")—which gives us a sense of the popular ideas about computing against which he may have been reacting. In the context of such reductive exaggerations, his "new" and yet still traditional philology would use computer automation, but with a reassuring emphasis on humanistic insight as providing the ultimate end and framework for the processing of linguistic details. As he repeatedly noted, Busa's own literary data processing always required moments of human intervention, when the machines were stopped and the philologist sorted the cards into lemmas, a step the machinery could not complete. In another publication on the Dead Sea Scrolls, for example, he declared that the goal of the indexing work was literally instrumental and documentary—"diplomatic" in the technical sense of the term, a method for producing accurate documents:

> The aim was to furnish an instrument and a documentation and conse-quently to avoid any interpretation or any personal points of view, to render therefore the information of the index completely adherent to the original and giving every aspect of every wording [in] the manuscript.[33]

And yet, despite this, Busa also seems at times to put empirical methods into pro-ductive tension with broadly humanistic meanings, and to suggest that comput-ing might facilitate the human production of meaning. At a March 26, 1958 press conference on the Dead Sea Scrolls held at IBM he predicted that the indexes they were making would have "a stimulating effect on research in the humanities" in general. Standing at the lectern with the giant IBM 705 as his backdrop, he told the audience that computing "opens new approaches to a researcher, not by substituting a machine for his mind, but by allowing his mind to develop through discipline, flexibility and creative power."[34] As Willard McCarty has said, "During these early decades, Father Busa was among the very few who insisted that the point was not saving labor but 'more human work, more mental effort.'"[35]

The index by itself, as a product, might have shed no new light on the Dead Sea Scrolls directly, as Paul Tasman admitted. But, despite his and Busa's sugges-tions to the contrary, as they emerged (but failed to be completed or published), the partially completed Dead Sea Scrolls indexes turned out not to be something preliminary, done once and for all, then used as a tool for traditional interpretation. Their acts of making the texts—with the attempted collaboration of a far-flung group of co-researchers—generated dynamic feedback as they configured and reconfigured bits of textual data. The feedback may have been epiphenomenal, as it were, but it pointed the way to another conception of the role of computing. The process, *as* a process, shed new light on the Dead Sea Scrolls *as a problem*—and on the value of such methods to expose and worry such problems, rather than simply to solve them. Father Busa seems to have been alert to these kinds of emer-gent possibilities, though he didn't explicitly engage them in his own research. In a kind of automated variation on the hermeneutic circle, he described the human imagination as a necessary component in the data-processing system, with the computer as a prod to human thought, the whole interaction stimulating further questions for research.

Like most such circular models, this represents without fully containing the tensions out of which it arose in the first place. Busa's new philology exempli-fied rather than resolved the tension between merely instrumental computing, data processing *per se*, and a more capacious vista of the "new dimensions" that computer processing might open up for human understanding—or as a challenge to human understanding. In one sense, his ideas just reflected a widespread ambivalence about computing at the time (one which persists today): was it a potential augmentation of human intellect, as Douglas Engelbart famously put it,[36] or a mere tool promising nothing more than greater efficiencies of time and labor (and often at an immediate cost in jobs and human control)?

In this context, it's worth hearing the homiletic remarks of Archbishop Montini of Milan at the December 17, 1956 dedication ceremony of CAAL in Gallarate (the Archbishop served as Honorary President of the Center's Advisory Board).[37] Before offering a blessing on the new Center, with its IBM punched-card machines ceremoniously displayed for the occasion, the future pope referred to the computer metaphorically as a "maidservant of Man," a figure oddly reminiscent of the "Oracle on 57th Street" cartoon and other feminized allegories of computers. On this occasion, the larger point of the gendered and class-based image is clear: the preeminence of the human in the human-machine relationship, master to maidservant. And yet, note the trajectory of the Archbishop's remarks, where they end up:

> The machine exists for Man. Now this maidservant of Man is learning to perform more exalted tasks; not merely saving him from bodily fatigue, multiplying the efficiency of his arm and, by lessening his labour, enormously increasing its fruits, but by narrowing the space that separates him from the points that concern his observation and his presence and widening the sphere of his movements and his senses in space: and finally, by facilitating his higher, sublime activity—that of Thought.

From being only a maidservant (an anthropomorphized version of the "mere tool" argument) the computer becomes—or may become as it learns to perform "more exalted [in technical terms, 'higher level'] tasks"—something like a mind-expanding collaborator, a conceptual rather than merely mathematical augmentation of human thought. That possibility arises out of quantification, because the computer treats the texts as data, encodes them as such, and processes them in ways that exceed our merely empirical, natural, semantic understanding. So, in an iterative process, computing might open human understanding ("Thought") to new dimensions of the texts, quantitative dimensions, yes, but also, at least potentially, at scales that reveal new qualitative or conceptual dimensions to explore.

The immediate assumption might be that the Archbishop has just grafted metaphysical language onto the arguments about the computer's being an assistive "maidservant" or instrumental tool. But I think this is to underestimate the importance of dialectical thinking in the Jesuit tradition. Montini's homily represents a view in which technology is expected not just to aid but to spur and provoke human cognition, in something of a productively oppositional relationship. Although Montini's invocation of "Thought" might seem at first to recall

IBM's "THINK," it's actually more in tune with the philosophy of that plaque in the SSEC room at IBM: "to explore the consequences of man's *thought* to the outermost reaches of time, space, and physical conditions" (see Chapter 2; my emphasis). In the implied scheme, the computer facilitates such flights of abstract thought across multiple dimensions: focusing attention of the researcher ("narrowing the space that separates him from the points that concern his observation") and opening vistas hitherto imperceptible ("widening the sphere of his movements and his senses in space"). That dimensional oscillation is itself an echo of the philological tradition. Stephen Ramsay observes that, "even in Busa's highly conventional methodological project, with its atomized fragmentation of a divine text, we can discern the enormous liberating power of the computer."[38] He means in part the ability of computing to generate a wide range of new dimensional perspectives through iterative acts of algorithmic reconfiguration.

Indeed, we can discern in Father Busa's own terminology hints of this possibility, this more radical role for the computer in relation to a new philology. In one later essay Father Busa defines philology as the "sciences defining how we speak and how we write";[39] elsewhere he points out that the "analysis of language," which is formalized in philology, "is as old as knowledge of human knowledge,"[40] but computing and the automation of analysis offers philology a new purchase, a renewed relevance. In the inaugural Busa Award lecture in 1998, he was still speaking in similar terms:

> Traditional morphology, syntax, and lexicon, must be re-established, reformed, re-formatted, re-formulated, but not abandoned, for computer use. Computers, which God wanted His children to give themselves, mark the beginning of a new era, as I said. They should mark also, and promise, a new era in language knowledge, i.e. an enhancing of scientific quality, a leap of dimensions, a deepening, an enlarging of information about human expression.[41]

The ultimate goal is still "inner human expression," which we might associate with authorial intention, for example. But "human expression" itself is experienced through signs—inscriptions and artifacts—and it is to these that philology has always attended first, as in an archaeological dig. Computers expose new dimensions in the composition of the strata of the cultural record, as it were. That archaeological metaphor is mine, but Father Busa ends his speech with a different metaphor of digging, the analysis of caves. His image is of a "computerized speleology," the purpose of which is "to retrieve deep roots of human language." The results of this philological delving and analysis, he says, would be to reveal something "fundamental in all disciplines. At this level, humanities are the prime source and principle for all sciences and technologies."[42]

Busa's speculation about computerized philology—and its place between the humanities and the sciences—was remarkably consistent over the years. In 1962, he used an odd, but characteristically comic, metaphor, that of an interdisciplinary choir (perhaps we are meant to imagine a kind of monastic setting): "It will not be long before the tenor voices of philologists will sing the praises of automation in the gardens of humanism, accompanied by the baritone comments of mathematicians."[43] This new role for the ancient practice, to celebrate automation (by making use of it), has come about because of a shift in the media landscape in which Father Busa has himself taken part: "the automation of accounting"—the use of those punched-card machines with which he started in 1949—has "caused the world-wide evolution of the means of information."[44] The voices (all in conventionally male registers, it's worth noting) of the imagined choir represent both philology's conversion to automation or mechanization, and the elevation of automation as a technique within the walls of the hitherto-cloistered humanities. The new philology affects the humanities as a whole by bringing computing into the academic garden, which perhaps occasions a subsequent *felix culpa*, a fortunate fall of philology (and the humanities in general) out of the garden and into the material world of interdisciplinary methods (the two cultures singing together). "The science of philology was not born with the computer," he says elsewhere. "The new philology will be a continuation from its predecessors, but with *a quality-leap and new dimensions*."[45] That last phrase—"a quality-leap and new dimensions"—which we see repeated in Busa's publications over the years, is crucial, and it's difficult to parse. It would seem, at least, to exceed the merely assistive advantages of office machinery. New dimensions might seem to mean simply quantitative expansion, the production of indexes and concordances in many fewer person-hours—in other words, increased efficiency. Or it could be a topological metaphor for mathematical dimensions on counterintuitive scales. Or, more far-reaching, it could signify the kind of otherness associated in Busa's day with the weird dimensions of the new physics.

Efficiency was always the starting place for Father Busa's calculations. And he often associated efficiency with the advantages of scale. But listen to the tone of the following description of even the "change" in mathematical "dimensions" brought about by computing:

> What has perhaps not yet sunk in, is the huge change in dimensions that has occurred: the computer enables us to perform a complete census on texts of tens and hundreds of millions of words. For so long the philologist, being able to work only with pen and paper, had to be happy with a mere sampling, like a bee flitting from flower to flower. We all know how unreliable sampling becomes as soon as semantics is called upon.[46]

The suggestion is implicit: because of a quantitative leap ("tens and hundreds of millions of words"), a potential qualitative one. Here Father Busa seems to recognize the potential for new *conceptual* dimensions, what Jerome McGann would later refer to as the quantum *n*-dimensionality of all texts.[47] The lofty, sometimes theological language can obscure the materialist basis of Busa's idea of "new dimensions." The computer has the potential to open up a series of alternative universes of meaning, yes, but in the way that data mining and data visualization can be said to do, by exposing multiple views of a textual corpus, for example, opening a range of perspectives to which scholars might not otherwise have access.

Although it grew out of the work on the *Index Thomisticus* and continued alongside it for some years, the Dead Sea Scrolls project in particular pointed in the direction of a new kind of computerized philology, one which exceeded Father Busa's own stated intentions in its reach (and which should resonate with a later generation of digital-humanities researchers, though they'd be unlikely to use the term "philology" for what they are doing). Stephen Ramsay's vision of one form of digital humanities work, "algorithmic criticism," does place it in relation to Father Busa's work, despite differing with Busa's theoretical premises regarding textual interpretation: "in the end, it is simply an attitude toward the relationship between mechanism and meaning that is expansive enough to imagine building as a form of thinking."[48] Almost despite itself, Busa's approach itself undermines its own more "positivistic claims" for computation, in which it implies that mechanization may be "the method by which humanistic inquiry may finally, after centuries of insecurity, claim its rightful place as a form of knowledge," as Ramsay puts it.[49] Instead, Busa's iterative analyses lead to viewing the artifacts of human culture as radically transformable, through a process of being disassembled, rearranged, and reassembled, over and over again.

And in fact that accurately describes what Busa and Tasman did with the texts of the Dead Sea Scrolls, on the model of the *Index Thomisticus*, but with already fragmented, materially recalcitrant artifacts. A 1957 article in *Der Spiegel* quoted an Italian newspaper as saying that Father Busa's method amounted to putting the philosophy of St. Thomas "through a meat grinder"—"Busa dismantled the 'thought process' in stages so that the machine could process the vocabulary [of Aquinas]."[50] It may seem a jarring image for textual work—sausage-making—and I can't say whether or not Busa sanctioned its use in the original source, but it's actually a surprisingly apt metaphor for the process of breaking down the text in order to reconstitute it in another form. The Busa Archive contains at least one set of pages from a published edition of the Dead Sea Scrolls texts that was used at CAAL. It's thoroughly marked up by hand, with words circled, lines drawn out to symbols in the margin, and the pages disbound so they might serve as copy for punched-card operators. What happened to these printed books is symbolic of what was being done conceptually to the verbal texts that they conveyed. Literary data processing has a deconstructive or deformative effect. Father Busa referred to it in one publication as the "dissociation of the text into its first elements."[51] This was the first stage in the new philology, which may in the end have unexpectedly upstaged the final unity Busa wished to achieve.

Philology is a broad, even vague, term. As a broad set of practices, it long predates the modern formation of humanities disciplines and can be seen as their common ancestor, before they began to form and branch off around 1800.[52] In the nineteenth century it gave rise to what we now think of as literary and textual studies, as well as cultural studies and history—in other words, a good deal of the humanities as they were institutionalized. Literally meaning the love of words, philology developed as a set of practices for studying language closely—almost always in material and historical contexts. Growing out of biblical textual criticism and the editing of classical texts by Renaissance humanists, philology combined attention to the minute particulars of language (as embodied in texts) with historical attention to scrolls, manuscripts, codices, stones, parchment, paper, etc., by which those texts were conveyed. At its worst, it leapt from that evidence to very broad generalizations about the human race (including, notoriously, about race).[53] The scope of philology was never merely the contents of manuscripts or books but, for better or worse, also included cultural history. In the modern era this broader philology was modeled on the German idea of *Altertumswissenschaft* (the "science of antiquity"). As Jerome McGann has put it, philology always sets out "to investigate the relation of language and literature to society," and "purely linguistic scrutiny needs exposure to the social network, in all its particulars, that communicates with us from the past."[54] Attention to the minute particulars of language and their material inscriptions forms the basis of "disciplined philological study," and this is "prerequisite for dispelling the abstraction that characterizes most approaches to 'context.'"[55]

Philology's attention to material evidence has always allied it with antiquarianism and archaeology. Renaissance philologists studied ancient texts in Latin, Greek, or Hebrew. Their texts came to them on parchment or papyrus (or in layered, palimpsestic manuscripts, scraped and reused), often as the basis of early printed editions. Textual criticism developed basic techniques for sorting and analyzing such textual transmission and descent, corruption and attribution, through comparison, reconstruction, and emendation. In the twentieth century, linguistics "gradually turned away from comparative historical work toward investigating linguistic structure synchronically,"[56] and literary studies gradually turned away from an empirical attention to verbal texts toward more philosophically inflected theories. Textual criticism was absorbed into literary studies but relegated to a service role, presumed to be scientific in a weak sense (merely factive), and thus marginal to the humanities out of which it had emerged in the first place. At the end of the nineteenth and beginning of the twentieth centuries, as literary studies was being consolidated as an academic discipline, philology was caught between:

> scholars of English began to narrow their understanding of "philology" around the turn of the century. Philology came to mean mere "study of words" or "linguistic science" in opposition to study of the forms of literary works, to literary history, and to the exploration of the "spiritual and aesthetic" meanings of poetry and fiction. . . . This cramped construal of philology was largely a red herring . . . . But it led, in two of three decades

after 1910, to widespread repudiation by literary scholars of a straw man called philology . . . .[57]

When one of Father Busa's correspondents, as we saw in Chapter 3, complained of "philology overemphasized" and said that it was creating "a drift in the direction of pure mechanical verbalism," he had in his sights that straw man.[58] More specifically, he was attacking Busa's "mechanical" methods—which indicates that that for him computers were at the heart of the problem.

By contrast, Father Busa came to see computers as a spur and a challenge to philology itself:

> I repeat that the bottleneck of computational linguistics (formalization of the global meaning of semantic sets) does not come from computers nor from mathematics, statistics or symbolic logic. It depends on philology, understood as the science of expression. The creative imagination and penetrating intuition of the philologists is called upon to create new, deeper and vaster strategies of research.[59]

This exhortation to imagination is a response to the apparent public failure of machine translation in the 1950s and 1960s. Despite his philosophical idealism, for Busa the computer's ability to engage and reorder the artifacts of material culture makes it a powerful spur: "Working on physical entities which the philologist uses and classifies, the computer has served above all to demarcate the borders between the graphic and the semantic."[60] Busa frames the problem in linguistic terms—the border between signs and meanings, graphic and semantic—but holds up the computer as a philological tool, in the process acknowledging philology's own fundamental tension—between engaging the materialities of artifacts (including graphical signs or inscriptions) and cultural expressions and meanings (the semantic).

Geoffrey Harpham has argued that *traditional* philology "cannot be considered a worthy model for contemporary scholarship," because of its historical connections to racism, starting with early philhellenism and leading to celebrations of Aryanism.[61] Citing Edward Said, Nietzsche, and Paul de Man as examples, Harpham sees philology as divided between "a technical and systematic investigation of texts, beginning with the establishment of the correct text, by restoration if necessary, and emphasizing accurate description and linguistic analysis,"[62] and a dangerously over-general focus on history and human culture.

> Philology became new or modern when it found a way to conjoin a limited empiricism to a speculative practice with no limits at all, when it discovered the route that led from the close study of the text to the language of the text, and from there to the author, the culture the author inhabited, other cultures, the origins of cultures, and finally to human origins and the mysteries surrounding those origins.[63]

Harpham concludes, however, that historical and critical judgment can make it possible to "assume the full burden of the history of philology," including being "instructed, inspired, and challenged by the genuine achievements of the greatest scholars of the philological tradition . . . ."[64] The history of philology is a history of divided focus, an attention at two different scales: the minute particulars of material inscription and the social and cultural contexts for those inscriptions. Father Busa called it "the science of expression," and the tensions implicit in that phrase remain active in philological approaches today.

One could say that the computer's affordances and constraints themselves mirror the tensions in philology. Indeed, Matthew Kirschenbaum's influential description of the computer's ability to shift between a "forensic materiality" and a "formal materiality" is another way to formulate such tensions.[65] Kirschenbaum's analysis of "mechanisms" in textual studies, bibliography, and media archaeology is fundamentally philological. As he shows, a computer is a machine for processing material inscriptions, its own or prior, archival instances—magnetic bits on tape, patterns of punched holes in cards, printed or scripted letterforms on paper, stone, printing or calligraphy—in the form of abstract logical models and quantified data. At its best, computing allows for modeling a system in which artifactual materialities and their data interact with one another in an iterative series of exchanges with their human interpreters. One definition of humanities computing is that process of exchange itself, as opposed to using computers to solve problems or complete puzzles.

I've argued elsewhere that a new form of digital humanities emerged around 2004–2008 in response to the "eversion of cyberspace," the turning inside out of the supposedly transcendent and otherworldly digital network (as it was imagined in the 1980s and 1990s) and its spilling out into the material and social world (from which it was never really separate in the first place).[66] Jentery Sayers summarizes the same historical moment in this way:

> During the 2000s, a material turn occurred in digital humanities research, with an emphasis on how new media are not ephemeral info-dust. They are inscribed onto platters, embedded in infrastructure, transmitted through wires, and grounded in platforms. Put this way, the material turn responds, if only tacitly, to critical theories of technology, virtuality, and cyberspace that, during the 1980s and 1990s, largely ignored the particulars of how new media actually work. With this turn, we observe what I call a "digging condition" across digital humanities: scholars are now approaching media archaeologically, scraping data, emulating obsolete programs, reanimating dead tech, and unpacking the hidden lives of objects.[67]

Sayers sketches here a kind of media archaeology, but his language also invokes cultural archaeology more broadly, its challenging encounters with the difficult-to-fathom, discontinuous, layered traces of material culture. Likewise,

Jerome McGann has said that "the philologian's focus is material culture," which is to say, "the documentary records that, fashioned and refashioned over time, get remembered, maimed, forgotten, and re-remembered."[68] At the same time, the humanities are "fundamentally self-reflexive," self-generating "autopoetic" systems for further generating meanings out of their encounters with those records.[69] The dialectical interaction between the stuff of material culture and the interpretations produced by humanistic discourse is the essence of philological research.

There's no question that Father Busa often used the language of problem-solving and industrial efficiencies to justify computerization, and he was openly committed to a scientific approach to language. I have been told anecdotally by more than one person who worked with him, especially later in his career, that he was skeptical of semantics itself and of structural theories of all kinds, as opposed to rigorous measurement and empirical observation. Nonetheless, the historical record, particularly in the first decade of his work (which has been the focus of this book), makes it clear that his practice embodied the productive tensions I've been describing. Perhaps in part under the influence of the engineer Paul Tasman, the early punched-card work was defined as instrumental, yes, but also as a process of experiment and discovery, leveraging the powers of computing in ways that, it turned out, might reveal unimagined and otherwise hidden dimensions in cultural materials. It's in this sense that Busa's mechanization of the study of human expression experimented with a new philology: a computerized (rather than merely a computer-assisted) philology. In those experiments, despite Busa's and Tasman's repeated efficiency topos (computers are for saving human time and labor), the machine performs as a mechanical, electronic partner with the human in a "dynamic heterarchy," to return to the term of N. Katherine Hayles, in a system of feedback and feedforward loops.[70]

So, what precisely did Busa and Tasman do in their work with the Dead Sea Scrolls? They applied the same techniques they had first developed for the *Index Thomisticus*: copy was marked up linguistically, individual words were transcribed from the copy, punched, verified, and sorted, and the result of this atomization and reconstitution of the texts was printed out. In the case of the Dead Sea Scrolls, however, no *final* printout for publication was ever made.

Another key difference was the use of the magnetic tape–based IBM 705 for analyzing the language of the Scrolls. Cards were punched by the student-operators at CAAL in Gallarate, then brought to New York, where their data were transferred to tape for processing—the various steps of sorting and rearranging—on the large-scale 705 Electronic Data Processing Machine (EDPM).[71] One photograph in the IBM Archives (see Figure 2.1, p. 53) shows Father Busa at the helm of an IBM 705, reading papers in front of him, four tall tape drives against the wall behind him. Another shows Tasman and Busa standing together at the typewriter-printer of the 705, comparing the printout of an index—its ordered columns visible in the photograph (it could print at 600 characters per minute)—to a long photostatic facsimile of a scroll, unrolled between them across the top of the metal console (see Figure 5.1). Less than a decade after walking past the large SSEC in the IBM showroom, Father Busa was able to use a room-sized electronic computer in his own work—and his correspondence shows him eagerly anticipating being able to do so. December 3, 1957, for example: "God willing, I shall be in N.Y. next January [1958] for processing with IBM 705 the indexing of the Dead Sea Scrolls (non-biblical texts only: 35,000 words)."[72] And indeed, as I've indicated, in March 1958 a press conference was held in IBM's showroom and Data Processing Center at 590 Madison Avenue to showcase the work on the Dead Sea Scrolls as a "method of literary analysis." The lectern was set up in front of the IBM 705 that was being used to process and print the indexes to the scrolls, and the audience of reporters, scholars, and clergy were surrounded by the machine's components, tape drives, console, and printer. Both Tasman and Busa gave presentations, and an IBM operator sat at the console, ready to demonstrate the machine (see Figure 5.2).

The IBM 705 was introduced in 1954, primarily for business purposes, in a line with the 701 Defense Calculator and the first such large-scale model at IBM to use magnetic tape and designed for business users, the IBM 702. The 705 was named and marketed as a programmable Electronic Data Processing Machine.[73] It operated on a program read into magnetic core memory made from addressable ferrite rings arranged in a grid, each of which could be set to a magnetic charge. The system could take input from magnetic tapes or punched cards, or, in some cases, directly from the manual switches on the console. The component devices could be used in combination, for card-to-tape, tape-to-card, or tape-to-printer

FIGURE 5.1 Paul Tasman and Roberto Busa comparing printout from IBM 705 EDPM with a Dead Sea Scrolls facsimile, 1958 (IBM Archives).

FIGURE 5.2 Roberto Busa presenting the Dead Sea Scrolls project (with Paul Tasman) at a press conference, IBM World Headquarters, New York, March 26, 1958 (IBM Archives).

input/output. One form of output was the paper printout I described Busa and Tasman consulting, but output could also go onto reels of tape or punched cards. The use of magnetic tape marked a major advance over working with cards alone, just in terms of capacity and speed. The data on 25,000–50,000 cards could be stored on a single reel of tape, then processed very quickly in serial fashion (along the length of the tape, instead of by shuffling stacks of cards) at 240,000 calculations per minute.

For Busa and Tasman, using the IBM 705 EDPM was the final step in the processing of the texts of the scrolls. Busa arrived in New York in January 1958. A piece of printout on continuous-feed paper from just a few weeks later, February 17, 1958, shows a typical automated login response, what may well be the result of Father Busa's first login to the big machine. "HELLO," it begins,

> I AM THE 705 DATA PROCESSING MACHINE
> I CAN WORK RAPIDLY AND ACCURATELY
> AS A DEMONSTRATION OF MY SPEED, I AM NOW GOING TO
> MULTIPLY 31684327591 BY 84365239428
> THAT WAS FAST, WASNT IT
> THE ANSWER IS 2673055883329901457948 [...][74]

Then the machine showed off its calendar data: "GIVE MY OPERATOR THE DAY YOU WERE BORN AND I WILL GIVE YOU SOME INTERESTING INFORMATION"—reminding the overworked Jesuit that he was "EXACTLY 44 YEARS 02 MONTHS 20 DAYS OLD AS OF TODAY FEB 17 1958," then running more calculations, including exactly how many hours he had spent in his lifetime sleeping, working, eating, based on averages. At that point, however, Father Busa's schedule was anything but average. "GOOD LUCK," the printout ends (as well it might).

Despite some of the carefully posed photographs with Father Busa alone at the console, of course Paul Tasman was ultimately in charge of the machine. Tasman went on to document the whole process in detail in several publications, most fully in an illustrated pamphlet published by IBM World Trade Corporation in 1958, *Indexing the Dead Sea Scrolls by Electronic Data Processing Methods*. The abstract to the pamphlet says that the procedures allowed for "30,000 words from the centuries-old Dead Sea Scrolls" to be "electronically catalogue[d] and and cross index[ed]." The abstract ends with another example of the familiar topos of scholarly humility, saying that the method's greatest importance is that "literary data processing has freed the scholar from tedious, repetitious clerical work and returned him to his real vocation—scholarly research." But this gesture of casting the method as humbly assistive sits a bit oddly alongside the claim that the machines provide scholars a means for both "*interpreting* and translating" the scrolls (my emphasis). Through combined human-machine analysis, a "variety of analytical indexes" can be prepared—in fact, potentially any number of such indexes—which can then be used by "scholars and researchers" to study the scrolls. The description of the method that follows makes it clear that the production of these indexes, and the possibilities of conceiving of and producing many more, has itself already become a new form of studying the scrolls.

Tasman always stressed the need for establishing "analytical ground rules" at the start of any project, by which he meant an intellectual understanding between scholars and technical experts about the goals of analysis, what precisely they hoped to get out of the processing.[75] It sounds obvious until one realizes that it forms the basis for the first active, concrete step: marking up the text by hand. Markings provide practical instructions for the punching of cards, as Tasman (always the engineer) observes. But marking a text is also, historically, the most fundamental philological act, as Jerome McGann has argued.[76] Figuratively and literally, the first step in any scholarly engagement with a text is to mark it. Marking places of interest or lines of doubtful authority, using marginal symbols, goes back to antiquity and Zenodotus's editions of Homer around 275 BCE, and to Alexandrian textual critics who built on his practice.[77] The earliest marks, the *asteriskos* (*), *diplē* (>), and *chi* (χ), were like the sigla used in the modern textual-critical apparatus. These marks and their descendants, the printer's marks used to prepare manuscripts for typesetting, are conceptually related to formalized systems of text markup used in computing, from SGML to TEI XML to Markdown, for example.

Tasman and Busa came up with a custom set of arbitrary marks, noted in published reports by both of them, including the venerable asterisk (*), which meant a word that appears in both the Dead Sea Scrolls and the bible, a virgule (/) to represent a canceled word, a percent sign (%) to represent a "scribal peculiarity," and an em dash (—) to represent a lacuna or gap in the manuscript.[78] Both Busa and Tasman printed as an illustration a page of the marked Hebrew text of the Habakkuk Commentary, where it's obvious that they started with a printed and published edition. The textual apparatus of the printed edition at the foot of the original page is visible in the illustrated image, but crossed out, since it doesn't figure in to the (re)purposes of the literary data processing.[79] As I noted, they worked with long, scroll-like photostatic copies of the Dead Sea Scrolls. They also relied on early printed editions—as I've said, typically disbound—then literally marked up by hand. Beyond potentially communicating to other scholars (who would share the key to the symbols), the markup communicated, via the intermediation of human keypunch operators, with the machines, as Tasman says, providing them with "sufficient intelligence" for processing the indexes.[80]

Operators punched the text and its accompanying data onto the cards. The encoded punched holes "can be understood by a machine and later converted [in turn] to magnetic tape."[81] The holes were punched in four zones of the cards, each zone custom-labeled with a printed Latin word representing the category: UBI (where), INITIA (beginning), ORDO (order), and VERBUM (word)—this last the space where the data represented about the word by the custom marks summarized above is recorded.[82] These categories were recorded on the cards for the first pass. "Later," Tasman says, "as a result of some of the data processing activity," additional data could be added to the cards through re-punching: numbers representing the word's alphabetic place in the list of graphically different words and the word-family to which it belonged (the lemma).[83] Finally, scholars could bubble-in with a special pencil the oval spaces in a new mark-sensing area on the edge of the card. The whole process is algorithmic, in the sense that it proceeds according to a step-by-step instruction set, and it crosses platforms iteratively, moving from paper text to punched card to magnetic tape (where each card occupies one unit-record of 80 characters), then (potentially) back to punched cards and then to tape again, and, when indexing is completed, using the IBM 717 printer-component to print out the results on continuous-feed paper.[84]

For the Dead Sea Scrolls, there were a possible six different kinds of indexes, the words sorted according to different principles and steps, including for example, screening for linguistic duplication in different word forms, culminating in the concordance proper.[85] These lists were compiled from four separate runs of the data through the IBM 705, which required programming the machine (from a sort-program deck of punched cards), at one point merging data from two different tapes onto a third, and, for the final concordance, collating two different tapes. When printing the contextual phrases that surround each indexed word, additional markup added to the text (in the form of hyphens) is read by the machine to designate "thought groups" or semantic segments of text.[86] Tasman's pamphlet includes one image of a single punched card with Hebrew language printed on it, another (also used in Busa, 1958; see note 39) of ten IBM punched cards spread out as if in a file, representing ten words from one line in one column of the *Manual of Discipline*, and a section of the printout of an alphabetic word list, as well as photostatic images from relevant portions of the original scrolls.

Tasman says the process responds to "the scholar's problem, textual criticism," by which he means "the restoration of the text, as far as possible, to the original form and meaning intended by the author"[87]—a formulation generally in keeping with modern author-centered Anglo-American theories of text editing at the time, to be eventually associated with W. W. Greg and Fredson Bowers.[88] But it's also consistent with the longer tradition of philology broadly conceived, especially when it comes to the reconstruction and decipherment of ancient texts. This is evident in the approach to the Dead Sea Scrolls fragments as a jigsaw puzzle with missing or scrambled pieces, and in the need to grapple with ancient languages.

These textual problems were anything but new when it came to the Dead Sea Scrolls. The centuries-old tradition of philology already included methods for systematizing the processing of ancient texts—indeed, more or less "mechanical" methods. In the middle of the twentieth century, after all, Busa had begun his work by applying the technology of handwritten paper index cards, an ancient method for sorting data about texts, whether for search and retrieval in libraries or for making indexes, dictionaries, and concordances. The Preliminary Concordance to the Dead Sea Scrolls was prepared using essentially the same method. Like this longer-lived form of (relative) "mechanization," the use of punched-card machinery and computers accelerates the process of analysis and increases the accuracy and flexibility of the work. But Tasman also notes that computerized mechanization makes texts "rapidly explorable."[89] He's probably referring to the convenience of better search and retrieval, but it's a suggestive term nonetheless in the context of these archaeological artifacts only recently discovered. Philology has always been concerned with "the documentary records" of inscriptions embodied in material artifacts that get "fashioned and refashioned over time, get remembered, maimed, forgotten, and re-remembered,"[90] and so the central role of philological practices in the humanities is couched in ambiguous terms of "the Human Sciences"—which should sound familiar to those who have read Busa's and Tasman's publications—which "are always enlisted for various instrumental social purposes," but are also "fundamentally self-reflexive," if also, "in social terms, conservative."[91] It is in this context that Father Busa argued for a new, computerized philology that would focus on what computing might prompt the researcher to question and to think about from new perspectives. As the Dead Sea Scrolls work went on, it was revealed (despite Busa's and Tasman's original intentions) to be a kind of open-ended series of nested analyses, the kind of processing that might have been used to expose multiple possible dimensions—both material and cultural—of the ancient texts.

Tasman's and Busa's work on the Dead Sea Scrolls continued into the mid-1960s. It led to Father Busa's helping Hebrew University in Jerusalem set up a literary data processing center of its own, as part of the larger plan for a network of centers. As late as September 1, 1964, Busa wrote to Dr. B. Shahevitch, Secretary of the World Union of Jewish Studies in Jerusalem: "I am glad to inform you that we are continuing the electronic processing of the Dead Sea Scrolls. We did punch and lematize [sic] all the words of the Scrolls published until the Spring of this year 1964. We did not publish anything of it. Of course we hope to publish everything pretty soon."[92] Despite this hope, however, they never did publish any Dead Sea Scrolls concordances. Although the Archive contains marked-up texts, printout of some portions of indexes, as well as punched cards and tapes, within a few years, the work came to a halt. Dead Sea Scrolls scholar Professor Lawrence Schiffman tells me that he knew of Tasman and Busa's work in the later 1960s, when he was at Brandeis working on his own computer-assisted study of linguistic roots in Hebrew, and that he requested but was "never able to get the work."[93] In fact, in a series of exchanges between 1968 and 1970, Father Busa explained to another scholar at Brandeis that the lemmatization had not been done but "the texts are complete on cards"; then Schiffman wrote on March 11, 1970, to request the "material as it now stands on any IBM compatible magnetic tape," even offering to pay the cost of copying and shipping the tapes. Busa replied on April 27, 1970, that the request had finally found its way to him, as forwarded mail to Boulder, Colorado, where CAAL had moved in the previous year.[94] But that's apparently the end of it. The tapes were never shipped or, at any rate, never reached Schiffman.

In a letter dated October 17, 1971, Father Busa responded to another, different request by reporting that he had stopped work on the Scrolls in 1967 for two reasons: "we became too busy with the Corpus Thomisticus . . . and it was too hard to get scholars qualified and available to lemmatize the words."[95] Ultimately, he says, the processing of the *Index Thomisticus* "became too demanding in human time and in costs," so that his "financing committee did not allow [him] to complete and to publish the whole."[96] An interesting bit of evidence confirms one way in which Busa and Tasman tried to get the lemmatization done: a booklet was printed by CAAL, dated June 8, 1958, to be distributed to a group of select academics, presumably experts in ancient philology (I did not see the list of recipients in the Archive). "Dear Professor," it begins, and then lays out a formal request for collaborative lemmatization and sorting of homographs in the Dead Sea Scrolls texts, with instructions on how to list and report the lemmas. The introduction promises collaborators that they'll receive credit in the published volume, even a chance to contribute to the Introduction and, it implies, shared co-authorship of the whole. This looks like a limited form of outsourcing—if not quite "crowdsourcing"—an attempt to distribute internationally the specialized work of humanities computing. The computing itself was centralized; it was the philology that required wider collaboration. Ultimately, the plan failed. As Busa said, they were unable to get the lemmatizing done on time and funding to continue was denied. The volume planned for publication was to have been dedicated to Thomas J. Watson, Sr., the CEO with whom Busa had originally reached an agreement almost exactly ten years earlier. It never appeared. By 1967, although the *Index Thomisticus* continued toward eventual publication, the Dead Sea Scrolls index had reached a dead end.

Whether as cause or effect of this failure to publish, Father Busa suffered from what he called a "nervous breakdown" in late 1958-early 1959, brought on, he said, by too much work, at a time when the Scrolls were dominating his workload. In a letter to Paul Tasman typed quickly on July 9, 1957, Busa described the pressure of the work itself as rabbinical in its meticulousness: "Now I feel as it I became a Rabby [sic]: day and nights on diacritical marks, photos of ma-nuscripts [sic], erased letters, infrared photos . . . I'll be very happy when finished . . . ."[97] Fifteen months later, on October 15, 1958—in a letter accidentally dated 1948 (it's tempting to read this slip as a kind of traumatized return to the first year of his work with IBM)—Father Busa responded to the bad news that one potential philologist-collaborator will not be contributing to the project because his own concordance, based on his PhD thesis, was slated for publication: "It appears every day more important to expedite this project."[98] Again in October, Busa says that he's "glad" that this young scholar was "able to get his index published before our index. At the same time there is there [sic] a reason more why we must avoid any further delay in our project."[99] Then, there is a relative lack of correspondence until spring of the following year. On April 18, 1959, Busa writes to Joseph Fitzmyer—the scholar who (ironically, probably unbeknownst to Busa) had recently begun to compile his own Preliminary Concordance—with apologies for the delay: "After a long period of excessive work and a nervous breakdown which was its result, I reassume [sic] the work of the Dead Sea Scrolls."[100] On May 11, 1959, Busa wrote to Chaim Rabin with the same explanation and apology: "After a period of excessive work, I got a nervous breakdown, which prevented me from doing anything on the Index of the Scrolls. Only now I reassume [sic] the work and start answering the mail that arrived in the meantime."[101]

The term "nervous breakdown" was widely used at the time. The Google Ngram viewer shows (within Google's corpus of published texts) that it peaked about 1946 but was still very common in the late 1950s. The phrase could cover a broad and indistinct range of symptoms and problems. Sometimes a euphemism for serious episodes of debilitating depression or anxiety, it could also describe milder, more common occurrences of exhaustion or collapse brought on by too much stress or too much work. Father Busa blamed his workload, as we've seen, and stress must have contributed to the breakdown. It occurred just after an extremely busy autumn, when he had faced significant deadlines for the Dead Sea Scrolls project, including trying to recruit and organize a team of collaborators, as well as the important public demo at Expo 58 in Brussels (September 3). And it came about only a few months before he successfully arranged for CAAL to make use of borrowed space at the Cuccirelli firm in Gallarate, what had to be a difficult interim solution before the Center was able to move more permanently in 1961 into the relatively spacious quarters on via Ferraris. The breakdown is a reminder of the human cost of all that relentless campaigning and networking by Father Busa in support of the precariously funded, complicated interdisciplinary work of establishing the first Literary Data Processing Center.

Almost exactly a decade later, another event—in this case a force majeure— further prevented any resumption of the stalled work on the Dead Sea Scrolls, and even impeded sharing the work that had been done up to 1967. In a kind of dark parody of all the successful travels through which Father Busa had built up his research project and the center(s) to support it over twenty years, on August 29, 1969, a truck carrying CAAL materials on the highway from Pisa to Milan, so that they could be flown from Milan to Boulder, was in an accident and caught fire. When the fire was put out, only part of its freight had survived. A large number of punched cards and reels of tape were burned. In fact, Busa later said that 307 magnetic tapes were destroyed; 20% of the material on the tapes as a whole had to be transferred again from the original punched cards—he estimated 2,000,000 of them. One reel of tape in the Busa Archive today poignantly hints at the story of the attempt to recover the data. It has a label at the center reading "IBM Data Processing Magnetic Tape." Attached labels read "BUSA," and, in Busa's own hand, "SCHEDE DSS CARICATE 'IN FURIA' NEL 1969 DOPO L'INCDENDIO"—"Dead Sea Scrolls [punched] cards loaded 'in a fury' in 1969 after the fire." In early 1972, Father Busa did manage to send some tapes and cards to Professor Larry Adams at Brigham Young University, explaining that they rep- resented "the records which may have not been loaded on tape after the fire: for sure at least some of those records are missing from the tapes: but I am not sure if all of them"; and, three years after the event in question, he added: "My material is still in a kind of mess after the fire . . . ."[102] The inscribed data had suffered the kind of loss, in general, through accidents of history and circumstance, that the Scrolls themselves so vividly represented, including in the end being imperfectly preserved in "languages"—in this case, encoded bits—that became increasingly difficult for posterity to read.

Because of the pressing work of completing the *Index Thomisticus,* the problem with getting proper lemmatization, the personal stress and breakdown all of this caused, and, later, the withdrawal of support from his financial committee, then accidents like the fire and the moves to America and back again to Italy, Busa's team never published indexes to the Dead Sea Scrolls. Any direct influence they might have had on Scrolls scholarship or humanities computing in the years that followed was therefore severely limited, a missed possibility, tantalizingly adjacent. In the meantime, scholarship on the Dead Sea Scrolls continued to unfold: in the 1950s and 1960s, one of the two consulting ancient Hebrew philologists who worked with Busa and Tasman, Father Pietro Boccaccio, S.J., with a co-editor, Guido Berardi, published annotated editions of the manuscripts from Cave 1 in the form of individual pamphlets.[103] A concordance to the already published non-biblical texts appeared, edited by the German scholar, Karl Georg Kuhn, in 1960;[104] volumes in a standard edition of the Dead Sea Scrolls texts began to come out from Oxford University Press; Wacholder and Abegg released their reverse-engineered, inverted-concordance texts (Abegg tells me he had no knowledge in 1990–1991 of Tasman's and Busa's work done thirty years earlier[105]); and, eventually, efforts to digitize the Scrolls resulted in facsimile images being made available online and new kinds of scholarly discoveries based on multi-spectrum imaging and computer-assisted DNA analysis, such as work by the team of Simon Tanner in the Centre for Computing in the Humanities at King's College London.[106]

On July 25, 1961, Busa presented his work at the Third World Congress of Jewish Studies held at Hebrew University in Jerusalem (he also gave a demo on the method, showing the use of punched-card machines fitted with Hebrew type).[107] A series of photographs and 35mm slides in the Busa Archive shows him at the conference and on tour in the region. One image is particularly striking: Father Busa, in a white robe, stands with a small party at an archaeological site in the desert, at what appears to be Qumran (Figure 5.3).[108] A brief letter from a student assistant in the summer of 1962 contains an anecdote that captures something of the adventure of that visit: "I hope you remember last summer in Jerusalem, and perhaps the motorcycle with side-car which took you to the reception of the president and the mayor."[109] Father Busa later cited the center at

FIGURE 5.3 Roberto Busa with others, International Congress of Jewish Studies, Jerusalem, July 25, 1961. (Possibly at Qumran site, Jordan.) (Busa Archive #420; single panel of multiple-photograph sheet).

Hebrew University in Jerusalem as among those begun on the model of CAAL and inspired by its example.

In autumn 2014 and spring 2015, on two separate visits to CIRCSE in Milan, I was taken to an office where my host opened metal cabinets full of cardboard file boxes containing decks of punched cards, printout in Hebrew on continuous-feed paper, and 35mm slides and glass transparencies of illustrations. It was at least part of what survived of the Dead Sea Scrolls project, archived in material form, among the only embodied forms it ever saw. In a way, that's the point: all that paper and tape and glass was the product but not the ultimate outcome of Tasman's and Busa's work on the Dead Sea Scrolls. Mostly as a result of accidents, personal and communal limits, material circumstance, and chance, the experiments themselves as they happened, the generative process of encoding, reordering, atomizing, and reconstituting the texts, along with the presentations, discussions, publications, and detailed methodological explanations, the discourse produced by the experiments—all of this experimentation and communication became the project, by default. The team failed to complete and publish the indexes, but the process of working on them was literally productive—of data, but also of the lineaments of a method, an extension of the method developed for the *Index Thomisticus,* toward a computerized philology. I certainly don't want to claim that this "anticipated" anything. Nonetheless, I think we can now recognize in this stalled late-1950s project a historical precedent for recent digital humanities lab work, tinkering, and experimental methods, the side of digital humanities that does things with material artifacts and documents rather than just producing new documents, and which foregrounds that experimental doing, the open-ended process, over discursive publications alone, as a legitimate possible outcome of humanities research.

The Dead Sea Scrolls were already embedded in complicated social contexts and scholarly controversies when Father Busa came to them. But their ineluctably artifactual qualities, their stubbornly material and fragmented state, made them a difficult test-bed. It's appropriate that they may have inspired those large drawings of textual fragments, looking like big puzzle pieces with symbols on them, that decorated the high walls of the factory workspace at CAAL in the 1960s. The most important legacy of that Center may be the example it set in grappling with the problem of how to study culturally embedded material inscriptions and the abstracted datasets to which they can be productively (if provisionally) reduced. This is what connects Busa's work with one important stream in today's digital humanities, which continues to explore methods for analyzing humanities data in the spirit of experimentation and discovery. The emphasis on discovery is a counterweight to the merely utilitarian problem-solving of the kind Father Busa himself explicitly promoted, especially early on.

The more immediate result of the Dead Sea Scrolls project was to extend the speculative and practical methodology of the *Index Thomisticus* (and, to a lesser extent, of the processing of texts by Goethe and others). If we go beyond the tangible results of the formidable print and electronic *Index Thomisticus*, Busa's work over the long term consisted in many cumulative machine-hours and (hu)man-hours spent in data processing, and in the very idea that such materials were amenable to being treated as data. That idea was Roberto Busa's and Paul Tasman's joint contribution to the emergence of humanities computing.

Paul Tasman's *New York Times* obituary referred to this as his life's work at IBM.[110] His March 2, 1988 obituary in the local paper for Palm Beach, Florida, (where he had retired), described the work on the *Index* as a "unique union of modern technology and ancient medieval mysticism," and mentioned that Father Busa, "the man with whom he had shared that long effort," was by his bedside when Tasman died; in fact, he officiated at the funeral.[111] Back in May 12, 1952, in New York City, as they were getting ready for their first big demo at IBM, Father Busa had inscribed the front cover of a copy of the *Varia Specimina Concordantiarum*: "Dear Mr. Tasman, This book testifies the 'modus operandi' by which Our Lord the Great Collator merged our work and our friendship."[112] Collated like punched cards, merged by divine will, according to the metaphor, like separate data streams, the two remained active collaborators for decades. For his part, Paul Tasman saw their "unique union" as contributing to the development of information retrieval and natural language processing. Looking back in 1967, he characterized his work with Father Busa as "a sort of mixed marriage" in that he had to teach Busa about the IBM machines and Busa had to teach Tasman about linguistics. The phrase "mixed marriage" jokingly refers to religious denominational differences, but more seriously refers to the disciplinary differences between Busa and Tasman, the philosopher-linguist and the computer engineer. These differences had to be negotiated in order for the work to proceed year after year, though the iterative practice of computerized philology, all those cards and tapes sent through the machines. But the differences between the two researchers were never entirely erased or even fully sublimated in the collaboration. Like traditional philology, computerized philology embodied significant tensions about treating texts as artifactual objects, often fragmented and decontextualized, materially embodied and yet capable of being abstractly modeled, inscribed and yet open to ongoing analysis and interpretation. In this way, understanding the history of the first decade of Father Busa's work can help us to better understand the emergence of humanities computing and, by extension, today's digital humanities, which continues to explore ways to study material artifacts, including texts, and the multidimensional data that can be derived from them.

Notes

1 "IBM computers help men find secrets in scrolls, history in the stars—and answers to literary puzzles," promotional advertisement, *Natural History: The Journal of the American Museum of Natural History* 74 (1965), 57.
2 IBM ad, *Natural History*.

3 For the basic outlines of the discovery of the scrolls, see "Discovery and Publication," The Leon Levy Dead Sea Scrolls Digital Library (Israel Antiquities Authority), http://www.deadseascrolls.org.il/learn-about-the-scrolls/discovery-and-publication.

4 Stephen Sennott, "Shrine of the Book," *Encyclopedia of Twentieth Century Architecture* (New York: Taylor & Francis, 2004), 1206; and "Discovery and Publication," http://www.deadseascrolls.org.il/learn-about-the-scrolls/discovery-and-publication.

5 Stephen Ramsay, *Reading Machines: Toward an Algorithmic Criticism* (Champaign: University of Illinois Press, 2011).

6 See Joseph Fitzmyer, S.J., "The Concordance, the Computer and the Battle for the Dead Sea Scrolls," *America: The National Catholic Review* 165.11 (October 19, 1991), 270–72. Fitzmyer says they were tasked earlier, but the Preliminary Concordance was first undertaken in 1957–1958, just at the time Father Busa was in correspondence with him.

7 On the Preliminary Concordance and Abegg's reverse-engineering of Dead Sea Scrolls texts (and how it meant that "the scroll monopoly was broken"), see Hershel Shanks, *Freeing the Dead Sea Scrolls: And Other Adventures of An Archaeology Outsider* (New York: Continuum Books, 2010), 144–47, 152–54.

8 Paul Tasman interviewed by Lawrence Saphire for IBM Oral History of Computer Technology (interview TC-99, August 14, 1968), 6, IBM Archives, cited courtesy of International Business Machines Corporation.

9 *The Universe*, January 4, 1957, Busa Archive (Stampa Estera 1700, 1950–1963).

10 Roberto Busa, "The Index of All Non-Biblical Dead Sea Scrolls Published Up To December 1957," *Revue de Qumrân* 1.5 (1959), 187–98 (187).

11 For example, a notice in *The Presbyterian News* 22.6 (December 1956), which also mentions the "giant electronic computer" provided by IBM. Father Busa mentions the two philologists, as well as Arthur K. Watson and Paul Tasman, and their counterparts at IBM Italy, G. Vuccino and Clemente Folpini, in "The Index of All Non-Biblical Dead Sea Scrolls," 187.

12 Photograph #31 (September 24, 1956), Busa Archive.

13 Letter from Roberto Busa to Dr. Larkin Kerwin, November 26, 1957; letter from Roberto Busa to Thomas A. Sebek, December 3, 1957, Busa Archive (Gall. Rel. Cult. 1940, USA tab).

14 Fitzmyer, "The Concordance, the Computer and the Battle for the Dead Sea Scrolls." Fitzmyer arrived in Jerusalem as a junior scholar in July 1957 and worked on the index through July 1958 (271).

15 Paul Tasman, *Indexing the Dead Sea Scrolls, by Electronic Literary Data Processing Methods.* (New York: IBM World Trade Corporation, 1958), 11. Besides journal publications, Tasman lists books by C. Rabin, M. Burrows, E. N. Sukenik, Barthelemy-Milik, and Avigad-Yadin.

16 Shanks, *Freeing the Dead Sea Scrolls*, 144–47, 152–54.

17 Email exchange with Martin Abegg, February 17, 2015.

18 Ben Zion Wacholder and Martin Abegg, eds., *A Preliminary Edition of the Unpublished Dead Sea Scrolls: The Hebrew and Aramaic Texts from Cave Four.* 2 fascicles (Washington, D.C.: Biblical Archaeology Society, 1991–1992).

19 Notably, Joseph Fitzmyer, as explained in "The Concordance, the Computer and the Battle for the Dead Sea Scrolls."

20 Shanks, *Freeing the Dead Sea Scrolls*, 153–54.

21 Fitzmyer, "The Concordance, the Computer and the Battle for the Dead Sea Scrolls."

22 Fitzmyer, "The Concordance, the Computer and the Battle for the Dead Sea Scrolls," 271.

23 Letter from Roberto Busa to Larry Adams, October 17, 1971, Busa Archive (Rel. Cult. USA 1, 1952).

24 The *Index Thomisticus* relied on published scholarly editions, as well, mostly the Leonine edition, a reprint of the Parma edition, and the Marietti edition, with a few other texts (according to a note in the Archive by Busa.)

25 Paul Tasman, "Literary Data Processing," *IBM Journal of Research and Development*, 1.3 (1957), 249–56 (256).

26 Ramsay, *Reading Machines*, 1.

27 Ramsay, *Reading Machines*, 1.

28 Ramsay, *Reading Machines*, 2.

29 Tasman, *Indexing the Dead Sea Scrolls*, 12.

30 Ramsay, *Reading Machines*, 2.

31 Roberto Busa, "Informatics and New Philology," *Computers and the Humanities* 24.5–6 (December 1990), 339–43; citation for presentation of inaugural Busa Award, 1998, http://eadh.org/awards/busa-award/busa-award-winners.

32 Busa, "Informatics and New Philology," 342, 340.

33 Busa, "The Index of All Non-Biblical Dead Sea Scrolls," 187.

34 "Revolutionizing Research: IBM and the Dead Sea Scrolls," *IBM World Trade News* 10.5 (May 1958).

35 Willard McCarty, "The Digital and the Human. Remembering the Future of Digital Humanities," Roberto Busa Award lecture, 2013, https://www.youtube.com/watch?v=nTHa1rDR680.

36 Douglas C. Engelbart, "Augmenting the Human Intellect: A Conceptual Framework" (Washington, D.C.: Air Force Office of Scientific Research, 1962), http://dougengelbart.org/pubs/papers/scanned-original/1962-augment-3906-Augmenting-Human-Intellect-a-Conceptual-Framework.pdf.

37 "Philosophy on Punched Cards in Italy," *IBM World Trade News* 9.1 (January 1957).

38 Ramsay, *Reading Machines*, 3.

39 Roberto Busa, "Half a Century of Literary Computing: Towards a 'New' Philology." *Historical Social Research* 17.2 (1992), 124–13 (125).

40 Roberto Busa, "The Use of Punched Cards in Linguistic Analysis," in Casey et al., *Punched Cards: Their Applications to Science and Industry* (New York, Amsterdam, London: Reinhold, 1958; second edition, 1967), 357–73 (357).

41 Roberto Busa, "Picture a Man . . . " (Busa Award Lecture, Debrecen, Hungary, 6 July 1998), in *Literary & Linguistic Computing* 14.1 (April 1999), 5–9 (6).

42 Busa, "Picture a Man...," 7.

43 Roberto Busa, "L'analisi linguistica nell'evoluzione mondiale dei mezzi d'informazione," in *Almanacco Letterario Bompiani 1962* (1962), 103–107; trans. Philip Barras, in Marco Passarotti, et al., eds., *One Origin of Digital Humanities* (Forthcoming, Springer Verlag).

44 Busa, "L'analisis linguistica nell'evoluzione mondiale dei mezzi d'informatione," 106.

45 Busa, "Informatics and New Philology," 339 (my emphasis).

46 Busa, "Informatics and New Philology," 339.

47 Jerome McGann, *A New Republic of Letters: Memory and Scholarship in the Age of Digital Reproduction* (Cambridge, MA and London: Harvard University Press, 2014) Kindle edition, 90–112.

48 Ramsay, *Reading Machines*, 85.

49 Ramsay, *Reading Machines*, 85.
50 "Elektronen-Gehirne: zum Ruhme Christi," *Der Spiegel* 14 (April 3, 1957), 62, quoting *Corriere della Sera*.
51 Busa, "The Use of Punched Cards in Linguistic Analysis," 363.
52 James Turner, *Philology: The Forgotten Origins of the Modern Humanities* (Princeton and Oxford: Princeton University Press, 2014), 235.
53 See Geoffrey Galt Harpham, "Roots, Races, and the Return to Philology," *Representations* 106 (Spring 2009), 34–62.
54 McGann, *A New Republic of Letters*, Kindle edition, 1, 3.
55 McGann, *A New Republic of Letters*, Kindle edition, 112.
56 Turner, *Philology*, 231, 250.
57 Turner, *Philology*, 272.
58 Letter from Father David L. McGlow[?], S.J., n.d. Busa Archives. (Gall. Rel. Cult. 1940, USA tab).
59 Busa, "Informatics and New Philology," 342–43.
60 Busa, "Informatics and New Philology," 339.
61 Harpham, "Roots, Races, and the Return to Philology," 34, 37–38.
62 Harpham, "Roots, Races, and the Return to Philology," 39.
63 Harpham, "Roots, Races, and the Return to Philology," 39.
64 Harpham, "Roots, Races, and the Return to Philology," 56.
65 Matthew G. Kirschenbaum, *Mechanisms: New Media and the Forensic Imagination* (Cambridge, MA: MIT Press, 2008).
66 Steven E. Jones, *The Emergence of the Digital Humanities* (New York: Routledge, 2014).
67 Jentery Sayers, lecture, "The Digging Condition: The Material Turn in Digital Humanities," February 26, 2015, http://sc.edu/about/centers/digital_humanities/future_knowledge_archive/sayers_videopage.php.
68 McGann, *A New Republic of Letters*, Kindle edition, 66.
69 McGann, *A New Republic of Letters*, Kindle edition, 8.
70 N. Katherine Hayles, *Electronic Literature: New Horizons for the Literary* (Notre Dame, IN: Notre Dame University Press, 2008), 45.
71 "Revolutionizing Research: IBM and the Dead Sea Scrolls," *IBM World Trade News* 10.5 (May 1958).
72 Roberto Busa, letter to Thomas Sebek, December 3, 1957, Busa Archive (Gall. Rel. Cult. 1940, USA tab).
73 Specifications of the IBM 705 EDPM from IBM Archives, http://www-03.ibm.com/ibm/history/exhibits/mainframe/mainframe_PP705.html.
74 IBM 705 EDPM printout, stored with Dead Sea Scrolls materials, Busa Archive.
75 Transcript of Paul Tasman Interview by Lawrence Saphire for IBM Oral History of Computing Technology (interview TC-99, August 14, 1968), 38–39, IBM Archives, Courtesy International Business Machines Corporation.
76 Jerome McGann, "Marking Texts of Many Dimensions," in Susan Schreibman, Ray Siemens, John Unsworth, eds., *A Companion to Digital Humanities,* http://digitalhumanities.org/companion/.
77 Turner, *Philology*, 11.
78 Tasman, *Indexing the Dead Sea Scrolls*, 3.
79 Tasman, *Indexing the Dead Sea Scrolls*, 3.
80 Tasman, *Indexing the Dead Sea Scrolls*, 4.
81 Tasman, *Indexing the Dead Sea Scrolls*, 4.
82 Tasman, *Indexing the Dead Sea Scrolls*, 5.

83 Tasman, *Indexing the Dead Sea Scrolls*, 5.
84 Tasman, *Indexing the Dead Sea Scrolls*, 5.
85 Tasman, *Indexing the Dead Sea Scrolls*, 6–7.
86 Tasman, *Indexing the Dead Sea Scrolls*, 9.
87 Tasman, *Indexing the Dead Sea Scrolls*, 2.
88 See for example Fredson Bowers, "Some Principles for Scholarly Editions of Nineteenth-Century American Authors," *Studies in Bibliography* 17 (1964), 223–228; and W.W. Greg, "The Rationale of Copy-Text," *Studies in Bibliography* 3 (1950), 19–36.
89 Tasman, *Indexing the Dead Sea Scrolls*, 2.
90 McGann, *A New Republic of Letters*, Kindle edition, 66.
91 McGann, *A New Republic of Letters*, Kindle edition, 7.
92 Letter from Roberto Busa to B. Shahevitch, September 1, 1964, Busa Archive (Gall. Rel. Cult. Est. 1943, Israel tab).
93 Email exchange with Lawrence H. Schiffman, March 3–4, 2015.
94 Roberto Busa letter to D. E. Sarna, March 9, 1968; Lawrence H. Schiffman letter to Roberto Busa, March 11, 1970; Roberto Busa to Lawrence H. Schiffman, April 27, 1970, Busa Archive (Rel. Cult. USA 1 1952).
95 Letter from Roberto Busa to Larry Adams, October 17, 1971, Busa Archive (Rel. Cult. USA 1, 1952).
96 Letter from Roberto Busa to Larry Adams, March 13, 1972, Busa Archive (Rel. Cult. USA 1, 1952).
97 Letter from Roberto Busa to Paul Tasman, July 9, 1957, Busa Archive (unaccessioned Dead Sea Scrolls materials). The letter is dated from Turin, where Father Busa had traveled to work with an expert in ancient Hebrew philology.
98 Letter from Roberto Busa to Dr. E. Aikele, IBM Deutschland, October 15, 1958 (first typed: "1948," corrected to "1958"), Busa Archive (unaccessioned Dead Sea Scrolls materials).
99 Letter from Roberto Busa to Mr. J.M. Smith, IBM (Grand Rapids, MI), October 15, 1958, Busa Archive (unaccessioned Dead Sea Scrolls materials).
100 Letter from Roberto Busa to Joseph Fitzmyer. April 18, 1959, Busa Archive (unaccessioned Dead Sea Scrolls materials).
101 Letter from Roberto Busa to Chaim Rabin (Hebrew University, Jerusalem), May 11, 1959, Busa Archive (unaccessioned Dead Sea Scrolls materials).
102 Letter from Roberto Busa to Larry Adams, March 13, 1972, Busa Archive (Rel. Cult. USA 1, 1952).
103 Corrado Martone, "Qumran Research in Italy," in Devorah Dimant, ed., *The Dead Sea Scrolls in Scholarly Perspective: A History of Research (Study of the Texts of the Desert of Judah)* (Leiden and Boston: Brill, 2012), 601–10 (606).
104 Karl Georg Kuhn, *Konkordanz zu den Qumrantexten* (Göttingen: Vandenhoeck & Ruprecht, 1960), cited by Fitzmyer (1991). Kuhn had been an antisemitic specialist on "the Jewish Question" under the Nazis; see Jörg Frey, "Qumran Research and Biblical Scholarship in Germany," in Devorah Dimant, ed., *The Dead Sea Scrolls in Scholarly Perspective: A History of Research (Study of the Texts of the Desert of Judah)* (Leiden and Boston: Brill, 2012), 529–64 (541).
105 Email exchange with Martin Abegg, February 11–17, 2015.
106 See Simon Tanner and Greg Bearman, "Digitising the Dead Sea Scrolls," in *Archiving 2009* (Arlington, VA: The Society for Imaging Science and Technology, 2009), 119–23, http://www.academia.edu/813028/Digitizing_the_Dead_Sea_Scrolls.

107 As recalled in email from Roberto Busa to Mr. Harbin, December 24, 1997, Busa Archive (Rel. Cult. USA 2, 1953).

108 Photograph #420. Busa Archive (available on the website for this book http://priestandpunchedcards.tumblr.com). I'm comparing one panel of the multi-panel sheet, which appears in my illustration, with another, which shows the backdrop of the archaeological site without the people, and appears to be Qumran, or another desert site like it. Busa's talk was later printed in the proceedings of the Congress, "The Index of All Non-Biblical Dead Sea Scrolls Published Up To December 1957," *Revue de Qumrân* 1.5 (1959): 187–98.

109 Letter from Uzzi Ornan to Roberto Busa, July 22, 1962, Busa Archive (Gall. Rel. Celt. Est. 1943, Israel).

110 "Paul Tasman, Executive, 74," obituary, *New York Times,* March 7, 1988, http://www.nytimes.com/1988/03/07/obituaries/paul-tasman-executive-74.html.

111 "IBM exec indexed the words of Aquinas," obituary, *Palm Beach Post*, March 2, 1988, 1. Father Busa's officiating at the funeral is mentioned by Tasman's granddaughter, Amy Sklar, in her blog entry, "Hail Mary," October 23, 2014, http://www.fromthereservoir.com/new-blog/2014/10/22/hail-mary.

112 Roberto Busa inscription to Paul Tasman, May 12, 1952 (personal copy), quoted courtesy of Professor Jordan Nash, grandson of Paul Tasman.

WORKS CITED

Primary Source Collections

Busa Archive, Università Cattolica del Sacro Cuore, Milan, Italy.
IBM Archives, Somers, New York.
Columbia University Rare Book and Manuscript Library, New York and Computer History website, ed. Frank da Cruz: http://www.columbia.edu/cu/computinghistory/index.html.
Fordham University Archives and Rare Books, New York.
A. Wayne Brooke Papers, North Carolina State University, Raleigh, NC.

Other Sources

Abbate, Janet. *Recoding Gender: Women's Changing Participation in Computing.* Cambridge, MA and London: MIT Press, 2012.
Atkinson, Paul. *Computer* (Objeckt) London: Reaktion Books, 2010.
Bashe, Charles J. "The SSEC in Historical Perspective." *Annals of the History of Computing* 4.4 (October–December 1982): 296–312.
Bashe, Charles J., Lyle R. Johnson; John H. Palmer; Emerson W. Pugh. *IBM's Early Computers.* Cambridge, MA: MIT Press, 1986.
Black, Edwin. *IBM and the Holocaust: The Strategic Alliance Between Nazi Germany and America's Most Powerful Corporation.* 2001; expanded edition, 2012.
Bogost, Ian and Nick Montfort. "Platform Studies," http://platformstudies.com.
Borgman, Christine L. *Big Data, Little Data, No Data: Scholarship in the Networked World.* Cambridge, MA and London: MIT Press, 2015.
Bowers, Fredson. "Some Principles for Scholarly Editions of Nineteenth-Century American Authors." *Studies in Bibliography* 17 (1964): 223–228.
Brennan, Jean Ford. *The IBM Watson Laboratory at Columbia University: A History.* http://www.columbia.edu/cu/computinghistory/brennan/.
Buckland, Michael K. "Emanuel Goldberg, Electronic Document Retrieval, and Vannevar Bush's Memex." *Journal of the American Society for Information Science* 43.4 (May 1992): 284–94.

Busa, Roberto, S.J. "L'analisi linguistica nell'evoluzione mondiale dei mezzi d'informazione." In *Almanacco Letterario Bompiani 1962* (1962), 103–107. Trans. Philip Barras, in Marco Passarotti, A. Ciula, and Julianne Nyhan, *One Origin of Digital Humanities: Fr. Roberto Busa, S.J. in His Own Words*. Forthcoming, Springer Verlag.

Busa, Roberto, S.J. "The Annals of Humanities Computing: The *Index Thomisticus*." *Computers and the Humanities* 14.2 (1980): 83–90.

Busa, Roberto, S.J. "Announcements: Complete Index Verborum of Works of St. Thomas." *Speculum* 25.3 (July 1950): 424–26.

Busa, Roberto, S.J. "Foreword: Perspectives on the Digital Humanities." In Schreibman, Susan, Ray Siemens, and John Unsworth, eds. *A Companion to Digital Humanities*. Oxford: Blackwell, 2004. Accessed online: http://digitalhumanities.org/companion.

Busa, Roberto, S.J. "Half a Century of Literary Computing: Towards a 'New' Philology." *Historical Social Research* 17.2 (1992), 124–133.

Busa, Roberto, S.J. "The Index of All Non-Biblical Dead Sea Scrolls Published Up To December 1957." *Revue de Qumrân* 1.5 (1959): 187–98.

Busa, Roberto, S.J. "Informatics and New Philology." *Computers and the Humanities* 24.5-6 (December 1990): 339–43.

Busa, Roberto, S.J. "*Mechanisierung der philologischen Analyse.*" *Nachrichten für Dokumentation* 3.1 (March 1952): 14–19. Transl. Philip Barras, in Marco Passarotti, A. Ciula, and Julianne Nyhan, eds. *One Origin of Digital Humanities: Fr. Roberto Busa, S.J. in His Own Words*. Forthcoming, Springer Verlag.

Busa, Roberto, S.J. "Picture a Man . . ." (Busa Award Lecture, Debrecen, Hungary, 6 July 1998). In *Literary & Linguistic Computing* 14.1 (April 1999): 5–9.

Busa, Roberto, S.J. *Sancti Thomae Aquinatis Hymnorum Ritualium Varia Specimina Concordantiarum: A First Example of Word Index Automatically Compiled and Printed by IBM Punched Card Machines.* Archivum Philosophicum Aloisianum. A cura della Facultaà di Filosofia dell'Istituto Aloisianum S.J. Serie II. N. 7. Fratelli Bocca: Milan, 1951.

Busa, Roberto, S.J. *La Teminologia Tomistica dell' Interiorita. Saggi di metodoper una interpretazione della metafisica della presenza.* Bocca: Milan, 1949.

Busa, Roberto, S.J. "Les Travaux du Centro per L'automanzione dell'Analisi Letteraria di Gallarate." *Cahiers de Lexicologie* 3 (B. Quemada, 1961; Paris: Didier, 1962): 64–68.

Busa, Roberto, S.J. "The Use of Punched Cards in Linguistic Analysis." In Robert S. Casey, James W. Perry, Madeline M. Berry, and Allen Kent, *Punched Cards: Their Applications to Science and Industry*. New York, Amsterdam, London: Reinhold, 1958; second edition, 1967. Pp. 357–73.

Bush, Vannevar. "As We May Think." *Atlantic Monthly* (July 1, 1945), http://www.theatlantic.com/magazine/archive/1945/07/as-we-may-think/303881/.

Chun, Wendy Hui Kyong. "On Software, or the Persistence of Visual Knowledge." *Grey Room* 18 (Winter 2005): 26–51; http://www.brown.edu/Departments/MCM/people/chun/papers/software.pdf.

Clark, Ken. Interviewed by Lawrence Saphire for IBM Oral History of Computer Technology (Box 1, Folder 18, August 8, 1967). A. Wayne Brooke Collection, NCSU.

Cortada, James W. *Before the Computer: IBM, NCR, Burroughs, and Remington Rand and the Industry They Created, 1865–956*. Princeton, NJ: Princeton University Press, 2000.

Dobbs, Michael. *Six Months in 1945: FDR, Stalin, Churchill, and Truman—World War to Cold War*. New York: Alfred A. Knopf, 2012.

Donohue, John W. *Jesuit Education: An Essay on the Foundations of Its Idea*. New York: Fordham University Press, 1963.

Drucker, Johanna. "Humanities Approaches to Graphical Display." DHQ 5.1 (2011), http://www.digitalhumanities.org/dhq/vol/5/1/000091/000091.html.

Dyson, George. *Turing's Cathedral: The Origins of the Digital Universe*. New York: Pantheon Books, 2012.

Eames, Charles and Ray. *A Computer Perspective: Background to the Computer Age*. Cambridge, MA: Harvard University Press, 1973.

Eames, Charles and Ray. *The Information Machine*. (Film, 1958). https://www.youtube.com/watch?v=djT-HNnWX8w.

Eckert, Wallace. Interviewed by Lawrence Saphire for IBM Oral History of Computer Technology (Interview TC-1, Box 1, Folder 15, July 11, 1967). A. Wayne Brooke Collection, NCSU.

Emerson, Lori. *Reading Writing Interfaces: From the Digital to the Bookbound*. Minneapolis: University of Minnesota Press, 2014.

Engelbart, Douglas C. "Augmenting the Human Intellect: A Conceptual Framework." Washington, D.C.: Air Force Office of Scientific Research, 1962: http://dougengelbart.org/pubs/papers/scanned-original/1962-augment-3906-Augmenting-Human-Intellect-a-Conceptual-Framework.pdf.

Engelbourg, Saul. *International Business Machines: A Business History*. New York: Arno Press, 1976.

Fitzmyer, Joseph A., S.J. *A Guide to the Dead Sea Scrolls and Related Literature*. Grand Rapids, MI: Wm. B. Erdmans, 2008.

Fitzmyer, Joseph A., S.J. "The Concordance, the Computer and the Battle for the Dead Sea Scrolls." *America: The National Catholic Review* 165.11 (October 19, 1991), 270–72.

Frey, Jörg. "Qumran Research and Biblical Scholarship in Germany." In Devorah Dimant, ed., *The Dead Sea Scrolls in Scholarly Perspective: A History of Research (Study of the Texts of the Desert of Judah)*. Leiden and Boston: Brill, 2012, 529–64.

Fritz, W. Barkley. "The Women of ENIAC." *IEEE Annals of the History of Computing* 18.3 (1996): 13–28.

Greenhalgh, Paul. *Fair World: A History of World's Fairs and Expositions from London to Shanghai, 1851–2010*. Winterbourne, UK: Papadakis, 2011.

Greg, W.W. "The Rationale of Copy-Text." *Studies in Bibliography* 3 (1950): 19–36.

Grosch. Herbert. *Computer: Bit Slices From a Life*. Third Millenium Books, Novato, California, 1991; 3rd ed., 2003. Columbia University Computing History, http://www.columbia.edu/cu/computinghistory/computer.html.

Gürer, Denise. "Women in Computing History." *ACM SIGCSE Bulletin* 34.2 (ACM Press, 2002): 116–20.

Haigh, Thomas and Mark Priestley. "Innovators Assemble: Ada Lovelace, Walter Isaacson, and the Superheroines of Computing." *Communications of the ACM* 58.9 (September 2015): 20–27. DOI: 10.1145/2804228.

Harpham, Geoffrey Galt. "Roots, Races, and the Return to Philology." *Representations* 106 (Spring 2009): 34–62.

Harwood, John. *The Interface: IBM and the Transformation of Corporate Design, 1945–1976*. Minneapolis: University of Minnesota Press, 2011.

Hayles, N. Katherine. "Cybernetics." In W.J.T. Mitchell, and M.B.N. Hansen, eds., *Critical Terms for Media Studies*, Chicago: University of Chicago Press, 2010, 144–56.

Hayles, N. Katherine. *Electronic Literature: New Horizons for the Literary*. Notre Dame, IN: Notre Dame University Press, 2008.

Heide, Lars. *Punched-Card Systems and the Early Information Explosion, 1880–1945*. Baltimore: Johns Hopkins University Press, 2009.

Hicks, Marie. "Only the Clothes Changed: Women Operators in British Computing and Advertising, 1950–1970." *IEEE Annals of the History of Computing* 32.2 (October–December 2010): 2–14. http://www.mariehicks.net/writing/Hicks_Only_the_Clothes_Changed_Annals_32_4_Final.pdf.

Hindley, Meredith. "The Rise of the Machines: NEH and the Digital Humanities: The Early Years." *Humanities* 34.4 (July/Aug. 2013). http://www.neh.gov/humanities/2013/julyaugust/feature/the-rise-the-machines.

Hockey, Susan. "The History of Humanities Computing." In *A Companion to Digital Humanities*, eds. Susan Schreibman, et al. Oxford: Blackwell, 2004, 3–19. http://digitalhumanities.org/companion.

Hodges, Andrew. *Alan Turing: The Enigma*. Princeton, N.J.: Princeton University Press, 2014. Kindle edition.

Hutchins, John. "ALPAC: The (in)famous report." *MT News International* 14 (June 1996): 9–12. http://www.hutchinsweb.me.uk/MTNI-14-1996.pdf.

Hutchinson, Lee. "Tripping through IBM's astonishingly insane 1937 corporate songbook." *Ars Technica* (August 29, 2014), http://arstechnica.com/business/2014/08/tripping-through-ibms-astonishingly-insane-1937-corporate-songbook/.

IBM Archives website, http://www-03.ibm.com/ibm/history/history/decade_1940.html.

"IBM computers help men find secrets in scrolls, history in the stars—and answers to literary puzzles." Advertisement in *Natural History: The Journal of the American Museum of Natural History* 74 (1965).

IBM 100 history website, http://www-03.ibm.com/ibm/history/ibm100/us/en/.

Jockers, Matthew L. *Macroanalysis: Digital Methods & Literary History*. Urbana, Chicago, Springfield: University of Illinois Press, 2013.

Johnson, Steven. *How We Got to Now: Six Innovations That Made the Modern World*. New York: Riverhead Books, 2014.

Johnson, Steven. "The Long Zoom." *The New York Times Magazine* (October 8, 2006). http://nytimes.com/2006/10/08/magazine/08games.html/.

Jones, Steven E. *The Emergence of the Digital Humanities*. New York: Routledge: 2014.

Judt, Tony. *Postwar: A History of Europe Since 1945*. New York: Penguin Books, 2005.

Kirschenbaum, Matthew G. *Mechanisms: New Media and the Forensic Imagination*. Cambridge, MA: MIT Press, 2008.

Koh, Adeline. "Niceness, Building, and Opening the Genealogy of the Digital Humanities: Beyond the Social Contract of Humanities Computing." *differences* 24.1 (2014): 93–106. DOI: 10.1215/10407391-2420015.

Kuhn, Karl Georg. *Konkordanz zu den Qumrantexten*. Göttingen: Vandenhoeck & Ruprecht, 1960.

Levy, Steven. *Insanely Great: The Life and Times of Macintosh, the Computer That Changed Everything*. New York: Penguin, 1994.

Lipstadt, Hélène. "'Natural Overlap': Charles and Ray Eames and the Federal Government." In *The Work of Charles and Ray Eames: A Legacy of Invention*. New York: Harry Abrams, in cooperation with The Library of Congress, 1997, 151–177.

Lubar, Steven. "'Do Not Fold, Spindle, or Mutilate': A Cultural History of the Punch Card." *Journal of American Culture* 15.4 (Winter 1992): 43–55.

Maney, Kevin. *The Maverick and His Machine: Thomas J. Watson, Sr. and the Making of IBM*. Hoboken, NJ: John Wiley & Sons, Inc., 2003. Kindle edition.

McCarty, Willard. "The Digital and the Human: Remembering the Future of Digital Humanities." Roberto Busa Award lecture, 2013. https://www.youtube.com/watch?v=nTHa1rDR680.

McCarty, Willard. "What does Turing have to do with Busa?" *Proceedings of the Third Workshop on Annotation of Corpora for Research in the Humanities* (ACRH-3). Eds. Francesco Mambrini, Marco Passarotti and Caroline Sporleder. Sofia: Institute of Information and Communication Technologies, Bulgarian Academy of Sciences, December 12, 2013: 1–14. http://www.mccarty.org.uk/essays/McCarty,%20Turing%20and%20Busa.pdf.

McGann, Jerome J. "Marking Texts of Many Dimensions." In Schreibman, Susan, Ray Siemens, and John Unsworth, eds. *A Companion to Digital Humanities*. Oxford: Blackwell, 2004, http://digitalhumanities.org/companion/view?docId=blackwell/9781405103213/9781405103213.xml&chunk.id=ss1-3-4.

McGann, Jerome J. *A New Republic of Letters: Memory and Scholarship in the Age of Digital Reproduction*. Cambridge, MA and London: Harvard University Press, 2014. Kindle ed.

Martone, Corrado. "Qumran Research in Italy." In Devorah Dimant, ed. *The Dead Sea Scrolls in Scholarly Perspective: A History of Research*. Leiden and Boston: Brill, 2012, 601–610.

Morozov, Evgeny. *To Save Everything, Click Here: The Folly of Technological Solutionism*. New York: Public Affairs, 2013.

Norman, Jeremy. History of Information website, http://www.historyofinformation.com/.

Nyhan, Julianne. Arche Logos blog, http://archelogos.hypotheses.org/127.

Nyhan, Julianne and Melissa Terras. Forthcoming, *Uncovering Hidden Histories of the Index Thomisticus: Busa's Female Punched Card Operators*.

Nyhan, Julianne, Andrew Flinn, and Anne Welsh. "Oral History and the Hidden Histories Project: Towards Histories of Computing in the Humanities." DSH 30.1 (April 2015). Published online, July 30, 2013. DOI: http://dx.doi.org/10.1093/llc/fqt044 71–85.

O'Malley, John W., S.J. *The Jesuits: A History from Ignatius to the Present*. Lanham, MD and London: Rowman & Littlefield, 2014. Kindle edition.

On Guard! (film, IBM Military Products Division), 1956. https://www.youtube.com/watch?v=YPQMwmdkVVU.

Parikka, Jussi. *What is Media Archaeology?* Cambridge, UK: Polity, 2012.

Pugh, Emerson W. and Lars Heide. "STARS: Early Punched Card Equipment, 1880–1951." IEEE Global history Network. Engineering and Technology History Wiki, http://ethw.org/index.php?title=Early_Punched_Card_Equipment,_1880_-_1951&redirect=no.

Ramsay, Stephen. *Reading Machines: Toward an Algorithmic Criticism*. Champaign, IL: University of Illinois Press, 2011.

Risam, Roopikah. "Revise and Resubmit: An Unsolicited Peer Review." Blog, April 20, 2015, http://roopikarisam.com/2015/04/20/revise-and-resubmit-an-unsolicited-peer-review/.

Rockwell, Geoffrey and Stéfan Sinclair. "Past Analytical: Towards an Archaeology of Text Analysis Tools." Digital Humanities 2014 conference, Lausanne, Switzerland, October 7, 2014. http://www.researchgate.net/publication/273449857_Towards_an_Archaeology_of_Text_Analysis_Tools.

Rodgers, William. *Think: A Biography of the Watsons and IBM*. New York: Stein and Day, 1969.

Rossiter, Margaret W. *Women Scientists in America: Before Affirmative Action, 1940–1972*. Baltimore and London: Johns Hopkins University Press, 1995.

Rydell, Robert W. *World of Fairs: The Century of Progress Expositions*. Chicago and London: University of Chicago Press, 1993.

Sayers, Jentery. "Making the Perfect Record." *American Literature* 85. 4 (December 2013), http://dx.doi.org/10.1215/00029831-2370230. SCALAR, http://scalar.usc.edu/maker/record/ibm-305-ramac-promotional-material-ca-1956?path=mediapath.

Shanks, Hershel. *Freeing the Dead Sea Scrolls: And Other Adventures of An Archaeology Outsider*. New York: Continuum Books, 2010.

Slocum, Jonathan. "An Experiment in Machine Translation." *ACL '80: Proceedings of the 18th annual meeting on Association for Computational Linguistics*: 163–64. http://www.aclweb.org/anthology/P80-1044. DOI: 10.3115/981436.981487.

Snow, C.P. *The Two Cultures: And A Second Look*. 1959; Cambridge, UK: Cambridge University Press, 1979.

Sobel, Robert. *IBM: Colossus In Transition*. New York: Bantam Books, 1983.

"Solving the Equation: The Variables for Women's Success in Engineering and Computing." American Association of University Women report (2015), http://www.aauw.org/research/solving-the-equation/.

Tanner, Simon and Greg Bearman. "Digitising the Dead Sea Scrolls." In *Archiving 2009*. Arlington, VA: The Society for Imaging Science and Technology, 2009. Pp. 119–123. http://www.academia.edu/813028/Digitizing_the_Dead_Sea_Scrolls.

Tasman, Paul. *Indexing the Dead Sea Scrolls, by Electronic Literary Data Processing Methods*. New York: IBM World Trade Corporation, 1958.

Tasman, Paul. "Literary Data Processing." *IBM Journal of Research and Development*, 1.3 (1957): 249–56.

Tasman, Paul. Interview by Lawrence Saphire for Oral History of Computer Technology. (Interview TC-99, August 14, 1968). Somers, NY: IBM Archives.

Terras, Melissa. Blog, http://melissaterras.blogspot.com/2013/10/for-ada-lovelace-day-father-busas.html.

Tollenaere, Félicien de. English typescript draft for *Nieuwe wegen in de lexicologie*. Amsterdam, Noord-Hollandsche Uitg. Mij., 1963. Busa Archive.

Turner, James. *Philology: The Forgotten Origins of the Modern Humanities*. Princeton, NJ: Princeton University Press, 2000.

Vanhoutte, Edward. "The Gates of Hell: History and Definition of Digital | Humanities | Computing." In *Defining Digital Humanities: A Reader*, Melissa Terras, Julianne Nyhan, and Edward Vanhoutte, eds. Farnham, Surrey, UK: Ashgate, 2013. Pp. 119–156.

Wacholder, Ben Zion and Martin Abegg, eds. *A Preliminary Edition of the Unpublished Dead Sea Scrolls: The Hebrew and Aramaic Texts from Cave Four*. 2 fascicles. Washington, D.C.: Biblical Archaeology Society, 1991–92.

Watson, Thomas J., Jr. and Peter Petre. *Father, Son & Co.: My Life at IBM and Beyond*. New York: Bantam Books, 1990.

Werner, Sarah and Matthew G. Kirschenbaum. "Digital Scholarship and Digital Studies: The State of the Discipline." *Book History* 17 (2014): 406–58. https://muse.jhu.edu/journals/bh/summary/v017/17.kirschenbaum.html.

Wiener, Norbert. *Cybernetics: Or Control and Communication in the Animal and the Machine*. Cambridge, MA.: MIT Press, 1948.

Winter, Thomas Nelson. "Roberto Busa, S.J., and the Invention of the Machine-Generated Concordance." *The Classical Bulletin* 75.1 (1999): 3–20. http://digitalcommons.unl.edu/classicsfacpub/70/.

Zielinski, Siegfried. *Deep Time of the Media: Toward an Archaeology of Hearing and Seeing by Technical Means*. Cambridge, MA: The MIT Press, 2008.

INDEX